The Curriculum Challenge

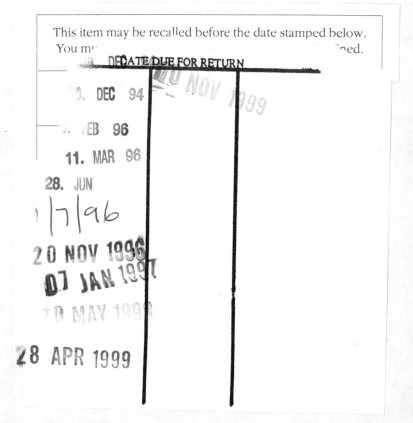

This book is dedicated to
Clare, Sue and Maggie

The Curriculum Challenge:
Access to the National Curriculum for Pupils with Learning Difficulties

Edited by

Rob Ashdown, Barry Carpenter
and Keith Bovair

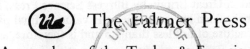 The Falmer Press

(A member of the Taylor & Francis Group)
London • New York • Philadelphia

UK   The Falmer Press, 4 John Street, London WC1N 2ET

USA   The Falmer Press, Taylor & Francis Inc., 1900 Frost Road, Suite 101, Bristol, PA 19007

First published 1991, reprinted 1991

British Library Cataloguing in Publication Data
The curriculum challenge: access to the National Curriculum for
  pupils with learning difficulties.
  1. Great Britain. Schools. Students with special educational needs.
  Education
  I. Ashdown, Rob   II. Carpenter, Barry   III. Bovair, Keith
  371.90941

  ISBN 1-85000-880-9
  ISBN 1-85000-881-7 (pbk.)

Library of Congress Cataloguing-in-Publication Data
is available on request.

Jacket design by Caroline Archer

Typeset in 11/13pt Bembo
by Graphicraft Typesetters Ltd, Hong Kong

Printed in Great Britain by Burgess Science Press, Basingstoke
on paper which has a specified pH value on final paper
manufacture of not less than 7.5 and is therefore 'acid free'.

Contents

Contents

List of Abbreviations

AT	Attainment Target
CDT	Craft, Design and Technology
DES	Department of Education and Science
EDY	Education of the Developmentally Young
ERA	The Education Reform Act, 1988
ESG	Educational Support Grant
ESN (S)	Educationally Subnormal (Severe)
FE	Further Education
GERBIL	Great Education Reform Bill
HMI	Her Majesty's Inspectorate
ILEA	Inner London Education Authority
INSET	Inservice Training
LEA	Local Education Authority
LMS	Local Management of Schools
MLD	Moderate Learning Difficulties
NCC	National Curriculum Council
PE	Physical Education
PMLD	Profound and Multiple Learning Difficulties
PSE	Personal and Social Education
SAT	Standard Assessment Task
SEAC	School Examinations and Assessment Council
SEN	Special Educational Needs
SLD	Severe Learning Difficulties
TGAT	Task Group on Assessment and Testing
TRIST	TVEI-Related Inservice Training
TVEI	Technical and Vocational Education Initiative

List of Abbreviations

Acknowledgements

We decided to collaborate on this project because of our wish that all pupils should have access to a National Curriculum that is stimulating and meaningful. We have been closely involved in the implementation of the National Curriculum as Headteachers of special schools for pupils with learning difficulties, and latterly, for one of us, as an Inspector for Special Needs. In one way or another we have been responsible for the organization and delivery of INSET initiatives relating to the National Curriculum. However, we have not worked in a vacuum. During this time our views and practice have been and are being continually reshaped by the stimulus and example of many colleagues in Cambridgeshire, Warwickshire, Humberside and Solihull. Also, we have found the opportunity to communicate more widely with the various contributors to this book extremely fruitful.

We are particularly grateful to Christine Cox of Falmer Press for her support for this project. We would also like to thank Jeremy Fathers of the Blythe School, Coleshill, for his logistical support and Enid Sowerby of St. Luke's School, Scunthorpe, for her assistance with typing manuscripts of several chapters.

This project would not have been possible without the tolerance of our families including eleven children in all who must have often felt fatherless. Special thanks are due to our wives, Clare, Sue and Maggie, for their forgiving natures and their understanding.

Extracts from Crown copyright material which appear in this book are reproduced with the permission of the Controller of Her Majesty's Stationery Office. Extracts from material of the National Curriculum Council are reproduced with their kind permission.

Introduction

Keith Bovair

The introduction of the National Curriculum has presented many challenges for all those concerned with education of children and young people. (A major question has been how to guarantee access to the National Curriculum for individuals with special educational needs) This book seeks to illustrate how this is possible in the case of those pupils with severe learning difficulties (SLD). In doing so, the book offers principles and examples of good practice which are relevant to the education of all pupils with special educational needs (SEN), not just this small group. Indeed, readers will find that this book contains powerful mesages for educators of all pupils in all types of schools.

Over approximately the past fifteen to twenty years we have seen the provision for children and young people, who are now described as having severe learning difficulties, move from the medical/care model of treatment in various settings to the education of these individuals in schools. This advancement has led to creative thinking in many quarters in the field of education that ensures greater access to a wider curriculum for these pupils.

There have been various reports and Acts over these years which have shown positive attitudes and intentions to ensure the right of access for pupils with SLD. Not only has their education taken place in specialist schools and units, but also within ordinary educational settings, promoting their acceptance within their communities.

With the evolution of the 1988 Education Reform Act (ERA) and the introduction of a National Curriculum, practitioners in the field of special education were initially facing possible pressure to retreat into the isolation of specialist settings, because it appeared at first that this legislation would totally exclude the pupils with SEN. There was no indication where these pupils fitted into the grand blueprint of the new ERA. Through vocalization of concerns and intense lobbying, documentation from government bodies was modified to state that the National Curriculum was a curriculum for all pupils.

For too long, the field of special education has been an appendage to educational planning and provision; something that is considered almost as an afterthought. When access has been offered, it has been like a ledge to which practitioners have had to lift the pupils. Because we need to keep things on the level, we present this book to ensure that the National Curriculum is a curriculum for all and that there is a continuum of educational provision for all pupils.

In each of the four sections of this book, we have drawn on practitioners in the field of education and voluntary agencies, who have worked to ensure that the right of access exists to a broad and balanced curriculum for pupils with special needs. All the contributors discuss principles and strategies of relevance to all educators working with children and young people, even in those chapters which are written with a focus upon pupils with SLD. They have tackled a cross-section of subject areas, themes and issues to give examples of current thought and practice and to show how the requirements of the National Curriculum can enhance good practice and contribute to the process of curriculum development.

Finally, it should be recognised that, although the contents of the book were accurate at the time of publication, the reader should not assume that the examples based on current DES/National Curriculum Council material will remain as quoted here. This is a time of rapid educational change: the National Curriculum is undergoing revision in the light of practice. However, the content of the book remains valid and will do so for years to come.

Section One

Assessing the Challenge

1   The Curriculum Challenge

Rob Ashdown, Barry Carpenter and Keith Bovair

Towards the National Curriculum

There have been several periods of rapid change during the history of education of pupils with severe learning difficulties (SLD). For instance, the Education (Handicapped Pupils) Act of 1970 profoundly affected the lives of pupils of the former Junior Training Centres and hospital schools and the staff who worked with them. Another major development has been the Education Act of 1981 which enshrined the radical new concept of special educational needs, increased the accountability of teachers of pupils with learning difficulties and forced a more rigorous examination of the education which was being offered to these pupils. Sweeping changes like these can always cause a considerable amount of anxiety and uncertainty for the people concerned, particularly the teachers. However, they were preceded by a reasonably thorough process of consultation with special educators, parents and interested lay people. Therefore, there was a consensus which held that these developments were desirable, no matter what reservations there may have been about the quality of the legislation and the level of resourcing from central government.

For some years now, the teaching profession has been rocked by a torrent of legislation culminating in the Education (No. 2) Act 1986 and the Education Reform Act 1988 (ERA). During this decade the voice of the teachers has barely been heard and, in fact, the minimal amount of time allowed by the DES for consultation with teachers has been almost derisory. There has been little or no effort on the part of the DES to achieve a consensus of opinion about these changes: the legislation is clearly yoked to the ideology of this particular government.

(Special educators have not escaped its effects. Often, we managed to do so in the past because special schools enjoyed a peculiar autonomy which ordinary schools did not, perhaps due in part to the mystique surrounding the specialist and also to the fact that, by and large, there were few pressures on us to teach our pupils to pass exams and gain employment after school. As a result, we are not used to being held to account in the same way that our colleagues in mainstream schools have been. Now, of course, accountability has arrived with a vengeance. A massive reappraisal of the curriculum has been forced upon all schools and teachers are wary about the effects of the introduction of Local Management of Schools (LMS) and increased use of their new powers by parents and governing bodies.)

The genesis of the National Curriculum may be traced back to a Labour Prime Minister, James Callaghan, who launched the 'Great Debate' about education at Ruskin College, Oxford in 1976. He used this platform to try to stimulate national debate about the issue of education, calling for a national consensus on aims and national policies on the curriculum. Thus, it is misleading to trace the movement towards a National Curriculum to a Conservative government clamping down on libertarian, socialist teachers and mediocre teachers. Rather it began in a climate when politicians of all hues were concerned that the nation was not educating its future labour force in a way which would promote the growth of industry capable of competing with other technologically advanced nations. However, it was only in the 1980s that a government came to power which has had the time and which has been increasingly prepared to use legislation to back up its political manifesto. The Education (School Information) Regulations 1981 (DES, 1981b) required that each LEA should produce a statement of the curriculum which would be offered in its schools. In 1984 *A Framework for the Curriculum* was published by the government (DES and Welsh Office, 1984a), identifying lists of skills, particular concepts and aspects of knowledge to be introduced as part of a core curriculum. As regards special education, the DES and the Welsh Office issued a note, *The Organization and Content of the Curriculum: Special Schools* (DES and Welsh Office, 1984b), which defined three broad ranges of approach to meeting special educational needs, with a 'developmental curriculum' being described as most appropriate for pupils with SLD. This curriculum was described as 'covering selected and sharply focused educational, social and other experiences with precisely defined objectives and designed to encourage a measure of personal autonomy' (DES and Welsh Office, 1984b,

p. 2). The main emphasis of this kind of approach was described as being upon:

> enabling pupils to take part in and derive satisfaction from the society in which they live to the greatest extent possible. The basic elements of this approach should be the acquisition of communication, self help, mobility and social skills, very basic literacy and numeracy, and an understanding of the world about them including simple science in its application to everyday life. (DES and Welsh Office, 1984b, pp. 3–4)

Her Majesty's Inspectorate (HMI) has been increasingly involved in the public debate about education. It has produced a series of discussion papers on aspects of the curriculum in the *Curriculum Matters 5–16* series. These have been described as being appropriate to all pupils and they certainly are relevant to pupils with SLD in that they affirm certain general principles about the content and organization of the curriculum. They continue the analysis of the curriculum in terms of the knowledge, skills, concepts and attitudes to be conveyed and they emphasize the need for curriculum continuity. From 1983, all HMI inspection reports have been published in order to ensure that there was public knowledge about the quality of education in schools. HMI also publish a variety of reports on aspects of the curriculum, some of which have been critical of special education provision, such as a report on the inadequate provision for science in special schools (HMI, 1986). HMI have recently published a summary of their findings from surveys of developments in the field of special education in the past decade (HMI, 1990).

Finally, there have been the various Education Acts. The Education Act 1981 (DES, 1981a) established and clarified how pupils with special educational needs can benefit from the education system. The Education Act 1986 gave parents and governors the opportunity to have a much closer involvement in schools and gave them decision-making powers as regards the schools in their community. But, of course, it is the passage of the Great Education Reform Bill (GERBIL) through parliament and the resultant ERA which has appalled so many people in the field of special education because they perceive it as a real threat to much of the solid achievement of the past few decades. Will Swann was not being light hearted when he quipped that 'The gerbil is too soft and cuddly a creature to give its name to this monster of an Education Bill which has now become an Act. I think of it more as a bad tempered, ill trained polecat' (Swann, 1988, p. 102).

The Pace and Scale of Change

The ERA has finally established that there will be a National Curriculum and made explicit the whole paraphernalia associated with it, such as the publication of test results and LMS, which are intended to raise standards where necessary, to increase the accountability of institutions, to involve the community and the parents and to secure the best possible return from finite resources. The government's philosophy of 'consumerism' holds sway and there can be no doubt that the whole field of special education can never be the same again. It remains to be seen whether market forces, that is, parents as consumers, will become focused enough to exert a strong influence upon teaching in schools. But there is no doubt in the minds of many writers that the ERA could have a disastrous effect upon special education especially as regards moves towards integration (for example, Wedell, 1988). However, no matter what opinion we may hold about the philosophy of the 'New Right' in the Conservative party and their educational initiatives, certain advantages in having a National Curriculum cannot be denied.

First, adequate research and consultation with educators could result in an agreed, soundly based curriculum framework and, secondly, there is official recognition that pupils with SLD are part of the general school population with the same entitlement to a National Curriculum as all other pupils (NCC, 1989). The National Curriculum framework might even make it easier to promote integration since there will be agreement between schools about how far pupils have progressed in relation to Statements of Attainment. Finally, the implementation of the National Curriculum has offered special educators considerable opportunities for professional development through the processes of curriculum review and development, moderation, new inservice education and training (INSET) initiatives, and the debate and dialogue between all teachers which is made possible by having a common terminology. Special schools may even be regarded as being in an enviable position in relation to mainstream schools because they may be left with greater autonomy to develop their curricula as long as they remain within the framework of the National Curriculum.

Unfortunately, these potential benefits are endangered at present by inadequate DES consultation with teachers of all pupils and the rapid pace of change which has been forced by the DES. The core subjects and some foundation subjects have been introduced for pupils with SLD only two years after the relevant National Curriculum Working Groups produced their first consultation reports. (Thus, there have been only eighteen months or less from the receipt in 1989 of the Statutory Orders for Mathematics, Science and English to the date prescribed for the implementation of these subjects for all pupils with statements of special educational needs. There has been or will be even less preparation time available for Technology, Geography and the other foundation subjects from the receipt of the Statutory Orders. Therefore, even though implementation of the National Curriculum is phased over several years, massive curriculum review and development have to be undertaken in periods of time which are too short for adequate preparation)

(The government's aims for the National Curriculum have been explained in the DES booklet *National Curriculum: From Policy to Practice* (DES, 1989a). It is a requirement that the curriculum for any school should be balanced and broadly based. It must promote the spiritual, moral, cultural, mental and physical development of the pupils and it should prepare pupils for the opportunities, responsibilities and experiences of adult life) Teachers of pupils with SLD have to meet these same requirements just as much as their colleagues in ordinary schools and colleges. The booklet emphasizes that the National Curriculum must be viewed as an entitlement of all pupils. Every maintained school is now obliged by law to provide a basic curriculum consisting of at least religious education, and for pupils of compulsory school age, the National Curriculum. Schools were not obliged to apply the National Curriculum to pupils with statements of special educational needs until Autumn 1990 but this 'year of grace' slipped by. The year was marked by a period of intensive curriculum development and review not only of the way in which the needs of individuals are met but also of whole school policies. The three core subjects of Mathematics, English and Science and the foundation subject of Technology were finally implemented in Autumn 1990. History, Geography and a modern foreign language are due to be implemented in Autumn 1991 and National Curriculum Working Groups for Art, PE and Music have been established. Of course, it must not be forgotten that provision for religious education too has been a requirement for all schools since the Education Act 1944.) Doubtless, every special school in England and Wales has its own working groups of staff carefully examining the various Working Group Reports, Statutory Orders and Non-Statutory Guidance, as well as the National Curriculum Council (NCC) curriculum guidance documents, and relating the contents of these to the school curriculum, making changes where necessary and producing school policies and schemes of work.

The pace and scale of change has alarmed many. In fact, there are reasons to suspect that there was inadequate consideration of pupils with special educational needs when the politicians and legislators first began to plan for the introduction of the National Curriculum. It is true that the most recent DES documents and NCC curriculum guidance do affirm their entitlement to the National Curriculum and acknowledge their needs. But the early DES documents about the National Curriculum contained little more than one or two paragraphs about pupils with special educational needs. As Wedell (1988) shows, GERBIL attracted a great deal of debate in parliament because of the lack of mention of these pupils and some significant changes were made before it was finally enacted.

It was made plain in documents from the DES and NCC, notably *National Curriculum: From Policy to Practice* (DES, 1989a) and the NCC *Curriculum Guidance Two: A Curriculum for All* (NCC, 1989), that the teachers have the responsibility for ensuring access to the National Curriculum. Unfortunately, curriculum guidance on planning to meet special educational needs within the National Curriculum has been limited largely to statements of principle and a few practical examples of generating sequences of supplementary experiences within Level 1. Of course, careful wording of the Statutory Order for each subject has meant that the National Curriculum can be interpreted as applicable to virtually all pupils. But, inevitably, it has fallen to the special educators, who never really asked for a National Curriculum, to take on board the unlooked for burden of making good its deficiencies. There have been a series of local initiatives and monitoring groups exploring the applicability of the National Curriculum to the pupils with SLD. Innovative practice has been cited by the HMI in its review of special education developments (HMI, 1990).

Special educators have some freedom to exercise their professional judgment and exempt pupils from or make modifications to parts of the National Curriculum. The DES and NCC documents mentioned above insist that there is expected to be minimal use of arrangements for exceptions and that when these occur they will be sensitively and positively applied. But will they? Bovair has pointed out that:

> Once doors are created people use them. A door is a two-way route (and this will be pointed out to those contesting any exclusion) by which a child can leave or return to the ordinary

education system. This will be fine, as long as no one drops the latch. (Bovair, 1990, p. 3))

Much effort has been made to reassure teachers that existing good practice need not be compromised. *National Curriculum: From Policy to Practice* (DES, 1989a) and interviews with Kenneth Baker (Baker, 1987; 1988), then Secretary of State at the DES, may have helped to allay the concerns of teachers of pupils with special educational needs. Much emphasis has been given to the facts that the ERA does not specify teaching methods and teaching materials and it does not require that timetables should be subject based or that specified amounts of time should be spent on each subject. In truth, the Statutory Orders issued to date do not appear to be a straitjacket. Nevertheless, despite the bland reassurances of the politicians, the introduction of the National Curriculum is not something which can be ignored and we will have to cope with the new demands.

Paradoxically, despite a general broadening of the curriculum, it seems most unlikely that there will be a dramatic change in the educational programmes and educational provision available for pupils with SLD in those schools where good practice was already in evidence. Therefore, for this group of pupils at least, there is a hollow ring to claims of the politicians that the ERA is the most sweeping and most radical reform of the education service since the Education Act 1944. Indeed, progress in curriculum development largely depends upon the goodwill, hard work, imagination and efficiency of the teaching force. At times, the parents of pupils with SLD have more restricted consumer powers than parents of other pupils. They cannot so easily pick and choose the school to which their child will go and publication of test results will have little meaning for these consumers, if indeed they are reliable indicators of the performance of ordinary schools. The checks and balances built into the ERA and the Education Act 1981 are simply no absolute guarantee of consumer satisfaction and the consumer has a limited capacity to force change. Also, it is doubtful whether the HMI and the LEAs' own advisory teams will have the time and resources to control the development of an appropriate curriculum for such pupils. Ultimately, all depends upon the ability of the teachers to act as advocates for their pupils, to objectively appraise their own performance and to pursue curriculum development doggedly when very much thrust back onto their own resources.

Clearly, the primary task of schools is that of curriculum development. Of necessity, the process of curriculum audit will remain an ongoing one and the school development plan must be revised annually if it is to become an effective management tool. There will always be the need for regular review of the curriculum by each school to make explicit details about the curriculum that is on offer, to identify areas in need of development and to identify any mismatch between the school curriculum and the National Curriculum. To their lasting credit, teachers of pupils with SLD have always responded to new challenges and, without doubt, they will respond to the new challenge of giving all pupils access to a meaningful National Curriculum. Nobody wants to return to the pre–1971 days when pupils with SLD were viewed as incapable of benefiting from the curriculum on offer in schools. Indeed, we must recognize that there is always a danger, no matter how remote it may seem at this time, that widespread demands for exceptional arrangements for pupils with SLD for exemptions or modifications could reinforce the unwelcome notion that these pupils do not require an education at school. Thankfully, there is recognition that these pupils are working at least within Level 1; there is no pre-Level 1 or Level 0 in the National Curriculum. In fact, there is much enthusiasm among special educators for the notion of developing adequate Level 1 curricula by defining the Statements of Attainment and extending the Programmes of Study. Clearly, successful schools with well-developed curricula (for example, Archer, 1989; Etherington, 1990) have much to offer the NCC should it decide to publish further information in this area.

Exploring the Whole Curriculum

The report of the Warnock Committee on special education needs (DES, 1978), emphasized that the goals of education were the same for all pupils. This is absolutely true, provided that these goals are then balanced and brought into harmony with the individual needs of the pupil. Meeting individual needs is about careful planning and room organization coupled with a positive, caring ethos where pupils are able to feel confident and safe.

The strength of special educators has been their ability to respond to the needs of the individual. With the stress in the National Curriculum on a differentiated curriculum all teachers need to be aware of the individual learning needs of pupils in their classes. For all too long, we have looked for the source of learning difficulties 'within' the pupil. Now, through the National Curriculum, we are having to reappraise the whole curriculum and examine our teaching styles.

As Smith (1982) says, 'If children find learning difficult, it could well be that there is something wrong with the way we are asking them to learn, rather than something the matter with their innate capacity for learning'.

King argues that through our audit of the curriculum we will come to realize the potential of differentiation as the key to a whole range of curriculum experiences for pupils: 'Differentiation is about meeting the needs of all learners and requires a concern with the pupil, the task and the learning context' (King, 1990). No longer must we view differentiation as the territory of those who teach the less able. All learners are different and all teaching needs to be differentiated. It is through the strength of differentiation that pupils with SLD will be given access to the curriculum and that continuity and progression will be ensured.

A major concern of teachers has been that the National Curriculum will become a curriculum straitjacket. The reality of this concern has caused a biased focus on only the core and foundation subjects which in turn has given rise to 'Mad Academic Disease' (Wragg, 1990). The antidote is the 'Whole Curiculum' — a curriculum diet that feeds and sustains the whole pupil rather than causing global mal-nourishment through experiences which fail to give sustenance. For, as John MacGregor, when Secretary of State for the DES, has affirmed; 'the National Curriculum *is not* inflexible nor is it all-embracing. It *is* a sure and rigorous foundation upon which all teachers can build using their professional skills and judgment and to which other important elements ... must be added' (MacGregor, 1990, p. 4).

Curriculum Compatibility

A driving force in the traditional design of the special education curriculum has been the goal of personal autonomy for each pupil. To make the pupil as independent as possible was seen as a primary target and significant attention has been given to the design and composition of the curriculum for the latter years, culminating in such strategies as the 'Leavers' Programme'.

This goal of autonomy must be retained. How do we go about this in the context of a National Curriculum which seems to be heavily skewed towards academic capabilities? We must now seek to chart a route in the 'new' curriculum that will enable the pupil with SLD to achieve maximum personal autonomy. The independence of the pupil must be an outcome of the educational process. It must remain high on the agenda of all involved in the education of pupils with SEN but, as usual, teachers will be the advocates, in particular, for this cause. Indeed, many young people with learning difficulties are realistic about their own aspirations for independence post-school in the areas of work, leisure and housing. *Circular 22/89* (DES, 1989b) now provides them with a strategy, through the Annual Review procedure, where they can vocalize and negotiate their ambitions which will lead them to their autonomy.

The ERA places a statutory responsibility upon schools to provide a broad and balanced curriculum which prepares pupils for the opportunities, responsibilities and experiences of adult life. Here we find, implicit in the ERA, the primary motivating goal of special education. HMI similarly emphasizes that we must ensure that the curriculum serves the pupil in 'promoting personal development and preparing that pupil for adult life' (HMI, 1990).

Curriculum Guidance Three: The Whole Curriculum (NCC, 1990) illuminates the context in which the National Curriculum must be set. Through its discussion of cross-curricular skills, dimensions and themes, it puts to rest many of the fears of the special educator that the pupil with learning difficulties may be forced to follow an arid academic curriculum. The need for all elements of the curriculum to contribute to the personal and social education (PSE) of all pupils is stressed in this document. PSE has a major role to play in the education of all pupils, but for the pupil with special needs it is vital that it is dealt with thoroughly and in considerable depth.

The skills identified by the NCC as having cross-curricular application are also highly pertinent to the educational objectives embedded in the individual learning programme of the pupils with SEN. These skills can be fostered across the whole curriculum and comprise communication, numeracy, study, problem-solving, personal and social and information technology skills. The development of these skills in young people is directly aligned to preparation for adulthood for, as the NCC states, 'What is beyond dispute is that in the next century these skills, together with flexibility and adaptability, will be at a premium' (NCC, 1990, p. 3).

The cross-curricular themes outlined by the NCC are particularly noteworthy for the special educator. It is to be regretted that these were not issued prior to the publication of the core subjects in the National Curriculum, for it is here that curriculum compatibility can be achieved. The cross-curricular skills, dimension and themes should form the bedrock upon which we set the core and foundation subjects of the National Curriculum. Mirrored in the details explaining careers education and guidance, economic and industrial understanding and so on, we can find many of the curriculum activities which we have considered crucial to the education of the pupil with learning difficulties. What is more, these activities are given status and are accepted in their own right as valid and valuable. We are no longer left thinking that subversive activity will be necessary to facilitate these targets for our pupils with special needs.

It will be possible to state openly where the themes are contributing to the total educational package for the pupil. Indeed, the curriculum weighting towards these themes may be greater for the pupil with special needs. Whilst it is appreciated that cross-curricular themes are intended to be delivered across the core and foundation subjects, it may be necessary to elaborate, consolidate and extend some of the key messages in these themes through discreet sessions in order to maintain consistent relevance to the pupil's individual needs.

Readers should refer to *Curriculum Guidance Three: The Whole Curriculum* (NCC, 1990) to examine the details and implications of this document for pupils with special needs. However, a few phrases from the document which offer 'light in our darkness' and words of reassurance may be helpful here.

First, in the latter years of special education a key experience has been, wherever possible, work experience. The theme of economic and industrial understanding says that 'pupils should have direct experience of industry and the world of work' (p. 4).

Secondly, self-esteem is of paramount importance to the pupil with special needs; often their educational failure at some point in their school career may have jeopardized this. It is heartening, therefore, to read that careers education and guidance 'aims first of all to help pupils develop self-awareness' (p. 4). This is fundamental to the personal growth and development of all pupils and may be achieved through a variety of strategies according to the nature of the pupil's learning difficulties. For the student with emotional and behavioural difficulties, it may be through counselling approaches; for the pupil with profound and multiple learning difficulties, it may be through the sensory curriculum.

Health education is seen as the umbrella for a range of issues, all of which are highly relevant to the pupils with special needs: education about sex, family life, safety, nutrition, personal hygiene. Apart from inculcating in the pupil the need for a healthy mind and body, this theme set about developing 'an appreciation and understanding of responsibilities to the community' (p. 4).

This leads well into the notion of responsible citizenship developed by the theme of education for citizenship. The outline of this theme, covering citizens' rights, leisure education, work and employment, family and parenting, is in itself a major component of some of the courses offered to students in their latter years of special education. It is encouraging to see these key elements so clearly endorsed and set against the scenario of a broader curriculum context than may traditionally have been envisaged for the delivery of these crucial topics.

Finally, environmental issues are the responsibility of every citizen and those with learning difficulties should be no exception to this. Environmental education 'is concerned with promoting positive and responsible attitudes towards the environment' (p. 6). As such, it is pertinent to develop positive and mindful attitudes in all pupils from an early age.

The National Curriculum poses a major challenge to all teachers, particularly those who serve the educational needs of pupils with learning difficulties. However, in the knowledge that these highly specific needs of the pupils can be set in the context of the whole curriculum, the challenge may seem less imposing and the curriculum route more viable.

Conclusion

Educators in the field of special education must take what is proposed in the National Curriculum and ensure that it is truly one of breadth, balance, relevance and differentiation. We have already established working relationships with our colleagues in mainstream settings through various joint inservice training (INSET) ventures, such as the Technical and Vocational Education Initiative (TVEI) and TVEI-Related Inservice Training (TRIST), for instance. The consortium model established in these ventures has drawn together all phases of education and has shown how we can work together because we often have a common ground.

The field of special educational needs was ignored in the beginning of the consultation leading to the ERA. The Special Educational Needs National Advisory Council pointed out this omission in their evidence to the government:

> The major developments from which we have drawn encouragement during the past decade include the Warnock Report (1978), the Education Act (1981), and the Third Report of

the Committee for Education, Science and Art (House of Commons, 1987), together with the positive responses to these of many LEAs and individual schools. Although the unevenness of responses and the inadequacy of funding for improved teacher–pupil ratios and inservice education leave much to be achieved, there was reason to hope that progress required by law would continue. However, our reading of the consultative document leads us to fear that the interests of children with special educational needs could suffer a setback. The consultation document makes only one reference to the individuals with LEA statements of special educational needs and provision. We ask that the existing legislation and related recommendations, together with the philosophy which under-lies these, are fully taken into account in legislation for a national curriculum and for the management of schools. (Haviland, 1988, pp. 60–1)

Such pressure from special educators led to an about turn and a declaration that the National Curriculum will be a curriculum for all.)

The National Curriculum now gives us a common language and a common framework to work within; the core subjects and the foundation subjects are all defined in the relevant documents. What special educators have to do is inject into the framework the means with which to individualize the learning experiences not only for pupils with SEN but for all pupils. We can establish a true curriculum continuum for pupils with SEN to move along. The old model of a resources continuum only identified the type of provision that could be offered; it was no easy task for a pupil to move in either direction to receive the appropriate educational provision for their level of ability and attainment.

Now having a common ground, a common language and a common framework establishes for us a common purpose. If there is a cross-section of educators having input into the variety of subject areas, discovering the ways and means to obtain access, the level of creativity will be heightened. Special educators can work with their colleagues in ordinary schools to develop a flexibility in the curricu-lum that will meet the individual needs of all pupils. They can break down learning experiences into accessible steps.

Showing that those pupils with SLD can be given access to the National Curriculum will be a means of ensuring that more is done to maintain all pupils within the framework of the National Curriculum and avoid use of the exception clause. There will be modification but that is nothing new to special educators. We have always modified the work we present to pupils. The degree of modifications may vary but exclusion from the National Curriculum should never occur. That is the challenge for the special educator; that is the challenge of this book.

References

ARCHER, M. (1989) 'Targetting change', *Special Children*, 33, October, pp. 14–15.

BAKER, K. (1987) 'The Education Secretary replies', *British Journal of Special Education*, 14, pp. 156–7.

BAKER, K. (1988) 'More replies from the Education Secretary', *British Journal of Special Education*, 15, pp. 6–7.

BOVAIR, K. (1990) 'Special educators — special education: THIS ISN'T KANSAS, TOTO!', in BAKER, D. and BOVAIR, K. (Eds) *Making the Special Schools Ordinary?* Volume 2, London, Falmer Press.

DES (1944) *The Education Act 1944*, London, HMSO.

DES (1970) *The Education (Handicapped Children) Act 1970*, London, HMSO.

DES (1978) *Special Educational Needs: Report of the Committee of Enquiry into the Education of Handicapped Children and Young People* (The Warnock Report), London, HMSO.

DES (1981a) *The Education Act 1981*, London, HMSO.

DES (1981b) *The Education (School Information) Regulations 1981*, London, DES.

DES (1986) *The Education (No. 2) Act 1986*, London, HMSO.

DES (1988) *The Education Reform Act 1988*, London, HMSO.

DES (1989a) *National Curriculum: From Policy to Practice*, DES/HMSO, London.

DES (1989b) *Circular 22/89: Assessments and Statements of Special Educational Needs: Procedures Within the Education, Health and Social Services*, London, DES.

DES AND WELSH OFFICE (1984a) *A Framework for the Curriculum*, London, HMSO.

DES AND WELSH OFFICE (1984b) *The Organization and Content of the Curriculum: Special Schools*, London, HMSO.

ETHERINGTON, C. (1990) 'Kingsley School makes an early start on the National Curriculum', *NCC News*, 3, pp. 8–9.

HAVILAND, J. (Ed.) (1988) *Take Care, Mr Baker*, London, Fourth Estate.

HMI (1986) *A Survey of Science in Special Education*, London, HMSO.

HMI (1990) *Education Observed: Special Needs Issues*, London, HMSO.

HOUSE OF COMMONS (1987) *Special Educational Needs: Implementation of the Education Act 1981, Third Report from the Education Science and Arts Committee*, Session 1986–87, London, HMSO.

KING, V. (1990) 'Differentiation is the key', *Language and Learning*, 3. pp. 22–4.

MacGREGOR, J. (1990) *Speeches on Education: National Curriculum and Assessment*, London, DES/HMSO.

NCC (1989) *Curriculum Guidance Two: A Curriculum for All*, York, National Curriculum Council.

NCC (1990) *Curriculum Guidance Three: The Whole Curriculum*, York, National Curriculum Council.

SMITH, F. (1982) *Understanding Reading*, 3rd Edition, New York, Holt, Rinehart and Winston.

SWANN, W. (1988) 'Integration? Look twice at statistics', *British Journal of Special Education*, 15, p. 102.

WEDELL, K. (1988) 'The new Act: A special need for vigilance', *British Journal of Special Education*, 15, pp. 98–101.

WRAGG, T. (1990) 'Time for a fling with the cabinet', *Times Educational Supplement*, 20 July.

2 Perspectives on the National Curriculum

Sue Fagg

A Historical Perspective

The last two decades have seen a revolution in the educational opportunities offered to children and young people with severe, complex and profound learning difficulties (see Chapters 3 and 19 in this volume). The Education (Handicapped Children) Act (1970) transferred responsibility for providing education for mentally handicapped children from the Health Authority to the Local Education Authority. Previously the establishments catering for mentally handicapped children had been called Junior Training Centres, but overnight in April 1971 they became special schools for the Educationally Subnormal (Severe) (ESN-S). This change required an assessment of what curriculum should be offered in a special school for ESN(S) pupils.

Staff who had previously worked in the Junior Training Centres as instructors were now called teachers (unqualified if, as was common, they held no Certificate in Education) and these staff were seconded over the next decade to a variety of full-time courses in teacher training. The schools were in a position where staff were returning after training with new ideas and questioning the content and methodology of the educational provision within their school. Models of good practice in existing special and mainstream schools were considered for their appropriateness, as were activities and practice which had accounted for successful learning in the past. Higher educational institutions offered the opportunity for continuing professional development through the provision of pertinent short courses and specialist lectures. Research in this field also increased, leading to an increase in publications directly related to the education of this group of pupils, and new methods of assessment and structures for the delivery of curriculum were developed. The Anson House Project (Hogg, 1979), the Pathways materials (Cheseldine and Jeffree, 1981) and the inservice programme for the Education of the Developmentally Young (EDY) (Foxen and McBrien, 1981; McBrien and Foxen, 1981) were among these. Reports produced by the DES were also influential in developments. For example, the Warnock Report (DES, 1978) stated the need for staff involvement and commitment in curriculum development, if the curriculum was to succeed. Four interrelated elements were identified: setting of objectives; choice of materials; choice of teaching and learning methods; and evaluation.

The 1981 Education Act (DES, 1981a) which arose from the Warnock Report had a great influence as it was specifically related to pupils with special educational needs (SEN) and directly involved parents and a multidisciplinary team in addressing the educational, health and social needs of a pupil. This Act with the subsequent production of educational statements brought a focus on the curricular needs of a pupil and the most appropriate way these could be addressed by choice of school and learning methodologies. At the same time DES *Circular 6/81* (DES, 1981b) referred to the necessity for all schools to produce curricular statements and subsequent evaluation.

During the whole of this period schools were working to address the curricular needs of their pupils by developing often very detailed curricular documentation in areas of core and experiential learning. The terminology used in this work was at times unfamiliar to parents as well as teachers in mainstream schools. The key curriculum areas being addressed were those of communication and independence, and fine and gross motor, cognition and acquisition skills. Over a period of time terminology and approaches changed and many curricular documents have been produced in an eclectic manner. The Fish Report (ILEA, 1985) helped to emphasize the need to consider the whole pupil. In some schools, there was a move away from curriculum being considered a within-child phenomenon, to an approach which sought to incorporate the ecology of the pupil.

The recent legislation which incorporates the National Curriculum will further influence developments, especially as many schools blend their existing curriculum documentation with the foundation subjects. The terminology of the National Curriculum will be adopted in many cases. The curriculum models which have been used as a basis for curriculum development since 1971 are an important consideration, for they provide an insight into the different approaches to teaching which are being used now at the inception of the National

Curriculum. Some of the curricular approaches and models are described below. With the advent of curricular change within the whole of education it would be surprising if further models utilizing some of the existing approaches did not evolve.

A Piagetian Approach

The substages of conceptual development as described by Piaget (1953) can be utilized to assist in the development of a cognitive curriculum. Cognitive development is broken down by Piaget into the following substages, each stage being linked to the development of a normal child and to its age. The substages are: the sensorimotor period, 0–24 months (this substage is divided into six stages); the pre-operational period, 2–7 years; the concrete operational period, 7–11 years; and the formal operational period, 11 years onwards.

As Gardener, Murphy and Crawford (1983) stated, the approach assumes conceptual development takes place through clear demarcated stages, intelligence being seen as an adaptive process that achieves equilibrium between the indvidual and his or her environment. The insistence that developmental stages follow in a constant order can be viewed as problematic for a pupil with SLD who frequently has additional physical disabilities. Experience for such pupils may be significantly different from that of their peers, and their limited movement may restrict their exploration in early stages of development, thus limiting their learning.

The pertinent factor about this approach is that unless a pupil has reached a certain stage of development it is unrealistic to teach certain skills. Hogg and Sebba (1986) illustrate that the approach is valuable in terms of assessment for pupils with profound and multiple learning difficulties (PMLD) who are learning within the sensorimotor period, often at the very early levels. Uzgiris and Hunt (1975) utilize Piaget's theory in their Six Scales for Assessment in Infancy. They are, however, reluctant to give age norms for the behaviours they are assessing through observation.

At a time when pupils with SLD are being offered educational opportunities that are being addressed in terms of normalization, an approach to curriculum that can discuss a pupil of 14 as being developmentally 15 months old, giving little consideration to the social experiences of the individual, should be viewed as somewhat unacceptable. Many pupils now receive their educational provision in a mainstream setting, and discussion in this way fails to take account of the great benefits gained by pupils interacting with their peers. Appropriate provision is not just a cognitive issue.

Carden (1986) illustrates that many have shown that Piaget does not represent the ultimate truth. However, if his theory is considered alongside another approach, perhaps an interactive one, it can be seen as valuable in terms of assisting the evaluation and assessment which must continually take place. This approach is pertinent when considering the development of mathematical concepts, and needs consideration when accessing pupils to this area of the National Curriculum (Aherne, Thornber, Fagg and Skelton, 1990).

A Developmental Approach

This approach has frequently resulted in the production of checklists in different curricular areas, for example, cognition, acquisition skills, communication. The checklists are primarily concerned with the developmental years 0–5 and are based on the skills observed and recorded in a child of average ability. Checklists are frequently used as an assessment tool, and after assessment a pupil's future teaching objectives can readily be planned. Piaget's approach is frequently adapted and incorporated to assist the understanding of early development within this approach when considering cognition and play (Hogg and Sebba, 1986).

Several checklists have been published; these act as a reference point for schools who wish to develop their own curricular documentation based on this model. One of the most influential of these documents was that produced by Rectory Paddock School (1983). Many of the ideas given in this document were current practice in schools throughout the country, but they had not previously been drawn together in such a practical format. No claim was made that the document was conclusive, and thus it helped people have the confidence and desire to carry out their own curricular development. Such developments frequently incorporated some of the strategies and content seen in the Rectory Paddock document, as well as personalizing the curriculum by ensuring the views of those involved with the curriculum development, and the pupils in the school for whom it was specifically written, influenced the content.

The developmental pattern suggested by Piaget, is not necessarily even for pupils with SLD. Physical and/or neurological damage may mean a stage of development is missed altogether. (Checklists utilized by a school that have been produced by others, although perhaps more accurate in their developmental steps, may lead to confusion. Staff may feel the step size is too large; this is a problem frequently associated with the Portage Guide to Early Education (Bluma *et al*, 1976), as the content of this document was not primarily planned with this client group in mind. As Dessent (1984) explains, the traditional Portage approach 'requires extension and modification to meet different realities'; if this occurs, its use with a wide-ranging client group is possible. Teachers now appreciate the importance of assessing and amending any form of approach in light of the specific individual needs of a pupil.

The checklist model is frequently utilized in curriculum planning but now often moves away from a solely developmental approach in an attempt to encompass the uneven developmental patterns found. (As the range of curricular content requiring accurate recording increases, the possibility of keeping within a developmental framework becomes more difficult, especially when a diversity of learning styles is utilized.)

The National Curriculum documentation can be seen as utilizing the idea of a checklist in terms of Attainment Targets, so, while amendment within the schools may occur, this approach can still be seen as valuable. Science Attainment Target 1, English Attainment Target 1 and Mathematics Attainment Targets 1 and 9 (DES and Welsh Office, 1989a, 1989b, 1989c) are based on a developmental process, and can be seen at Level 1 to include all pupils with severe learning difficulties if access is given by a developmental framework (Fagg, Aherne, Skelton and Thornber, 1990).

A Behavioural Approach

(The main feature of behavioural psychology is the attention given to overt behaviour. Many teachers will have some familiarity with this approach to learning having studied B.F. Skinner. However, it is frequently associated with the treatment of inappropriate behaviours rather than the acquisition of new skills (Porter, 1985). In the educational setting the essential elements include accurate and detailed assessment, exact definition of the behaviour to be learned and a task analysis of how this will occur, as well as recording the learning process of the pupil.)

The development of *Training Staff in Behavioural Methods* for the EDY course (Foxen and McBrien, 1981; McBrien and Foxen, 1981) increased rapidly the number of schools consistently utilizing this approach to learning. Within the course, which is planned for all classroom based staff, sessions deal with observation, taking a baseline, task analysis, the need for consistent reinforcement of the desired behaviour, prompting, chaining, shaping, recording and generalization as well as other more controversial areas. This whole school approach to learning led to a shared understanding and terminology among the staff, ensuring the educational input pupils received within the classroom from staff other than the teacher was valued and a team approach adopted. (EDY is being reviewed and updated at the present time by staff at Manchester University).

Many schools utilized this approach when staff were teaching on an individual basis but when working in groups some difficulties were experienced. In some instances schools adopted a classroom management structure that facilitated this approach, pupils when working in a group being given a series of tasks they had previously mastered in an individual setting. A member of staff would position themselves to ensure the individual within the group kept on task, prompting as required. This classroom management system while allowing a member of staff to be involved in individual work, did not allow any significant interaction within the group of pupils whose work tended to rely heavily on fine motor tasks.

A behavioural approach can be seen as one that provides the skills to teach an individual what the developmental approach highlights as the next step in learning. Within some aspects of National Curriculum this approach could be incorporated. Any schools utilizing a traditional classical approach throughout the day may need to consider whether the interactive learning proposed by the core documents is to be followed. Thinking and understanding are elements of the National Curriculum, but are not noticeable observable behaviours (Ainscow and Tweddle, 1979).

When completing an EDY course many experienced staff comment that much of the content is common sense. While reinforcing correct behaviour with food may be considered inappropriate and unhealthy, reinforcement of some kind is at the very heart of society and human interaction. If a task cannot be completed due to the level of difficulty, a simpler approach must be taken if success within the task is to be achieved. This is inherent in some aspects of the National Curriculum and teachers will be using task analysis to access success in the learning of many skills to ensure pupils make achievements within Level 1 and beyond.

An Objectives Approach

This approach can, perhaps, not easily be differentiated from the behavioural approach. 'One can define an objective with sufficient clarity if one can describe or illustrate the kind of behaviour the student is expected to acquire so that one would recognize such behaviour if one saw it' (Tyler, 1949). However, many schools using an objectives approach would not view themselves as behaviourists, the former approach having been taken to extremes within this area of special education, and it is therefore important to differentiate the two. Ainscow and Tweddle (1979) have strongly advocated this method for slow learners (historically in 1918 Bobbitt introduced objectives to the field of education). They asked the question, 'is it possible to help the young child with some learning difficulties by changing teaching methods and tactics, or by rearranging some aspects of classroom organization?' Each pupil with learning difficulties was seen to need a suitable teaching programme.

Stage 1 was seen as the identification of one or more teaching goals, a teaching goal being the description of priority teaching intentions. A decision regarding which basic skill areas should be for immediate attention is required of the teacher. Within these areas one or more priority teaching intentions are written. Stage 2 is the translation of goals into specific objectives. Objectives must all describe the desired pupil behaviour, behaviour being any observable action.

Teachers utilizing this method need to be able to formulate and implement carefully structured programmes. The objectives the teachers set act as a basis for assessment and record keeping. Utilizing this method ensures each pupil's learning within a class is differentiated. A procedure called the Early Learning Skills Analysis (ELSA) developed by Ainscow and Tweddle (1984) has furthered this approach. Although the approach is not primarily aimed at pupils with SLD, it links strongly with the behavioural approach and Skills Analysis Model.

Some schools have developed curriculum documentation based on the approach. This documentation can be seen as rather narrow if it does not incorporate materials relating to the philosophy, aims and extended content of a subject. The National Curriculum Science and

English documents (DES and Welsh Office, 1989a, 1989c) show a clear distinction between the Programmes of Study, which outline goals that should be incorporated into the individual schools' schemes of work, and the Attainment Targets, which state the objectives to be achieved.

An Interactive Approach

(This curricular model takes account of a pupil's total ecology. The term 'ecology' as Hogg (1979) defines it is used to denote the complex system in which an individual behaves and functions. Bronfenbrenner (1977) stated that at the centre are the immediate social and physical influences of home, family and friends. School can be seen in a wider community context and a more distant influence is that of the total society with its dominant cultural attitudes and philosophy of life. The pupil's ecology is formed from the number of interdependencies and interrelationships between an individual and her or his behaviour in the environment.)

Nind and Hewitt (1988) express the importance and success of this approach which can be strongly associated with a mother or father's spontaneous interaction with a young infant. A sensitive parent will wait for an infant's unprompted behaviour and then elaborate this response, thus a dialogue-like interaction can be set in motion. Such interaction can be seen as the development of good relationships between teacher and pupil, but additional structure is required to assist development (Hogg, 1979). Nind and Hewitt (1988) point out that such an approach is at odds with a clinical or behavioural curricular approach.

(If such a strucuture is used, the success is largely dependent upon the 'art' of the teacher (Eisner, 1985), this art extending beyond the interactive process to evaluation, the degree of preparation and sensitization and the need for structure. The family and support agencies a pupil is associated with need to be an integral part of the school to gain full understanding of a pupil's ecology, so that appropriate intervention procedures could be established.)

In a period of time when the need to promote self advocacy is recognized, this approach to learning and curricular planning has to be seen as valuable. Only by becoming familiar with the natural unprompted responses of individuals can their own feelings and views on different experiences and situations be gained, their likes and dislikes known.

A Process Model

Stenhouse (1975) proposed that there were four processes comprising education in schools. They are training, instruction, initiation into social norms and values and induction into knowledge. He maintained that the objectives model was appropriate for the first two but breaks down for the third and fourth. If a broad and balanced education is to be offered to all pupils as stipulated by the 1988 Education Reform Act (ERA), this model must be considered. Stenhouse considered that a process model was pertinent in areas of the curriculum that centre on knowledge and understanding. In this curricular design the process is specified, that is, the content being studied, the methods being employed, the concepts involved and an evaluation of the relevance of the activity. Unlike the objectives model the end product is not specified beforehand in terms of behaviours.

If pupils are to gain self advocacy skills, this approach is of obvious value. In terms of the National Curriculum great emphasis has been placed on active learning with the pupil responding as an individual: 'Pupils should observe familiar materials and events in their immediate environment, at first hand using their senses' (Science Attainment Target 1, Level 1, in DES and Welsh Office, 1989c). The teacher has to provide the learning opportunities rather than rigidly control the outcomes as can occur in a behavioural approach.

The Skills Analysis Model (SAM)

This model as described by Gardener, Murphy and Crawford (1983) was designed to incorporate the best elements and theories of different practices in a unified strategy. The model can be used to generate curriculum objectives for children of different ages and with differing needs. In this approach the necessity of involving all the school staff in curricular development is seen as an integral part of the model. No limitation of the schools' curriculum development plans, or rigidity, should be caused by the model. (See Figure 2.1.)

There are obvious possibilities when considering this model in the context of the National Curriculum. School staff would be able to ensure that existing school priorities were maintained if they did not fit into the National Curriculum. Staff using the model today are likely to move away from the strong behavioural emphasis, as would be necessary to incorporate the National Curriculum fully. If this

Figure 2.1: Summary of the Skills Analysis Model

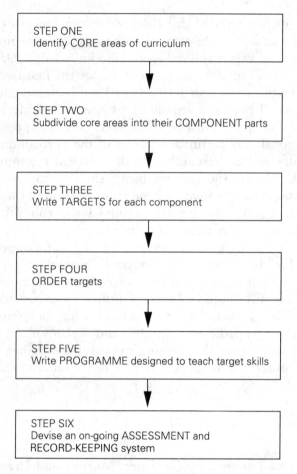

STEP ONE
Identify CORE areas of curriculum

STEP TWO
Subdivide core areas into their COMPONENT parts

STEP THREE
Write TARGETS for each component

STEP FOUR
ORDER targets

STEP FIVE
Write PROGRAMME designed to teach target skills

STEP SIX
Devise an on-going ASSESSMENT and
RECORD-KEEPING system

(From Gardner, Murphy and Crawford, 1983)

model is used on a behavioural basis, it is difficult to ensure all the open curriculum and desired experiential learning are included.

Curriculum Intervention Model

This model (Coupe, 1986) seeks to utilize many of the approaches previously described. The aims and philosophy of the school are an integral part of the model, acting as a foundation for subsequent goals and objectives. The curriculum document to be produced would include the 'what' of education. This model will need minor adjustment if the content of the National Curriculum and the philosophy and aims of recent DES legislation and National Curriculum Council (NCC) documentation are to be included. (See Figure 2.2.)

Part 2 of this model has to be seen as an integral part of the development of the curriculum document because the assessment, programme planning, recording and evaluation, the 'how' of education, will ensure that the curriculum documentation is continually amended and updated to meet the needs of the pupil group it serves. This continual evaluation by 'school staff, parents, governors and all interested agencies' could be utilized to incorporate assessment and recording ideas arising from national and local developments. In this way the curriculum for pupils with SLD could keep a close link with mainstream schools.

Curricular Content

The content of the curriculum in the 1970s and 1980s was determined largely by the staff of the school. Staff were directly influenced by pupils' needs, parents, publications and public opinion. Since this time there have been considerable changes, reducing the overriding influence of the staff and presenting increasing challenges to existing curriculum.

With improved post-natal care (Brudenell, 1986) more brain-damaged children are surviving and this has caused a gradual change in the school population. All teaching staff now need to address the needs of pupils with PMLD who may make up 25 per cent of the school population (Ouvry, 1987). The curriculum these pupils require is significantly different in terms of their access to learning, the multi-disciplinary team involved with the pupil and the necessity for very close parental links (Carpenter, 1989). If learning is to be fostered through interdependent interactions between the pupil and the environment, a close working relationship between the home and school is essential.

Legislation itself has ensured that all parents are closely involved with monitoring the education offered to their children. The 1981 Education Act required that all parents should make written contributions for their child's statement and this is again required when the child is reassessed during their thirteenth year or if reassessment is requested at any other time. (Parents are frequently given help by friends or professionals, preferably those not directly involved in the possible future educational provision, if they find writing such material difficult). Annual reviews are held for each pupil to which parents

31

The Curriculum Challenge

Figure 2.2: Curriculum Intervention Model

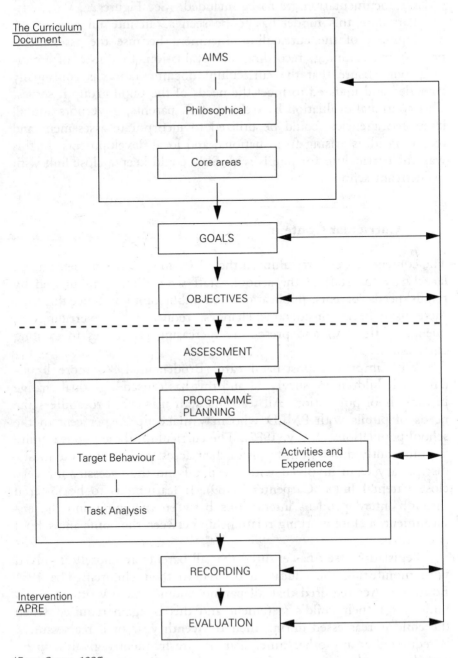

(*From Coupe, 1986*)

legally must be invited. This ensures that there is a forum within the education system for the curriculum each pupil is following to be discussed. Naturally all parents do not find this official meeting the easiest venue at which to express themselves. If regular contact is fostered between home and school, a continual sharing of ideas regarding appropriate areas of educational priorities for each pupil is possible (see Chapter 12 in this volume). Unless the content is agreed by parents, in many areas little generalization may occur. For instance, if a high proportion of time is spent on shopping skills, the parent needs to be in support of this activity and the teacher planning the activity familiar with the shopping facilities near the pupil's home.

Some pupils may attend reviews and have the opportunity to act as their own advocate in terms of curriculum content. This is particularly pertinent in the senior years where the Technical and Vocational Education Initiative (TVEI) can be a significant influence on the curriculum offered. TVEI has led to the development of Records of Achievement and students may now leave with a portfolio that clearly illustrates their achievements. (Records of Achievement have been developed and validated that are appropriate to students of all abilities). Since the development of the National Curriculum the position of Records of Achievement has been questioned (Munby, 1989). This form of curriculum development has been so successful in meeting students' needs in special and mainstream educational settings that it is likely to remain in many schools an area of high priority, although at present outside the government legislation.

The ERA and the subsequent legislation which includes the National Curriculum ensures that *all* parents have access to the curriculum their child is following, and also to information regarding the progress of their child. Many have argued that this recent legislation would not have a major impact on the curriculum offered in schools for pupils with SLD, but this is unlikely to be the case. DES *Circular 22/89* states:

Section III of the statement should specify, in accordance with section 18 of the 1988 Act:

(a) any exceptional arrangement modifying the application of the National Curriculum to the individual pupil. Modification may apply to the attainment targets, programmes of study, or to the testing and assessment arrangements, and

(b) any exceptional arrangements disapplying any aspect

of the National Curriculum from the individual pupil.

Where the exceptional arrangements apply only to specific foundation subjects or other aspects of the National Curriculum, these should be identified. If no modification or exemption is shown in Section III, maintained schools (except those established in a hospital) are obliged to offer all the subjects of the National Curriculum without modification for that pupil at a level appropriate to the pupil's ability unless the provisions of the National Curriculum are excluded or modified by virtue of other provisions made under the 1988 Act. (DES, 1989a, p. 18)

This legislation illustrates clearly the requirement that the education of all pupils should be considered in terms of the content of the National Curriculum. Should the content be deemed inappropriate in any area decisions regarding alternative provision are required.

Future Curricular Development

Few schools for pupils with SLD have clear curriculum documentation regarding all the foundation subjects. Curricular development was influenced by the *Curriculum from 5 to 16* (DES, 1985) which defined the following essential areas of learning:

aesthetic and creative;
human and social;
linguistic and literacy;
mathematical;
moral;
physical;
scientific;
spiritual;
technological.

The booklets within the HMI *Curriculum Matters* series were not felt to address in any depth the needs of this group of pupils, so consequently did not influence significantly the schools' desire to extend their curricular documentation to include these areas. A major influence was the gradual increase in teaching staff who had experience in mainstream schools or in other sectors of special education. Many of these staff would have been accustomed to having some whole school guidance regarding the expected content of areas of learning not seen as part of a core curriculum in this sector of special education. This collaboration between staff from differing backgrounds can lead to curricular documentation that incorporates foundation, core and extended areas of curriculum (Fagg, 1987). When such documentation is readily available to parents, professionals and visitors, the pupil with SLD is seen as part of the total education system, not a totally unique individual but a pupil whose needs are addressed by careful planning within the context of education enjoyed by his peers. Brennan (1979), in a criticism of teachers in special schools, advocates that most 'would benefit from wider acquaintance with the general literature on curriculum development'. If a broader view is taken of the curriculum, pupils will still gain pertinent skills yet enjoy a broad and balanced education. Some schools have traditionally offered a wide range of educational experiences, but many of these did not see fit to document them formally, documentation being based on the core areas of learning only. Billinge (1988) expressed an alternative viewpoint when describing the objectives model of curriculum development as a 'creaking bandwagon'. 'The point of view is expressed that SAM, and other behavioural objectives models, can lead to an unrealistic imbalance with an emphasis on what is being taught rather than what is being learned: approaches which ultimately degrade the learner, the teacher, and the learning process'.

The advent of the National Curriculum, with the emphasis on schools producing their own schemes of work which will incorporate the National Curriculum Programmes of Study and associated Attainment Targets, as well as areas of learning deemed appropriate by the school but not part of the National Curriculum, will ensure that schools look beyond the objectives approach. Baker and Bovair (1989) believe the National Curriculum will ensure that all pupils are entitled to take part in a broad range of experiences. *Curriculum Guidance Two: A Curriculum for All* (NCC, 1989b) gives guidance on how this may be achieved by careful planning. Resources are not infinite and may indeed be very limited in a small all-age special school. Plans to develop access to resources in terms of teachers with expertise in some curricular areas, as well as facilities, may have to be made. Far from curtailing integration opportunities for these young people, it would appear the development of links with other schools would be likely to lead to a broader and more balanced curriculum. *Planning for School Development* (Hargreaves *et al.*, 1989) gives specific directives to help governors, headteachers and teachers move forward into this new educational era.

Change can be exciting and stimulating but it may also result in casualties if not planned carefully. Change in a special school must always involve consultation with parents, the whole school staff and any support agencies involved in the school. In terms of curricular change this group of people is likely to keep at the forefront of their minds the need for the curriculum for pupils with SLD to incorporate throughout communication skills, independence skills and the opportunity to develop self advocacy skills. Recent legislative changes now ensure the development of the school curriculum is not the sole responsibility of school staff. The 1980 Education Act established a place for teachers and parents on the governing body, and obliged the governors to publish information about the school and its curriculum. The Education (No. 2) Act 1986 included community representation on the governing body and, looking forward to the 1988 Education Act, gave the governors the responsibility of making sure that the curriculum of the school reflected the requirements of the various Education Acts. Cooperation and consultation that includes shared learning experiences between the school staff and governors in terms of the National Curriculum is obviously the way forward. Curriculum is now influenced by far more variables and new models will arise.

One Way Forward

Halliday (1988), when discussing curriculum development, points out the need to consider the influences upon the curriculum. A curriculum is written for pupils and the physical, sensory, medical, emotional, linguistic and intellectual needs of the group need to be considered. All aspects of the National Curriculum need to be considered for every pupil. Some may well question the issue of a modern foreign language, but do we not teach a significant number of our pupils in a modern foreign language every day? The pupils whose mother tongue is Gujerati, and whose intellectual impairment is such that their understanding of that language is as yet at an early level, could surely benefit from work carried out in another language — their own.

The staff in any school are the major resource and the characteristics associated with a teacher include open-mindedness, flexibility of style, enthusiasm, care and understanding, ability to self evaluate, planning and recording skills, teamwork and motivation. The school itself has characteristics worthy of consideration, and learning should be:⁾

> pupil centred and relevant;
> experiential not passive;
> problem solving;
> positive and success based;
> enjoyable yet challenging;
> preparing for the next stage in life;
> broad, balanced and differentiated;
> easily accessed. (Halliday, 1988)

(The school itself should be dynamic not static, being influenced by parents, governors, LEA, national government, and thus be similar to mainstream schools.)

Planning for Balance in the Curriculum

This model (see Figure 2.3), having considered much of the above, can be seen to readily incorporate the National Curriculum within the existing school practice. The curriculum should balance the needs the individual pupil shares with his or her peers within the community and the special educational needs. Linking throughout the model helps ensure that the work of pupils is continually evaluated, this evaluation itself reflecting on the success, relevance and balance of the curriculum offered.

There can be no final answer to curriculum development in any school. The National Curriculum itself, now an area of vital importance, is likely to be amended as time goes on. Documents produced in relation to these materials, such as *National Curriculum: From Policy to Practice* (DES, 1989b) and *Curriculum Guidance One: A Framework for the Primary Curriculum* (NCC, 1989a) ensure that the curriculum remains dynamic as educationalists discuss changes and how these can be implemented with success for the pupil within the classroom.

Curriculum development goes on but, perhaps, it is now no longer only in the hands of the school but of society. As Pring (1989) points out, 'the principles of curriculum development are: breadth, differentiation, continuity — and agreement on essential areas of knowledge, understanding and skills'. Only time and evaluation will enable us to understand how much the whole school curriculum has been influenced by the National Curriculum. If schools are to ensure

Figure 2.3: *Planning for balance in the curriculum*

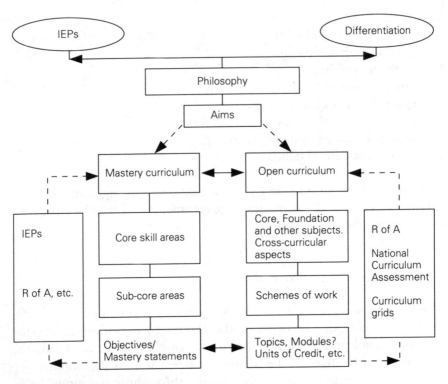

IEP — Individual Educational Programme
R of A — Record of Achievement
– – – – implies means of evaluation

(From Halliday, 1990)

their existing good practice is not lost by staff being unduly influenced by all the changes, curriculum planning is essential within the school and in consultation with colleagues locally and nationally.

References

AHERNE, P., THORNBER, A., FAGG, S. and SKELTON, S. (1990) *Mathematics for All*, London, David Fulton.

AINSCOW, M. and TWEDDLE, D. (1979) *Preventing Classroom Failure*, Chichester, John Wiley and Sons.

AINSCOW, M. and TWEDDLE, D. (1984) *Early Learning Skills Analysis*, London, David Fulton.

BAKER, D. and BOVAIR, K. (Eds) (1989) *Making the Special Schools Ordinary?*, Volume 1, London, Falmer Press.

BILLINGE, R. (1988) 'The objectives model of curriculum development: a creaking bandwagon?', *Mental Handicap*, 16, pp. 26–9.

BLUMA, S., SHEARER, M., FROHMAN, A. and HILLARD, J. (1976) *The Portage Guide to Early Education*, Wisconsin, Cooperative Education Service.

BRENNAN, W.K. (1979) *The Curricular Needs of Slow Learners*, London, Evans/Methuen Educational.

BRONFENBRENNER, V. (1977) 'Toward an experimental ecology of human development', *American Psychologist*, 32, pp. 513–31.

BRUDENELL, P. (1986) *The Other Side of Profound Handicap*, Basingstoke, Macmillan.

CARDEN, N. (1986) 'The development of cognition and perception', in COUPE, J. and PORTER, J. (Eds) *The Education of Children with Severe Learning Difficulties*, Beckenham, Croom Helm.

CARPENTER, B. (1989) 'The curriculum for children with profound and multiple learning difficulties: current issues', *Early Child Development and Care*, 46, pp. 87–96.

CHESELDINE, S.E. and JEFFREE, D.M. (1981) *The Path Project: Handicapped School Leavers and their Families*, Manchester, Hester Adrian Research Centre, Manchester University.

COUPE, J. (1986) 'The Curriculum Intervention Model', in COUPE, J. and PORTER, J. (Eds) *The Education of Children with Severe Learning Difficulties*, Beckenham, Croom Helm.

DES (1970) *The Education (Handicapped Children) Act 1970*, London, HMSO.

DES (1978) *Special Educational Needs* (The Warnock Report), London, HMSO.

DES (1981a) *The Education Act 1981*, London, HMSO.

DES (1981b) *Circular 6/81: The School Curriculum*, London, DES.

DES (1985) *The Curriculum from 5 to 16*, London, HMSO.

DES (1986) *The Education (No. 2) Act 1986*, London, HMSO.

DES (1988) *The Education Reform Act 1988*, London, HMSO.

DES (1989a) *Circular 22/89: Assessments and Statements of Special Educational Needs: Procedures Within the Education, Health and Social Services*, London, DES.

DES (1989b) *National Curriculum: From Policy to Practice*, London, DES.

DES AND WELSH OFFICE (1989a) *English in The National Curriculum (Key Stage 1)*, London, HMSO.

DES AND WELSH OFFICE (1989b) *Mathematics in the National Curriculum*, London, HMSO.

DES AND WELSH OFFICE (1989c) *Science in the National Curriculum*, London, HMSO.

DESSENT, T. (1984) *What's Important About Portage?* Windsor, NFER.

EISNER, E.W. (1985) *The Educational Imagination on the Design and Evaluation of School Programs*, 2nd edition, New York, McMillan.

FAGG, S. (1987) *Piper Hill School Curriculum*, Manchester, Manchester Education Committee.

FAGG, S., AHERNE, P., SKELTON, S. and THORNBER, A. (1990) *Entitlement for All*, London, David Fulton.

FOXEN, T. and MCBRIEN, J. (1981) *Training Staff in Behavioural Methods, Trainee Workbook*, Manchester, Manchester University Press.

GARDNER, J., MURPHY, J. and CRAWFORD, N. (1983) *The Skills Analysis Model*, Kidderminster, BIMH.

HALLIDAY, P. (1990) *Planning for Balance the Curriculum in Salford: Towards a Senior Curriculum*, Salford, Salford Local Education Authority.

HARGREAVES, D., HOPKINS, D., LEASK, M., CONNOLLY, J. and ROBINSON, P. (1989) *Planning for School Development: Advice to Governors, Headteachers and Teachers*, London, DES.

HOGG, J. (Ed.) (1979) *The First Two Years*, Hertford, Barnardo.

HOGG, J. and SEBBA, J. (1986) *Profound Retardation and Multiple Impairment*, Volumes 1 and 2, London, Croom Helm.

ILEA (1985) *Educational Opportunities for All?* (The Fish Report) London, Inner London Education Authority.

MCBRIEN, J. and FOXEN, T. (1981) *Training Staff in Behavioural Methods; Instructors Handbook*, Manchester, Manchester University Press.

MUNBY, S. (1989) 'The month records died', *Times Educational Supplement*, 29 September.

NCC (1989a) *Curriculum Guidance One: A Framework for the Primary Curriculum*, York, National Curriculum Council.

NCC (1989b) *Curriculum Guidance Two: A Curriculum for All*, York, National Curriculum Council.

NIND, M. and HEWITT, D. (1988) 'Interaction as curriculum', *British Journal of Special Education*, 15, 2, pp. 55–7.

OUVRY, C. (1987) *Educating Children with Profound Handicaps*, Kidderminster, BIMH.

PIAGET, J. (1953) *The Origin of Intelligence in the Child*, London, Routledge and Kegan Paul.

PORTER, J. (1985) 'Beyond a simple behavioural approach', in COUPE, J. and PORTER, J. (Eds) *The Education of Children with Severe Learning Difficulties*, Beckenham, Croom Helm.

PRING, R. (1989) *The New Curriculum*, London, Cassell Education.

RECTORY PADDOCK SCHOOL (1983) *In Search of a Curriculum*, Sidcup, Robin Wren Publications.

STENHOUSE, L. (1975) *An Introduction to Curriculum Research and Development*, London, Open University/Heinemann.

TYLER, R. (1949) *Basic Principles of Curriculum and Instruction*, Chicago, University of Chicago Press.

UZGIRIS, I.C. and HUNT, J.McV. (1975) *Assessment in Infancy: Ordinal Scales of Infant Development*, Urbana, University of Illinois Press.

WILSON, M. (1981) *The Curriculum in Special Schools*, London, Schools Council/Longman.

3   Access for Pupils with Profound and Multiple Learning Difficulties

Carol Ouvry

A Retrospective

With the passing of the Education Reform Act (ERA) in 1988 the pace of curriculum development in schools for pupils with severe learning difficulties (SLD) has suddenly accelerated. At the same time the content and ways of working have been called into question, particularly where pupils with profound and multiple learning difficulties (PMLD) are concerned, by the need to establish firmly the right for all pupils to participate in the National Curriculum, irrespective of the extent or degree of their disabilities.

Curriculum planning is an ever-changing process and this chapter attempts to examine the way in which the new developments in education relate to previous approaches in the teaching of pupils with PMLD, and to suggest ways in which implementation of the National Curriculum can make a positive contribution to the ongoing process of curriculum development.

Although precipitating rather abruptly a radical rethinking of the structure, content and methods of delivery, the National Curriculum can be seen as the latest in a series of phases in the teaching of pupils with PMLD which began in 1971 when provision for children and young people with SLD was transferred from the Health Authorities and became the responsibility of the Local Education Authorities.

A retrospective look at these phases will show how far we have come in these two decades in our knowledge and understanding of the complexity of the learning difficulties of this group of pupils, and may perhaps help us to view the current developments more as a springboard to further development than a threat to existing practice.

Phase I — Tender Loving Care

Initially, curriculum development focused on the majority of pupils in ESN(S) schools (Schools for the Educationally Subnormal (Severe) as they then were), and the learning needs of the minority of pupils with PMLD were largely unrecognized rather than ignored, as their need for care was so great and so obvious that this took priority over all else. In the 'special care' class, care and therapy (where appropriate) prevailed. Even those teachers who had a special education qualification were unprepared for the severity and complexity of impairments they were faced with in the 'special care' class, and there was no fund of experience relating to the teaching of these pupils for teachers to draw upon. In addition they were often quite isolated within the school both geographically and professionally, with few, if any, other colleagues with whom to discuss the particular problems of teaching this group of pupils.

The curriculum for the rest of the school rarely acknowledged the presence of these pupils and individual teachers were generally left to devise activities for the pupils in their class, and develop a curriculum which was seen as separate, more limited, and less rigorous than the main school curriculum. Teachers were feeling their way and this was a period of getting to know the pupils for the profession as a whole. It was as much a learning process for the staff as for the pupils.

Phase II — Stimulation

The limitations in terms of opportunity for learning became apparent in an environment where the emphasis was upon caring activities, and it became generally accepted that the pupils should be exposed to a highly stimulating environment to counteract the passivity, or learned helplessness, which is a common characteristic of many pupils with PMLD.

Sensory stimulation involving all the senses became the main approach and much time and ingenuity were devoted to devising equipment and activities which would be stimulating to the pupils and create an active and busy atmosphere. Classroom displays were designed to catch the attention, and a forest of mobiles might be suspended from the wall, ceilings or frames. All stimulation tended to be regarded as positive and any activity was better than no activity.

Since the pupils' attention control is likely to be at a very early stage of development in which they are unable to filter information or sustain attention in the presence of competing stimuli, this bombardment of the senses is likely to raise the general level of arousal and increase alertness (which may be positive in itself), but it will not necessarily result in any purposeful or functional behaviour or learning, because of the confusion which is counterproductive in terms of understanding the environment and learning new skills to use in the environment.

However, this approach did acknowledge the vital role of motivation and the need for greater opportunities for pupils to engage actively with their surroundings.

Phase III — The Behavioural Approach

The behavioural techniques which were adopted in ESN(S) schools in the 1970s were recognized as being equally appropriate for pupils with PMLD. They were seen as the remedy for the disadvantages of the stimulation approach in providing structure, purpose and precision in the teaching of pupils with PMLD. These techniques are so widely documented and used in schools for pupils with SLD that no description is necessary here.

The advantage of the behavioural approach lies in the fact that it provided a long term perspective and expectation of progress, and the analysis of tasks revealed the complexity of the demands which even apparently simple tasks make upon pupils with PMLD. This focused attention upon the sequence of development and the processes involved in learning, and the subtleties of presentation necessary to elicit the desired responses from the pupils. Individual teaching in a one-to-one situation became central to the pupils' individual programme and indeed is often still regarded as 'the programme'. The detailed recording methods showed that progress, even if slow, could be achieved by even the most disabled pupil if the expectations and presentation of the task were at the right level. This resulted in a more positive view of the curriculum, which was seen to be closer to that of the rest of the school as the same approach was used within the same framework, albeit at a different level, and what the teachers in the 'special care' class were doing became recognizable to all as 'teaching' as opposed to 'stimulating' or even 'entertaining'! The analytical approach and more positive attitudes have been reflected in a growing number of publications which illustrate individual teaching programmes (Kiernan, 1981; Kiernan, Jordan and Saunders, 1978; Simon, 1981), or which describe curriculum models which were specifically designed, or are particularly appropriate, for this group of pupils (McInnes and Tref-frey, 1982; Bailey, no date; Hogg and Sebba, 1986; Ouvry, 1987). This increase in published materials has been matched by an increase in the availability of commercially produced equipment and other resources.

There are other benefits associated with the use of behavioural techniques. Because behavioural techniques are precise and structured, it is comparatively easy to explain them and therefore to use other classroom staff as teaching assistants rather than welfare assistants, thus increasing the expertise and time available for direct teaching within the classroom. Careful classroom organization and deployment of staff is necessary, and different models have been used to make the best use of the skills and experience of everyone in the classroom. These include the use of designated key workers for one-to-one teaching, small group work and variations on the 'room management' system (Sturmey and Crisp, 1986) which is probably the most sophis-ticated of the models of organization currently used in schools.

However, too great a reliance upon behavioural techniques for curriculum delivery can lead to a very narrow educational experience. The very prescriptive method of teaching which demands that the pupil makes a response which is predetermined by the teacher does not encourage spontaneous behaviours on the part of the pupil and may prevent the teacher from building upon them. There are particu-lar difficulties in working with pupils with PMLD because of the commonly found characteristics of a low level of responding, incon-sistency of response from day to day, and often stereotyped patterns of responding (Porter, 1986), as well as the extreme difficulty in maintaining and generalizing skills. This unreliability makes it difficult to determine whether a pupil has achieved the objective, with the result that a pupil may continue to be on a particular programme for long periods of time.

Additionally, behavioural objectives are not equally applicable to all facets of the curriculum, and there is an experiential element to education as well as observable responses to a given situation. Billinge (1988) comments that there is a danger that 'areas of teaching which are difficult to account for in precise terms may simply be ignored', and frequently the periods between the individual sessions are con-sidered less important, although the potential for learning is now generally recognized, even if it is not always as carefully analyzed and planned. Although there is no suggestion that the behavioural approach does not have a place in the teaching of children with PMLD, it should be regarded as an extremely effective method when used appropriately and it should be used sparingly, as and when it seems to be the most likely way to help a child to learn.

Ager (1989) suggests that many of the principles underlying the behavioural approach — freedom from distraction, encouraging attitude, clear goals, accurate assessment — are all elements of good teaching practice. The precision of planning and observation required can also be an extremely effective learning situation for teachers, not least in getting to know the pupils and the unique combination of abilities and needs which each one presents. Experienced teachers will incorporate the individual objectives of pupils at appropriate levels into activities of all kinds. It may be helpful for teachers new to the field to use one-to-one teaching and behavioural methods, before they are able to broaden their approach to the use of group sessions and experiential activities, while still maintaining precision and individual objectives for all pupils within an apparently less structured session.

Phase IV — The Holistic Approach

During the last few years a broader approach which redresses the balance has been gaining ground. This considers all facets of the pupil's development and the pupil's environment as an interactive system. There has been an upsurge of interest and research relevant to the processes and necessary conditions for learning to take place in the early stages of development. This has demonstrated the extreme importance of an environment which provides a meaningful context and encourages interactions between the pupil and other people or objects in the surroundings. Although interactive and intuitive approaches have been used for many years, as in Sherborne Movement, there has been a renewed interest based upon research findings, and inter-personal interactions have, in some cases, become central to the whole curriculum (Nind and Hewitt, 1988) and are no longer linked to specific sessions or periods of the day.

The context for learning is also receiving much more serious attention to ensure that it provides the clues the pupils need for understanding of their surroundings and to make activities more meaningful. The permanent features of the environment form a stable and familiar background which the pupils can recognize and in which they feel at ease. This will prepare them for the familiar routines and activities, and allow them to focus on the experiences which are offered. The changing context will be related to the different activities throughout the day, and should be carefully planned to intensify the features which identify each situation, so that the pupils can recognize the activity, and anticipate their role, and thus enable them to be active participants. It is plainly much easier to create a meaningful and relevant context for group activities than it is when pupils are withdrawn for one-to-one work on their 'programmes', where the skill being taught quite often bears little relation to the situation in which it is taught.

There are various strategies and methods of analyzing activities which can help the teacher to ensure that the pupils have the maximum chance of situational understanding. Harris (1987) has described the characteristics of activities which enable them to be understood at a non-verbal level and refers to Nelson's concept of a generalized mental representation which children build up about activities to which they are repeatedly exposed. The implication is that if the activity and context are carefully planned and continuity maintained the pupils will, after a time, have a general feeling of what it is all about. Even if they are not able to understand the sub-routines which make up the activity at a more complex level, they are able to participate to some extent in any recurrent situation even if this involves an affective rather than a behavioural response.

Apart from each pupil's individual objectives, many of which can be embedded into a wide variety of situations, there are certain skills which are essential in all situations and form the foundations for further learning. These skills include the ability to focus and sustain attention, and to filter out competing stimuli which are not relevant to the situation; the ability to interact purposefully both with people, through commonly understood patterns of interaction, and with objects, by developing a repertoire of actions which are then available for purposeful goal directed behaviour.

Opportunities for encouraging the development of attention control, interaction patterns and appropriate actions at all levels exist in virtually all activities, although some obviously offer some opportunities to develop certain skills than others. Unlike the 'stimulation phase' with the implicit assumptions that learning would take place, we are now aware that careful planning and analysis of the environment and the activity is necessary to make this learning possible and effective.

This approach, which emphasizes the context for learning and the basic skills which form the foundation for learning, is essential in implementing integration schemes within the school where the time and opportunity for one-to-one teaching is more limited than in a special class which may be organized for this way of working, and it will also be valuable in the implementation of the National Curriculum and in ensuring that the curriculum on offer is both broad and balanced as required by the ERA.

These phases are not, of course, discrete periods one following the other, but have evolved gradually as models of good practice which have been widely adopted. They have overlapped and the best from each phase has been retained.

The National Curriculum

Although the National Curriculum can be seen as the latest phase in the process of curriculum development, it is unlike the previous phases in that it is being externally developed, and has very specific requirements which were not designed with the educational needs of pupils with PMLD in mind.

The early expectation, which was widespread, that certain categories of pupils, and among them those with PMLD, would not be required to follow the National Curriculum has now changed. The implications of wholesale exemption from the National Curriculum for any group of pupils, and particularly those with PMLD (and where do we draw the line?), are serious. Firstly, it would be an immediate reversion to the situation before the 1970 Education (Handicapped Children) Act, where our group of pupils (then ESN[S]) were excluded from education as provided for all other pupils.

Even with the best intentions regarding appropriate provision, how long would it be, with the current pressures on teacher time, before the exempted group were deemed not to need qualified teachers, in spite of evidence which shows that the learning needs are so complex that the intellectual, physical and emotional demands on teachers are particularly great? Loss of qualified teachers would inevitably result in a change of emphasis towards personal care and occupation in many situations.

The implications for resourcing an exempted group are also grave. When so many demands are being made to resource the National Curriculum, whether these are accommodation, equipment and materials, specialist staff, or inservice training, the chances of generous resourcing in any of these areas for an exempted group must be less likely. Many educationalists with no direct experience of these pupils might well be relieved if this was one group which they no longer had to consider within the National Curriculum.

Integration of pupils with PMLD into the regular classes within the SLD school, let alone the mainstream sector, would be likely to become much more difficult if they were following a different curriculum, and they might find themselves even more separate as their peer groups in regular classes drew closer to their mainstream counterparts, and they drew further away. Because they are a relatively small group of pupils, any group exemption would inevitably magnify the resulting segregation and increase their isolation, whereas the stated entitlement of all pupils to participate actively in the National Curriculum brings education for the pupils with PMLD firmly within the curriculum followed by all pupils, and should therefore be a positive impetus towards integration. Teachers must be committed to ensuring that the entitlement to participate in the National Curriculum is demanded and achieved, despite any adaptations necessary to ensure that it is appropriate and that their participation is accepted as valid.

However, avoiding the unwelcome consequences of exclusion from the National Curriculum is not, on its own, enough reason for insisting upon entitlement. There must be a positive gain in educational terms for pupils with PMLD.

A major concern for teachers is to retain the good practice while participating to the fullest possible extent in the National Curriculum. There are many issues involved, but as new regulations and guidance for pupils with special educational needs are made available, the ways in which flexibility and relevance can be achieved become clearer. The initially perceived threat of an irrelevant and unwieldy curriculum is diminishing, and the potential benefits, even for pupils with PMLD, are being recognized. The assertion, which is frequently repeated, that the National Curriculum is a necessary, but not sufficient, part of the whole curriculum is reassuring, as this creates the space to include the best of the existing PMLD curriculum. Our task is to integrate the national and the developmental curricula and incorporate them, with the special programmes already being carried out, into a coherent and relevant experience for pupils with PMLD.

There seem to be two major questions — can the National Curriculum be a positive influence in the process of curricular development for pupils with PMLD, and is it compatible with the approaches which are currently considered good practice for working with this group of pupils?

There are, of course, positive educational benefits from working within the National Curriculum, and with ingenuity it can be used as an agent of progress rather than as a limitation of effective development and delivery. The principles of entitlement to a broad and balanced curriculum which is relevant and differentiated, and provides both continuity and progress, are exactly what we would wish for pupils with PMLD. If the National Curriculum makes us re-examine our priorities and methodology and extend our thinking about the curriculum on offer, this can only be to their benefit.

Breadth and balance are issues which are particularly relevant to pupils with PMLD. Because of the very specific educational and developmental needs of pupils with multiple disabilities there is always the danger of focusing too narrowly on the more obvious areas of need, such as eating and drinking, the next step in physical development, or perhaps sensory awareness, and sacrificing other areas of development which are more difficult to define in behavioural terms and depend to a large extent upon experiential objectives and a context which is meaningful to the pupils. As we examine the Statements of Attainment for each Attainment Target, our concept of the possible curriculum content is widened. Even a quick glance through the associated Programmes of Study will suggest a number of new activities or ways of extending activities we already use, to increase the range of experiences and learning opportunities we offer.

However, there is no question that the curriculum must be guided by the learning needs of the pupils and not the need to conform to the National Curriculum. The curriculum on offer must reflect the collective learning needs of all the pupils in the class and will be composite, incorporating the relevant elements of the National Curriculum, the developmental curriculum and any additional elements necessary to cater for the individual needs of the pupils.

The National Curriculum states that all subjects should be studied for a 'reasonable time' and there is no prescribed proportion of time specified for any subject. This allows flexibility in planning the most effective delivery of the curriculum. Time is at a premium for pupils with PMLD as there are many calls upon it which are not, on the face of it, educational. These may include personal welfare, physiotherapy, and even the extra time taken to position a group for an activity or to move around the school. However, every activity has the potential for teaching and learning and we are used to capitalizing on this where pupils with PMLD are concerned. These activities should be subjected to the same analysis as the formal teaching sessions.

Balance should not be regarded as every subject being covered at any one time, or for equal periods of time, but should be seen in terms of each pupil's need. If a concentrated effort is called for to help the pupil to progress in any given area this should be a priority for the time being. However, a particular danger for pupils who are most severely disabled, and for whom progress is sometimes almost imperceptible, is that a very restricted 'programme' may be continued for over-long periods of time. Although it is necessary to allow enough time for learning to take place, the continuation of certain activities, sometimes for years, may well be counterproductive as motivation diminishes with over-familiarity and progress is not demonstrated. The decision to abandon a stated objective, however developmentally valid it may be, or to change the approach used, can be quite arbitrary and may be the result of a change of teachers, rather than a considered decision, and a system of monitoring programmes in the long term is essential. Because of the need for concentrated work and continuity over a period of time, some activities might be planned as modules so that breadth and balance are achieved over a longer period rather than being evident at any one point in time.

This modular approach is particularly useful when introducing new activities, perhaps associated with particular Attainment Targets, or when sharing scarce resources such as a swimming pool, riding or specialist teaching areas or equipment. It has the added advantage that a module can be repeated at a later stage, with any changes necessary to take account of progress in the meantime. This can overcome the potential conflict between breadth and balance on the one hand, and continuity and time needed to make progress on the other.

Progress in terms of acquiring demonstrable skills can be very slow, and in some areas progress might be defined in terms of a pupil gradually building up an increasingly wide range of experiences. The use of modules can provide the opportunity for progression from one activity to another in addition to achieving behavioural objectives. Thus the notion of modules and of the spiral curriculum, in which learning experiences are repeated, can reconcile continuity and progress with variety and an increasing range of experiences. 'Reasonable time' will relate the individual pupil's needs and progress, and the collective needs of the class, to the periods of time allotted to the various education experiences offered. Time can be considered in several dimensions: the individual teaching sessions; the daily or weekly timetable; the half-termly or termly schemes of work; even the academic year.

These principles stated in the ERA which relate to the National Curriculum are clearly compatible with, and indeed should enhance, good practice in teaching pupils with PMLD, but 'the right to share in the curriculum ... does not automatically ensure access to it, nor progress within it' (NCC, 1989, p. 1).

When we consider the curriculum content, the task of integrating the National Curriculum and the existing PMLD curriculum certainly seems formidable. However, the initial steps of curriculum matching and identifying similarities and differences between the two curricula is made easier by the fact that the structure of the National Curriculum, although more complex, resembles the curriculum structure already in use in many SLD schools. Although the core and foundation subjects do not all equate easily with existing areas of the PMLD curriculum, a more detailed consideration of the Attainment Targets and Programmes of Study shows that, in fact, those subjects which seem most obviously to match, such as English with Communication and Language, may prove more problematical because of the high level of knowledge and skills assumed to be acquired during the preschool years. Science, which is not likely to have been identified in the existing PMLD curriculum, makes no such assumptions (that scientific knowledge will be gained in preschool years), and it incorporates much of the work included in the early sensory and cognitive areas of the PMLD curriculum. Whether this will hold true for subjects as unfamiliar as History and Geography remains to be seen. We should, therefore, never assume that any subject, or part of a subject, should be automatically excluded from the curriculum on offer, and we must examine every Attainment Target and the associated Programmes of Study, before we make any decisions about the relevance for pupils with PMLD.

The Attainment Targets cause concern on several counts. Although the Statements of Attainment are written in the form of objectives, they are sometimes couched in less precise terms than is usually used in SLD schools. Words such as 'know', 'understand', 'identify', need to be qualified since the usual and assumed means of demonstrating this knowledge and understanding through language or actions is not available for this group. We are used to specifying responses, particular to each pupil, which we would accept as demonstrating such knowledge and understanding. However, it is no more difficult to be sure that a pupil knows and understands within the National Curriculum than it is to be sure in the existing curriculum.

The implicit assumptions of skills and knowledge already acquired during the preschool years makes Level 1 of many of the Attainment Targets out of reach of pupils with PMLD. The number of Statements of Attainment which are relevant and attainable exactly as they stand seems to be a relatively small proportion of the total. However, there are some which are already part of the PMLD curriculum, for example:

Science (DES and Welsh Office, 1989a):

AT 1.1a   observe familiar materials and events in their immediate environment at first hand using the senses;

AT 1.2b   identify simple differences, for example, hot/cold, rough/smooth;

AT 14.1   know that sounds can be made in a variety of ways.

English (DES and Welsh Office, 1989b):

AT 1.1c   respond appropriately to simple instructions given by a teacher.

There are many Attainment Targets which, flexibly interpreted, need little qualification and where learning routes within the Statements of Attainment seem quite clear:

Science (DES and Welsh Office, 1989a):

AT 3.1a   be able to name or label the external parts of the human body/plants, e.g. arm/leg, flower/plant/stem.

The learning route would involve developing awareness of, and imitation of, body movements involving trunk and limbs, and responding to facial features and expressions by taking part in a variety of movement activities focusing on body awareness and control. For many pupils, however, the part which relates to plants would probably have to be experiential rather than aiming at demonstrable knowledge.

Science (DES and Welsh Office, 1989a):

AT 3.2c   be able to give a simple account of the pattern of their own day.

Learning routes would involve anticipating the sequence of events within an activity, anticipating the sequence of activities within a session, a day, a week, using systematic cueing of regular activities and routines, and the use of objects or signs as symbols of events.

Some Attainment Targets are accessible in part on an experiential rather than an achievement basis, and this should be regarded as valid participation if this basis can be justified.

English (DES and Welsh Office, 1989b):

> AT 1.1a participate as speakers and listeners in group activities, including imaginative play.

Many group activities involve listening and possibly the expectation of vocal or physical response, whether this is a group drinks session, drama games (involving imaginative situations and different roles) or story telling with or without props.

Science (DES and Welsh Office, 1989a):

> AT 1.1 be able to describe familiar and unfamiliar objects in terms of simple properties, for example, shape, colour, texture, and describe how they behave when they are, for example, squashed and stretched.

Much of the perceptual work with pupils with PMLD involves becoming aware of the properties of various objects and substances. However, this AT requires us to do more than give a random selection of 'feelies' or toys to a pupil and we should spend time in selecting particular properties and providing similarity or contrast within those properties to provide a more structured learning situation.

There are, of course, a number of Attainment Targets which on consideration may be judged not to be relevant to pupils with PMLD, either because they demand a level of cognitive development beyond their capabilities or because they are unlikely to be relevant to any of the pupils in their present or future lifestyle:

Mathematics (DES and Welsh Office, 1989c):

> AT 2.1a count, read, write and order numbers to at least 10; know that the size of a set is given by the last number in the count.

Any pupil, however multiply disabled, who could recognize and differentiate between 2D symbols or manipulate numbers in this way would be totally misplaced in a group of pupils with PMLD in a special school.

There are surprisingly few Attainment Targets in the core subjects at Level 1 which can be considered to be totally inappropriate, and even these may act as facilitators of new approaches or new avenues of experience and thus contribute to the breadth of the learning experience.

Having examined the Attainment Targets and the Programmes of Study for each subject, some method of recording is necessary, not only as evidence of what parts of the National Curriculum are on offer to the pupils but as a reference source when devising each pupil's individual programme or amending the Statements of Special Educational Need. The format used should be capable of showing which targets are appropriate as they stand; which need to be flexibly interpreted either by rewording or experiential participation; and which are to be lifted/omitted because they are deemed to be inappropriate.

In addition, the alternative curriculum which takes the place of those parts which have been lifted (DES, 1989b) or makes provision for those subjects outside the National Curriculum (NCC, 1990) must also be recorded and the links between the two curricula established. This will be likely to include those elements of the existing curriculum which are not addressed by the National Curriculum. In English, for example, this might be establishing those interaction patterns which are the foundations for interpersonal communication and the communication system whether formal or idiosyncratic, which takes the place of conventional speech. There will also be a need to include some elements of the PMLD curriculum such as Personal and Social Education (PSE), in particular self-help and independence skills, which have been identified as dimensions of cross-curricular teaching but for pupils with PMLD are an important part of the main curriculum. Special programmes such as physiotherapy, music therapy and other specialist input should also feature as being supplementary to the curriculum.

Another question which is quite frequently raised is whether it would be advantageous to create new levels appropriate to the earlier stages of learning covered by the developmental curriculum. In *Curriculum Guidance Two: A Curriculum for All*, it is suggested that 'some pupils will need specially designed schemes of work which provide access to Level 1 in foundation subjects or which break down the elements of Programmes of Study into a series of finely graded, age appropriate, achievable steps' (NCC, 1989, p. 8). There is certainly a need to identify progressive learning steps within Level 1 in order to show each pupil's stage of operating, and to allow progress to be demonstrated even if some pupils are working on activities associated with Level 1 in all ATs in all subjects for perhaps the whole of their school life. Some school curricula already specify steps which can be incorporated into Programmes of Study and schemes of work relating to National Curriculum subjects, and work is also being done on a series of developmental stages which can be applied across the curriculum and across the ability range of pupils with SLD. This model would identify the level that each pupil is operating at within each Attainment Target. However, there is, as yet, no suggestion that there should be a nationally accepted model. Although it might seem desirable and save time in the initial work necessary to implement the National Curriculum in the classroom, it would also mean the sacrifice of some of the flexibility and differentiation which is so vital when working with pupils with such complex needs.

Many people are extremely concerned about the fact that some pupils will never achieve, let alone progress beyond, Level 1 in most or all Attainment Targets. The notion of 'working towards' is unacceptable because of the implication that the work is sequential and the goal is that stated in the Statements of Attainment which may never be achieved, or may take many years to achieve. The notion of 'working within' Level 1 is much more flexible in that it implies that the work is related to and guided by the Statements of Attainment, but that the learning routes are not necessarily sequential and the goals may be experiential and affective rather than behavioural or skill orientated. The pupils will thus be participating in the National Curriculum but the schemes of work will be able to take their learning needs and experiences into account.

Perhaps the greatest concern of all is whether the requirements of the National Curriculum will make such demands that existing good practice, and the development of new approaches, will be severely constrained.

National Curriculum: From Policy to Practice (DES, 1989a) states that 'the use of subjects to define the National Curriculum does not mean that teaching has to be organized and delivered within prescribed subject boundaries, and cross-curricular themes and activities are particularly appropriate for these pupils for whom the processes of learning are similar within a variety of activities'.

The emphasis on cross-curricular teaching, particularly in the early stages of learning, is very encouraging, and the elaboration of the concept with the identification of dimensions, skills and themes is a useful framework for considering the teaching approaches and methods used in delivery of the curriculum as a whole.

The dimensions which are expected to permeate the whole timetable, are as valid for pupils with PMLD as for all other pupils. However, as mentioned previously, PSE is so vital for those pupils and the personal welfare needs make such demands upon the available teaching time that these aspects of it must be subjected to at least as rigorous analysis as other core curriculum areas. It is, nevertheless, quite reasonably also seen as an element of cross-curricular teaching in that the activities relating to PSE provide opportunities for working on targets in many other curriculum areas such as communication, gross and fine motor skills, perceptual and cognitive skills. It thus makes links between different parts of the curriculum, and the activities involved provide a meaningful context which enhances the pupil's situational understanding and facilitates functional learning and reinforcement of practical skills.

The cross-curricular skills identified — communication, problem solving and study skills — which are developed through all subjects are very broad but are equally valid for pupils with PMLD at their own level. The National Curriculum demonstrates the fact that there are certain skills which are incorporated into ATs in all subjects, for example, the ability to verbalize observations, report back on work of any kind. The holistic approach described in the introduction to this chapter also recognizes that there are certain essential elements which are foundations for learning in all subjects and situations. The skills identified by the National Curriculum can be further analyzed and linked with these elements: communication with interaction skills; problem solving is based on early interactions and manipulation of objects and situational understanding; study skills are dependent upon developing attention control as well as social interaction skills.

The themes are described as elements which enrich the educational experience of pupils, and several topics are identified which are 'more structured and less pervasive' than the other aspects of cross-curricular teaching, but still make links between different parts of the curriculum. Most of the themes specified can be seen to be, at the very least, useful avenues of experience.

The notion of linking all areas of the curriculum is particularly important for pupils with PMLD to avoid fragmented learning, isolated experiences with no functional meaning for the pupils, and to consolidate the basic skills needed for progress in all areas of the curriculum. In practice it is virtually impossible to isolate any one 'subject' in the existing curriculum although each activity will have its own emphasis, and this can be used to advantage to offer an integrated curriculum. For example, movement activities such as Sherborne Movement are ideal for establishing the early interaction patterns and intentionality which are the foundations for formal communication and decision making, as well as extending the pupils' experience of movement and encouraging physical skills. We must not neglect to record these facts to demonstrate the breadth of curriculum which can be delivered within the time limitations which are an inescapable feature when working with pupils with PMLD. The use of topics or themes is less common in the teaching of this group, but may well be an effective way of approaching new areas. Topics may be suggested by certain Attainment Targets or Programmes of Study, or a topic may be chosen and then related to the Attainment Targets which can be incorporated into it. If the same topic is followed throughout the whole school it will have a cohesive effect and increase the unity of purpose within the school.

The format for recording the curriculum on offer within the class, and the elements of this curriculum which are covered in each pupil's current programme, will be a matter for discussion within the school as a whole and possibly within the LEA. However, the records used for continuous assessment are likely to be based upon the existing recording systems which will, of course, need to be adapted 'to bring them in line not only with the Statements of Attainment themselves but with the small steps leading to them' (NCC, 1989, p. 12). Recording responses and progress of pupils with PMLD is notoriously difficult because of the variability of response from one day to the next, and because of the subtlety of changes in expression or the minimal movements which require a high degree of observational skill, knowledge of the individual pupil, and intuitive interpretation based on experience. It is difficult to do justice on paper to the abilities and personality of a pupil with extremely complex disabilities. A variety of records will be likely to be used — recording grids with a simple code, observation sheets, checklists and graphs, and periodic reports to summarize, such as those sent to parents as termly or yearly reports or prior to the annual reviews. However, other methods of recording provide valuable supplements — photographs, audio or video recording of particular experiences or periodic recording of repeated activities to show progress, however fine, and to register the range of experiences. Multi-media records of achievement might take time to set up, but once the various techniques become familiar to teachers and the deployment of staff organized, it may, in the long term, be a time-saving device, and offer a much more comprehensive record of achievements than 'paper and pencil' methods are able to provide.

Perhaps the biggest question is how Standard Assessment Tasks will relate to the work of pupils with PMLD. In *Curriculum Guidance Two* it states that 'standard assessment tasks are being developed to be

Figure 3.1:   The curriculum for pupils with PMLD

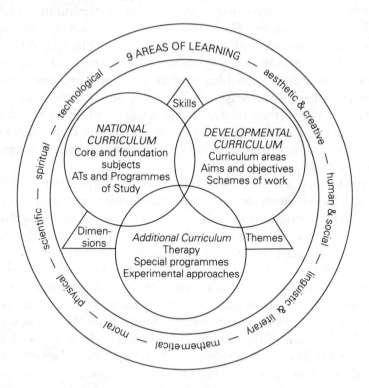

accessible to all pupils as far as possible' (NCC, 1989, p. 12). This certainly implies that there will be some pupils for whom they are not accessible and we must establish the validity of their National Curriculum studies even if the Standard Assessment Tasks are not applicable. The quality of teacher records and assessments will have to be particularly high if they are to be accepted as validating the work done. This is an area in which further research, guidance and inservice training are urgently needed, and requires local and even national attention.

Concerns are also expressed about the reactions of parents to the inclusion of their child within the National Curriculum. Will they view it as being totally irrelevant, or will it encourage unrealistic hopes of greater progress than their child is capable of? The answer must surely lie in the quality of their relationship with the school and the degree of confidence parents have in the teaching which their child already receives.

Helping parents to have appropriate expectations for their child has always required a high degree of sensitivity in order to sustain positive expectations of progress over a long period of time, whilst accepting the limitations of the child's disabilities. Teachers, and in particular head teachers, will need to be very clear in their own minds how the National Curriculum will fit in with the existing curriculum and the personal and therapy needs of each child (which many parents consider to be quite satisfactory already), and how it can strengthen and complement good practice. The annual reviews will, of course, continue to be the statutory forum for individual curriculum review but good staff-parent relationships will be more vital than ever to ensure that parents have enough information to allay their fears or temper their enthusiasm.

Parents will, of course, be involved in the revision of statements of special educational needs to take account of any modifications or lifting of the requirements relating to all or part of any subject of the National Curriculum, and the alternative curriculum to take the place of any parts which are lifted. The format for recording these changes in curriculum will need to be clear and as concise as possible while containing the necessary information. Each LEA will, no doubt, produce its own guidance for schools to ensure a common format across the range of special needs.

Conclusion

The National Curriculum is not the whole curriculum, neither is it totally different from the existing curriculum. There are elements which are part of both curricula and there are larger areas of less exact overlap. We must not forget the additional therapy, special programmes and new approaches of an experimental nature, for these are all learning situations and all contribute to the pattern of each pupil's educational experience. All these aspects are bound together by cross-curricular elements and in particular by those dimensions and themes which are already important parts of the existing curriculum, and those opportunities to acquire basic skills which are embedded in every activity and experience.

The whole curriculum will embrace all these features and contribute towards the nine areas of learning and experience identified in *The Curriculum from 5 to 16* (DES, 1985). From this curriculum the skilled teacher will select and blend the items which will contribute most to each individual's progress at any given time.

Participation in the National Curriculum can be used creatively to build upon and extend the best of existing practice and to act as an antidote to the tendency towards narrowness which is sometimes characteristic of the curriculum offered to pupils with PMLD. Teaching must still be focused on the learning needs of the individual pupil, but perhaps we need a more variable focus to ensure that the pupils are not unnecessarily limited in their experiences. The notion of the least restrictive environment accords well with the concepts of breadth, balance, differentiation, continuity and progression spelt out in the ERA.

To achieve this provision we must have a broad concept of how the curricula overlap and complement each other and maintain a perspective which places the individual needs of the pupils firmly in the centre of an enhanced educational experience.

It will take time before the models of practice devised for implementing the National Curriculum for those pupils with the most profound and multiple disabilities can be accounted as valid in practice, as catering for their needs and enhancing their learning, and valid in principle, as incorporating the content and achieving those principles set out in the Act and in the Orders within the curriculum and learning experiences offered to the pupils.

References

AGER, A. (1989) 'Behaviour teaching strategies for people with severe and profound handicaps: A re-examination', *Mental Handicap*, 17, 2, pp. 56–8.

BAILEY, I.J. (no date) *Structuring a Curriculum for Profoundly Mentally Handicapped Children*, Glasgow, Jordanhill College of Education.

BILLINGE, R. (1988) 'The objectives model of curriculum development: A creaking bandwagon?', *Mental Handicap*, 16, 1, pp. 26–9.

CARPENTER, B. (1987) 'Curriculum planning for children with profound and multiple learning difficulties', *Early Child Development and Care*, 28, 2, pp. 149–62.

CARPENTER, B. (1989) 'The curriculum for children with profound and multiple learning difficulties: Current issues', *Early Child Development and Care*, 46, pp. 87–96.

CARPENTER, B. and LEWIS, A. (1989) 'Searching for solutions: Approaches to planning the curriculum for integration of SLD and PMLD children', in BAKER, D. and BOVAIR, K. (Eds) *Making the Special Schools Ordinary?* Volume 1, London, Falmer Press.

DES (1970) *The Education (Handicapped Children) Act, 1970*, London, HMSO.

DES (1985) *The Curriculum from 5 to 16*, London, HMSO.

DES (1989a) *National Curriculum: From Policy to Practice*, London, DES.

DES (1989b) *Circular 22/89: Assessments and Statements of Special Educational Needs: Procedures within the Education, Health and Social Services*, London, HMSO.

DES AND WELSH OFFICE (1989a) *Science in the National Curriculum*, London, HMSO.

DES AND WELSH OFFICE (1989b) *English in the National Curriculum*, London, HMSO.

DES AND WELSH OFFICE (1989c) *Mathematics in the National Curriculum*, London, HMSO.

HARRIS, J. (1987) 'Interactive styles for language facilitation', in SMITH, B. (Ed.) *Interactive Approaches to the Education of Children with Severe Learning Difficulties*, Birmingham, Westhill College.

HOGG, J. and SEBBA, J. (1986) *Profound Retardation and Multiple Impairment Volume I: Development and Learning, Volume II: Education and Therapy*, Beckenham, Croom Helm.

KIERNAN, C. (1981) *Analysis of Programmes for Teaching*, Basingstoke, Globe Educational.

KIERNAN, C., JORDAN, R. and SAUNDERS, C. (1978) *Starting Off*, London, Human Horizons/Souvenir Press.

MCINNES, J.M. and TREFFREY, J.A. (1982) *Deaf-blind Infants and Children*, Milton Keynes, Open University Press.

NCC (1989) *Curriculum Guidance Two: A Curriculum for All — Special Educational Needs in the National Curriculum*, York, National Curriculum Council.

NCC (1990) *Curriculum Guidance Three: The Whole Curriculum*, York, National Curriculum Council.

NIND, M. and HEWITT, D. (1988) 'Interaction as curriculum', *British Journal of Special Education*, 15, 2, pp. 55–7.

OUVRY, C. (1986) 'Integrating pupils with profound and multiple handicaps', *Mental Handicap*, 14, pp. 157–60.

OUVRY, C. (1987) *Educating Children with Profound Handicaps*, Kidderminster, British Institute of Mental Handicap.

PORTER, J. (1986) 'Beyond a simple behavioural approach', in COUPE, J. and POSTER, J. (Eds) *The Education of Children with Severe Learning Difficulties*, Beckenham, Croom Helm.

SIMON, G.B. (1981) *The Next Step on the Ladder*, Kidderminster, British Institute of Mental Handicap.

STURMEY, P. and CRISP, T. (1986) 'Classroom management', in COUPE, J. and PORTER, J. (Eds) *The Education of Children with Severe Learning Difficulties: Bridging the Gap Between Theory and Practice*, Beckenham, Croom Helm.

TOMPKINS, A. and CARPENTER, B. (1990) 'A post-16 education project for students with profound and multiple learning difficulties', *Mental Handicap*, 18, pp. 105–8.

Section Two

Responding to the Challenge

4   Approaches to Science

Linda Howe

Introduction

The entitlement of all pupils to the scientific curriculum is clearly established. Science for all does not, however, mean that the same science should be provided for all pupils. This chapter examines how the framework of the National Curriculum for Science can be adapted in ways which make it relevant for pupils with a range of learning difficulties.

Why Provide a Scientific Curriculum?

Although some pupils may well experience difficulties in fully understanding the concepts or developing the skills involved in scientific tasks, there are many good reasons for including science activities in their curriculum. These include:

> pupils enjoy scientific activities;
> scientific activities are practical, first hand and relate to current experiences;
> scientific activities can be set in a range of contexts which allow safe exploration of the home and local environment without the pupils having to acquire facts or theories;
> scientific activities can be adapted to suit varying levels and can be carefully structured with easily achievable targets;
> scientific skills are not dependent on previously acquired language or number skills.

Teachers may also find scientific activities a useful tool for evaluating pupils' needs and monitoring progress.

Figure 4.1:   *The National Curriculum for Science*

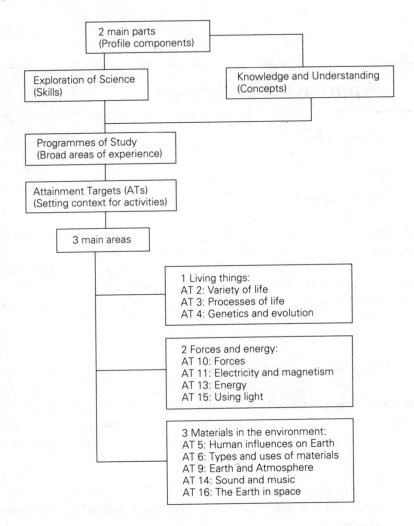

Examining the National Curriculum for Science

The National Curriculum for Science (DES and Welsh Office, 1989) outlines the areas of science which provide a broad and balanced minimum entitlement. In establishing Science as a core subject in the curriculum for pupils with severe learning difficulties (SLD), the framework provided by the Programmes of Study becomes the basis of planning schemes of work. Figure 4.1 shows the composition of the National Curriculum for Science with explanatory comments. It shows how the Programmes of Study and their corresponding Attainment

Targets can be grouped into three blocks: Living Things (containing three Attainment Targets); Forces and Energy (containing four Attainment Targets); and Materials in the Environment (containing five Attainment Targets). These three areas of study can be used to ensure that pupils receive a balanced range of scientific experiences. They can form a framework which sets the context for planning themes and activities on a termly or preferably on a two-yearly basis. Before examining how these areas can be used to plan balanced topics, it is worthwhile considering the sorts of activities which pupils with profound and multiple learning difficulties (PMLD) and pupils with SLD can undertake.

The following section contains a summary of the Key Stage 1 requirements for the three main areas of science together with a very small selection of examples of the many possible appropriate activities.

Living Things

Pupils should have opportunities to observe a wide variety of living things. They should help to care for living things and find out about their needs. Pupils should find out about themselves, their needs and the differences between themselves and other pupils. They should consider how to keep themselves healthy and identify parts of their bodies and plants. They should be aware of new and extinct life.

PMLD groups

Animals and plants, or parts of them, can be brought into the classroom. Pupils can feel, smell and look at a wide variety of life forms from worms to pets, from tree bark to holly leaves and from sea shells to sheep's wool. Tapes of animal noises or bird song can be used to extend the range of sensory experiences. Individuals from within and visiting the class can be named and different sizes of clothing tried on.

SLD groups

Pupils can visit farms, wildlife parks and bird gardens to find out about the different creatures, their homes and their food needs. They can grow seeds and care for these and classroom pets and mini-beasts. Weeds can be taken apart and sorted into sets of leaves, roots, and stems. Songs and games can help to identify body parts and clothes can be sorted into sets which fit and do not fit. Baby clothes can be tried on and pupils' appearance can be compared, using mirrors to look at selves. Favourite tastes can be looked at, (from food to TV programmes). Pupils can tear or cut out leaf shapes and visit the school grounds or local park to see how many of that shape of leaf they can find. Skill games, (for example, how many pegs can you get on a line in three minutes), develop an awareness of pupils' own capabilities.

Forces and Energy

Pupils should explore how pushes and pulls can make things move, speed up, swerve and change shape. They should find out that toys move in different ways and that some things use electricity and can be dangerous. They should use batteries, bulbs and magnets. Pupils should investigate the food we eat and hot and cold, including the effects of heating and cooling. They should explore different ways of making light and experience sorting colours, looking at shadows and exploring reflections.

PMLD groups

Pupils can be guided to touch warm hot water bottles and ice cubes. They can push shapes which will and will not roll, (for example, rolling pins and building bricks). Hands can be moved through water wearing different gloves (for example, rubber, woollen mittens, sheepskin) to feel different forces. Hands can also be moved through different substances with varying degrees of resistance (for example, sand and mud, fresh and very salty water, play dough and clay). Torches can be switched on and off in dark rooms or open boxes. Different tastes and sensations can be experienced by substances (for example, jelly and biscuits) being rubbed on lips or put in mouths.

SLD groups

Collections of things which will and will not roll can be sorted into sets, and things can be stopped from rolling or non-roll things made to roll (for example, paper plates stuck over the ends of cardboard boxes). Ways of making things roll further and faster can be found (for example, down slopes, on different surfaces). Coloured rollers can be made by filling clear plastic bottles with small coloured objects (for example, acquarium stones, water and glitter, beads, or coloured water and baby oil) or painting patterns on the outside. Noisy rollers are made by putting in stones or nails. These can be used to focus attention on the rolling object and observing what happens as it rolls.

Toys can be moved across different surfaces and along the ground, through the air and through water. Boats with sails for the water tray or paper fish shapes for a floor game can be made, and ways of making winds to move them can be explored. Moving tools such as hand whisks or drills can be used, and turning things like spinners, paper windmills and hanging spirals investigated. Torches can be switched on and off and made to work (for example, changing the batteries). Light patterns can be made by moving torches around in sieves and colanders in dark rooms. Pupils can explore what a magnet can and cannot pick up. Shadow games can be played to identify and explore shadows. Pupils can see what happens to their shadows when they move, make shadows with only one leg or work with a friend to make a two-headed shadow. Simple shadow puppets can be made by sticking cut or torn shapes on sticks and moved around or towards and away from a light source. Different foods can be tasted and matched to other foods with the same or similar tastes. Pupils can explore hot and cold by melting and keeping ice cubes, mixing different things in hot and cold water and dropping food colouring into different temperatures of water.

Materials in the Environment

Pupils should investigate everyday waste products and decay. They should compare different materials, their properties and uses and explore how these materials can be changed. They should observe the natural environment, including rocks, soil and seasonal weather changes and the way these affect our lives. Pupils should experience a range of sounds, know how they are made and make their own.

PMLD groups
Pupils can run or be guided to run hands over old and new or shiny and rusty objects. They can handle a variety of materials, or have things held against them, including card, plastics, cloth — rough and smooth, rubber and metal. They can push hands in different textures such as clay and stone, sand and mud, wet and dry flour. Pupils can be taken outside in a variety of weather conditions — sun, rain, snow, fog, wind. Tapes of a variety of sounds can be played including tapes of music, household noises and traffic sounds. Pupils can be guided to shake boxes and plastic bottles which are empty or full of stones, buttons, sand or bells.

SLD groups

Collections of boxes, tins, clothes and shoes can be sorted into old and new sets. The items for a meal can be unwrapped and the different types of things compared (for example, egg shells, cardboard boxes, bottles). Packets can be examined to see if they will fit inside each other, find how much each one will hold and tested to see if they can hold water, flour or biscuits. Pupils can explore which can be torn or what happens if they are squashed. Collections of different materials can be compared for feel (for example, hide some of one material from sight in a bag; can you feel which one it is?), strength and 'waterproofness'. Baked potatoes, ice cubes and slices of bread can be wrapped in various materials to compare insulation and how well they keep things fresh. Shakers can be made using different fillings (including some which do not produce sounds, like cotton wool) in plastic bottles with screw tops. Sounds in and around the school can be recorded on walks and visits.

Kites can be made and/or flown in different weather conditions. Pupils can feel varying strengths of wind by holding up sheets of card or strips of cloth on different days. Snow can be collected in buckets and brought inside to watch melting. Collections of different clothes can be sorted into warm/cold weather sets.

Some General Points Arising from these Activities

Many of the activities suggested for PMLD groups serve to broaden the range of sensory experiences offered. It must be noted that observation involves the use of all senses as appropriate and that touch sensations will involve other parts of the body apart from hands (for example, ice cubes on stomach).

Pupils need to experience contrasting things so that transparent collections should also contain non-transparent articles and shakers be made with quiet fillings.

Some pupils will need the basic activity extended to meet their needs such as using lengths of string to compare how far each roller travels or making a chart to show what they have found out.

Integrating Activities into Topic Work

Ensuring that pupils receive a broad and balanced curriculum involves careful topic planning. One way of guaranteeing a balance in the scientific curriculum is to plan topics which relate to each of the three main areas in each year.

Figure 4.2 shows how different topics fit into the main areas and Figure 4.3 shows how this has been used as a planning aid to set a two-year cycle of themes for a group of pupils. Where pupils are likely to transfer from one group to another either at the end of the year or more frequently, this process will involve two or more teachers planning cooperatively. Consequently, continuity is ensured and the plan becomes a vehicle for teachers to share ideas and discuss activities. Many of the usual classroom activities, including those from schools which have not previously identified the scientific as part of their curriculum, are also part of the National Curriculum requirements and these are shown in the centre part of Figure 4.3. By being identified in this way, they not only become an integral part of the school curriculum but also encourage the examining of ways of ensuring that these activities play a vital role in the SLD curriculum. Examples of how these experiences can be given a fresh outlook are shown below.

Sand and Water Play

Sand and water trays often contain only articles which are purpose made. Extending the range of equipment to include things which are unsuitable for them offers the opportunity to explore materials which are not strong enough for the purpose (for example, paper bags in the sand tray) or are not waterproof (for example, cardboard cereal packets in the water tray). Extra variety can be introduced by adding water to the sand tray and salt, soap or food colourings to the water tray.

Cooking

Careful consideration of the relevance of the type of cooking which takes place questions whether it is more appropriate for pupils to participate in an activity where trays of identical cakes are produced, or to offer the opportunity to explore more accessible foods. Investigations can include finding out what happens if you add too much or too little water to a mashed potato mix, and making patterns with various potato mashers or making and tasting different jellies. Other associated activities could include finding out what happens when you

Figure 4.2: A topic planning device

Areas of study	Topics which relate to areas of study		
1 Living things AT 2: Variety of life AT 3: Processes of life AT 4: Genetics and evolution	Ourselves Animals Growth Seeds School grounds	Farms Birds Flowers Families Local park	Trees Seasons Harvest Pets
2 Forces and energy AT 10: Forces AT 11: Electricity and magnetism AT 13: Energy AT 15: Using light	Food Flight Toys Ships Hot and cold Candles	Moving things Water Colour Travel Dark and light Bridges	Wheels Fairs Olympics Building
3 Materials in the environment AT 5: Human influences on Earth AT 6: Types and uses of materials AT 9: Earth and atmosphere AT 14: Sound and music AT 16: The Earth in space	Litter Under the ground Houses Rainy days Around us Seasides Changes	Packaging Seasons Wet and dry Making music Hard and soft Holes	Weather Clothes Shops Up and down
General topics which can relate to any of these areas	Stories My world Special days etc.	Nursery rhymes Our school etc. . .	

Figure 4.3: A 2-year plan for Key Stage 1

	Autumn Term		Spring Term		Summer Term	
Year 1	Colours (2)	Christmas (all)	New Life (1)	Eggs (2)	Under the ground (3)	Having a picnic (all)
Year 2	Toys (2)	Christmas (all)	Clothes (3)	Pets (1)	Weather (3)	Seaside (1)
Other Areas	Sand and water play Songs/music Home corner Weather records Gardening			Cooking PE Classroom pets/plants Art/craft Visits		

use metal, plastic or wooden spoons in hot water, or testing different ways of cleaning different kitchen surfaces.

Art and Craft

Pupils can mix their own colours from either liquid or powder paints. Activities such as marbling (dropping drips of waterproof inks onto water, stirring and laying absorbent paper on top) can stimulate excitement and curiosity, encouraging 'wanting to find out more' which is the first stage of investigating. Extending activities may include providing a wide variety of paper for painting, drawing and colouring on; what is it like to paint on blotting paper? Clay is a safe medium for exploring using a variety of tools either for cutting and shaping or making patterns. When dry and hard these patterns can be used to print with in a similar way to lino prints.

Home Corner

Science activities often involve an element of sharing activities or ideas. This can only be achieved if pupils have opportunities to play in a social way. 'Real materials' such as bowls of water, kitchen tools and items of clothing can greatly enhance the quality of experiences.

Children's Recording and Involvement in their own Learning Environment

The following is a case study of a class of 6- and 7-year-old children with SLD working on a topic of colour.

Involving children in their own learning can occur at many different levels. Classroom displays can result from children's activities or be used as a vehicle to create interest. A table was set up in the centre of the room before the children arrived. An arrangement of used, crumpled sheets of coloured wrapping paper was placed on the table. Coloured art feathers were 'hidden' on the sheets of paper — some are placed on complementary and some on contrasting colours. When the class was settled they were encouraged to find the feathers, which were stuck on a strip of paper as they were found, thus making a record of the order in which they were seen. The children were encouraged to say which colours were easiest and hardest to find (there was little response at this stage).

For the rest of the week the table, with the crumpled wrapping paper still on it, was moved to the side of the room and different coloured objects were placed on it each day, for example, toy cars or balls from the PE store. As the children entered the class each day, they were encouraged to see 'what is there today'. By the end of the week some of the children were going straight to the table as soon as they entered the room and were sorting the objects found into a line showing the order in which they were found. The results were photographed. During the week the children hid coloured cotton reels and made and hid paper caterpillars for each other to find. The caterpillars were pinned on the wall in the order in which they were found.

The next week the display was changed to include three brightly coloured bowls and a collection of the same coloured random objects. At various times during the day the children were encouraged to visit the table and place the coloured objects in the matching bowls. The class found out if they could feel colour by one child sitting with hands behind their back and another child placing a coloured ball in them. The child who was guessing either said which colour they thought the ball was or touched one which they thought was the same colour. A similar paired exercise was carried out with the children closing their eyes while a friend placed a coloured smartie in their mouth. A pre-drawn chart was filled in with one blob showing the colour guessed and one blob to show the actual colour. It was easily seen that most guesses, including those of the adults, were purely random! Photographs of the children's faces were taken as they tasted the smarties. The children investigated dropping water onto black felt pen blobs on blotting paper. The resulting patterns were displayed and the felt pens used, together with a few new ones, were left on the activity table with a plentiful supply of small pieces of blotting paper. Again the children were encouraged to visit the table throughout the day.

On another day the children were given a selection of coloured card and were asked to 'hide' a picture on it. Coloured crayons were supplied. The results varied from children who coloured randomly to those who carefully chose a colour to match their piece of card. The class then went to the school hall and sat in a row. One child started at the opposite end of the room and moved toward the rest of the class holding up their picture. The children put their hands up when they thought they could see the picture. The pictures were collected and mounted according to how far away they could be seen (it is worth noting that two of the pieces of card proved very hard to see, and close examination revealed that they had no picture at all). The children were mainly interested in the 'winner' which was a yellow picture on yellow card and when asked to try another picture several chose these two materials.

The work continued for the rest of the half term with the children making their own coloured sweets, putting drops of food colouring into cake mixture to see what happened to them in cooking and mixing the water obtained by boiling red cabbage with different liquids to explore colour changes. Each practical activity was photographed and the prints were put into individual folders.

Assessing Scientific Activity

Many of the problems experienced when assessing pupils' scientific achievement occur at the planning stage. If the aims of the activity are not clearly defined, then the assessment of individuals or groups of pupils becomes unfocused and in consequence more difficult to manage. Attempting to assess all the pupils who are engaged or all possible aspects of each activity is also difficult to manage and very time-consuming. The best classroom organization for assessment purposes are those times when another adult is present. The planned use of support staff can release the teacher to work with a small group or even one individual in order to make a close observation of that activity.

Figure 4.4 shows how charts of pre-determined criteria can be used as a focus for observing and drawing conclusions from pupils working. The context for each activity is given for future reference to remind the teacher of what the children were doing and to show the experience given. Where the whole staff or groups of colleagues meet to set the criteria they become a focus for discussion of possible outcomes and the assessment process becomes an integral part of planning. Teachers observe pairs of pupils working, moving around the groups so that all the pupils in a group can be observed in a given time. Pupils can often be involved in the process by the teacher identifying what she is looking for: 'I want to see how many parts of your face you can find'. A space at the bottom of the observation sheet is provided for the teacher to use when reflecting on the pupils' achievement, and planning the next stage.

Keeping Records of Pupils' Progress

The main types of record kept of pupils' scientific progress take two forms. There are those kept to show the experiences which the pupils

Figure 4.4: A example of a chart which can be completed when observing pupils working

Activity: Children looking in mirrors and being encouraged to touch different parts of face.		
	Child 1	Child 2
1 Child looks around randomly without appearing to focus on mirror		
2 Child looks at self in mirror but quickly loses interest		
3 Child shows interest in self in mirror and touches some parts of face		
4 Child shows sustained interest and touches named parts when asked		
Future work		

have had, either individually or as a group, and those which are compiled as the result of classroom observation or assessment tasks which show an individual's achievement. If the work for a group of pupils is planned carefully, the amended plan (showing the actual work covered, including omissions and digressions) can form a group or class record. This may take the form of a simple checklist which includes the relevant Attainment Targets.

Keeping records which give an accurate picture of the individual pupil in a way which can be easily understood by colleagues and parents requires a more complex record. Figure 4.5 shows a very simple way of involving the pupils in building up a profile of themselves. This record is designed to be completed once a term or as frequently as the school decides is appropriate. The first box is completed from the class or group plan and may be filled in before the sheet is copied for the whole class. As the pupil works throughout the term, photographs, tapes and any pictorial or written work are put into a folder. When completing the record this collection is spread

Figure 4.5: *An example of a profile of scientific work to be completed with the pupil*

Name _____	A piece of my work:
Date _____	
I have:	
(A space to list experiences cross-referenced to ATs)	
I think:	
(A space for the teacher to record the child's comments)	
My teacher thinks:	
(A space for teacher's comments)	
My parents/guardians think:	Why I chose this piece of work:
(A space for parents to add their comments)	

out and the pupil is given prompt questions such as, 'what were you doing here?' or 'which is your best one?'. The teacher then fills in any comments made by the pupil and adds her own. One piece of work is selected and stuck onto the record. The record can be shown to parents and guardians who are invited to make their own comments. Obviously, records for some pupils will require the use of pictorial symbols (for examples in other curriculum areas, see Staff of Blythe School, 1986).

Note

Some of this material has already appeared in the *Collins Primary Science Scheme*, authored by Linda Howe. She wishes to acknowledge the cooperation and support of Collins.

References

DES AND WELSH OFFICE (1989) *Science in the National Curriculum*, London, HMSO.

STAFF OF BLYTHE SCHOOL (1986) *Working with Makaton at Blythe School*, Camberley, Makaton Vocabulary Development Project.

5   A Sensory Science Curriculum*

Flo Longhorn

Introduction

A 'sensory curriculum' provides a rich sensory tapestry for the 'very special child' to weave his or her own unique patterns of learning. Now the golden threads of a National Curriculum can be woven into the tapestry, enhancing the learning experiences of the very special child. The National Science Curriculum is one such thread.

The very special child fits perfectly into Jacob Bronowski's (1908–1974) views of the discoveries of science:

> We build up a model of the world as we learn to link one message with another to relate what the ear hears with what the hand touches and the eye sees. Smells, tastes, visual patterns, sounds and tactile events are differentiated and organized in a unified whole. Both the ordinary human being and the scientist show similar experiences in this way. The discoveries of science are not here to be picked up. They come into being only by an activity enacted between the scientist and his selected environment. In an analogous manner, the child has to find reality for himself, by building up from simple to more complex experiences.

The pupils referred to in this chapter are individually described as 'the very special child'. This description applies to those who have

* This chapter should be read in conjunction with Longhorn, F. (1988) *A Sensory Curriculum for Very Special People: A Practical Approach to Curriculum Planning*, London, Souvenir Press (E & A) Ltd, in the Human Horizons Series.

profound and multiple learning difficulties (PMLD), usually linked to sensory and physical impairment. Of course, there are young people with PMLD in schools and other establishments who cannot be called children, but the sensory Science curriculum is just as relevant to them. Also, through the entitlement of the National Curriculum, other children and young people can now use a sensory approach to learning science — pioneered by the very special child.

What is a Sensory Science Curriculum?

The whole school curriculum now embraces the National Curriculum. A Science curriculum and a sensory curriculum are part of this whole curriculum. Blending the sensory and Science curricula together produces a 'sensory Science curriculum'. It enables the development of the senses of taste, smell, touch, vision, sound and bodily movement through science. It also enables science to offer new learning experiences using these in a scientific way. Generalizing these learning experiences, through a multisensory (intermodal) approach, enables the very special child to use the whole school curriculum more effectively.

The Links to the Sensory Curriculum

Many schools have developed their own unique sensory curriculum to meet the educational requirements of very special children. They have produced a written sensory curriculum; written, video, photographic and audio records; built-in assessments; sensory banks: human, material and environmental; and have expanded sensory learning into other areas. This means that sensory Science has a very firm base from which it can build.

The Link to the National Curriculum

All pupils are entitled to the National Curriculum, including very special children. Through a sensory approach, the Science curriculum validates all the work undertaken in the sensory curriculum. As this scientific link develops, there will be more access to other National Curriculum subjects — through a sensory approach.

The Link to the Science National Curriculum

Each school, under the direction of the headteacher, in conjunction with the governing body and the LEA, will develop its own approach to curriculum planning. Therefore sensory Science should be devised within this framework, relating especially to Science in the National Curriculum (DES and Welsh Office, 1989). There will need to be a flexible approach, in view of the importance of sensory learning for the very special child.

Why Develop a Sensory Science Curriculum?

The Right Reasons

A carefully planned sensory Science curriculum, threaded through the main sensory curriculum, offers the very special child the opportunity for:

> a broader base for sensory learning;
> equality of curriculum opportunity;
> access to a wider range of resources;
> enriched teaching through new sensory media;
> a continuity of sensory learning from 5–16;
> generalizing and integrating learning into other settings.

The Wrong Reasons

The major pitfall in planning a sensory Science curriculum is ignoring the statement:

> A school should bear in mind that the objective of the National Curriculum is to ensure that each pupil should obtain maximum benefit by stretching the pupil to reach his or her potential, but without making impossible demands. (DES, 1989, p. 12, para. 58)

Other pitfalls include: teaching to Science Attainment Targets and not to the pupil; offering an isolated and fragmented curriculum with no cross-curricular approach; tokenism, going through the motions of teaching without the rationale; and disapplication or modification for any pupil.

Who Can Use a Sensory Science Curriculum?

The answer to this question must be 'anyone', including all very special children.

Planning a Sensory Curriculum

The sensory Science curriculum should be planned and developed in coordination with all other areas of the combined school and National Curriculum. It is an extension of the sensory curriculum *not* a replacement. It should form part of a well balanced, overall curriculum whose main aim is to stretch every pupil to reach his or her maximum potential.

As well as use of the sensory banks already established in a school, consideration needs to be given to:

timetabling, ensuring sensory Science is a valued part of an individual, group or class timetable;

space, ensuring there is equal access to any Science resources in or out of school (these may include a sensory courtyard, kitchen, dark room or Science centre);

humans, ensuring there are enough humans available to help co-active learning situations;

materials, ensuring a budget is set for sensory materials including field trips;

thinking time, ensuring staff go on stimulating Science courses and then reflect on their adapted use to the very special child.

Where Does the Sensory Science Curriculum Begin?

The Very Special Child

Where Does the Sensory Science Curriculum End?

The Very Special Child

Careful observation of the very special child will give the starting point of his or her programme. Observation and assessment of the results of the sensory Science programme will give the next steps. Many activities may be repeated in a variety of ways — sometimes with no apparent results. If an Attainment Target is covered or partly attained, this is a *bonus* for the very special child.

Resources for a Sensory Science Curriculum

What is a Sensory Resource Bank?

A sensory resource bank matches and enhances the sensory curriculum. It offers a variety of sensory materials and experiences to explore and learn through the senses. The main resource bank may be kept in mobile trolleys, on a set of shelves on the wall or in a resource room such as a dark room. The resources are in sensory areas and are clearly labelled to the relevant sensory area such as taste, smell or sound. Each separate resource may be kept in a clearly marked tray, with zip bags labelled with the contents and the sensory area. Examples of the contents of a zip bag may be:

Sharp Smells	*Scratchy Touch*	*Crackle Sounds*
Vick	Brillo Pads	range of papers that glitter and
aftershave	pan scourers	make crackly sounds when
curry powder	pumice	pulled or waved
carbolic soap	stiff net	
mouth spray	scrub brush	
peppermint oil	toothbrush	
menthol oil	sandpaper	

Other sensory resources would be within the school such as the jacuzzi, music room, kitchen or the ball pool. Outside the school there is also a wealth of sensory resources such as the river, the café, the fairground or the market. It is important to ensure any work undertaken is 'age appropriate' to the child or young person concerned.

What is a Sensory Science Bank?

A sensory Science bank is an integral part of the whole school sensory bank. It provides a new dimension by offering a cross-curricular range of experiments and experiences that have a scientific outlook. Many of the sensory resources can already be used in a scientific way; the

National Science Curriculum and its Programmes of Study validate this approach offering extensions to structured sensory work.

It may be helpful to design a simple colour code system so that there can be easy identification of the key Attainment Targets being used. Examples might be:

Red   Attainment Target 1 — Exploration of Science (short description of the level can be written on the label)

Blue   Attainment Target 2 — Variety of Life

Yellow   Attainment Target 3 — Processes of Life

Some zip bags may have many stickers as they contain cross-curricular materials. For example, a resource tray of gold and silver materials may cover:

AT 1   Exploration of Science

AT 6   Types and uses of materials

AT 10   Forces

AT 14   Sound and music.

It is up to the adult working with the child to use the resource appropriately to the child's programme, not to an Attainment Target. An example of a child's programme, exploring sound and vibration, may include using the gold and silver tray to make sounds and vibrations, such as silver paper noises, silver balls in a noisy mobile and metal bars vibrating as they are rolled and banged together. This would provide for that particular child experience and experimentation in AT 14 — Sound and music — at the following levels of attainment:

1a   sounds in a variety of ways;

2a   sounds reaching the ear;

2b   simple music sounds;

3a   sounds through vibration.

Developing Science Resources for the Sensory Science Bank

The sensory Science bank should introduce new materials with a particular Science emphasis. These would be clearly identified through the simple colour codings, earlier described. Some examples of new resources may include:

Magnet Tray

iron filings and nails

oscillating magnets

metal bars and metal objects

cylindrical magnets

horseshoe magnets

rusty materials

wood objects

doodle filings game

fishing magnet pole game

fridge magnets

magnetic ladybirds

tin foil

magnet theatre

magnet door mechanism

All providing exploration and experimentation in magnetism (AT 11: 2a).

Fossil Tray

fossil stones

seashells

fossil rock

fossil bones

ordinary stones

gem stones

coal

dinosaur models

All providing exploration of the extinct life forms from a long time ago (AT 4: 3a).

Waste Tray

Contains all the waste found on an ecological walk in the park, leading to an environment friendly project in the park.

Experiencing how human influences affect the Earth (AT 5).

Spring Tray

coiled springs

Slinky

big/little springs

metal and plastic springs

springy paper

wood shavings

wind-up toys

insides of clocks

Jack-in-the-box

spring balance

Developing the understanding of properties of materials (AT 6).

Push and Pull Tray

Contains a range of simple toys that require pushing, pulling, and a small ramp, playdoh, plasticene and clay, air filled objects, such as a rubber ring, inflatables and balloons.

Developing and experiencing the knowledge of forces, their nature, significance and effects on the movements of objects (AT 10).

Sensory Science Environments

Sensory Science can be generalized outside school. The range of exploration and experimentation may include these environments, linked to Attainment Targets:

> pond dipping (ATs 5 and 2)
> the launderette (ATs 10 and 11)
> the bakery (AT 6)
> electrical shop (AT 12)
> farm (ATs 2 and 3)
> wet day snail hunt (ATs 2, 3 and 4)
> petrol station (ATs 5, 6 and 10)
> amusement arcade (ATs 12, 10 and 14).

Whole School Resources

It is important to ensure that whole school Science resources are not neglected. There are some excellent resource packs using modular or thematic approaches suitable for use with the very special child. One example is the *Ginn Science* pack which lists at Level 1 the following topics under various modules:

Ourselves and Healthy Living
Our bodies
Heads and faces
Touch

Other Animals and Plants
Plant growth
Pets
Playground birds

Materials and Their Uses
Keeping warm
Keeping cool
Building materials

Energy and Forces
Making things move
Floating and sinking
Water

Earth and Space
Winter
Summer
Soils and stones

Here are examples of *Ginn Science* Level 1 materials used in the module Materials and Their Uses:

pictures of clothes
cups, mugs or tubs of similar sizes but different materials
four similar-sized tin cans
hot water bottles
nails, a hammer and a plastic comb
pictures of houses and buildings
empty cylinders
empty boxes or packets in the shape of cubes, triangular prisms
   and cuboids
materials used in house-building such as brick, wood and slate
pieces of wood

Here is the list of general materials recommended for *Ginn Science* Level 1; it looks suspiciously like a good sensory bank!

Variety of papers, different colours and sizes
Different types of card
Painting and drawing materials
Glue
Scissors
Elastic bands
String
Paper-clips
Plasticine
Blotting paper
Cotton wool
Sawdust
Cocktail sticks
Straws
Sponge
Balloons
Chalk
Plaster of Paris or Polyfilla
Camera and film
Variety of cartons, tubs and containers, for example, for growing seeds, bulbs and corms
Plastic bags

Gloss paint and brush
Hammer and nails
Casings from used ball-point pens
PE hoop
Watering can and rose
Hooks
Sieves with different sizes of mesh
Water dropper
Salt
Food colouring
Magnifying glasses and lenses
Beads, marbles or ball-bearings
Selection of pieces of fabric
Articles of clothing
Large building bricks — cardboard boxes can be as useful as commercially made bricks
Wooden boards to act as ramps
Construction toys
Plastic aprons
Plastic sheeting, for example, plastic tableclothes or bin bags

Compost

Measuring sticks

Mirrors — plastic unbreakable ones or mirror tiles securely glued to pieces of wood

Slide projector or powerful torch

Blindfolds — scarves or cloths

'Feely' box or bag

Large piece of cloth, a sheet or curtain will do

Large water bath, basins and water containers

Variety of plastic containers such as washing up liquid bottles, lemonade bottles and plastic jugs

Sand-tray

Sand — different types if possible such as 'builders' sand and silver sand

Funnels

Approaches to Delivering the Sensory Science Curriculum

Spider's Web — Thematic Approach

The thematic approach lends itself well to the very special child's style of learning. It begins with the very special child at the centre of a web of learning, linking strands into other areas of the curriculum. Some schools have a termly theme, mapped out for the next few terms, to ensure continuity of Science themes.

Look at a web with sensory Science and a child at the centre (see Figure 5.1). If the word 'sensory' is removed, the programme remains the same. 'Sensory' adds a new dimension.

It is unusual for any topic at the centre of a web not to produce many strands. It is usual to find a sensory web running amok! 'Brainstorming' the term's theme is a good team builder, all staff working together. Figure 5.2 is a web on the sense of 'touch' showing project work undertaken and linking to Attainment Targets being experienced.

Delivery through the Sensory Science Resource Bank

The sensory bank should include a range of new Science trays which can be used as stimuli for experimenting and experiencing sensory Science. Care must be taken to ensure this is not a 'hit and miss' method. However, it is highly likely that the stimuli will lead into thematic work, under the guidance of staff. It is *not* for teaching *to* Attainment Targets.

Figure 5.1: Sensory Science and the very special child

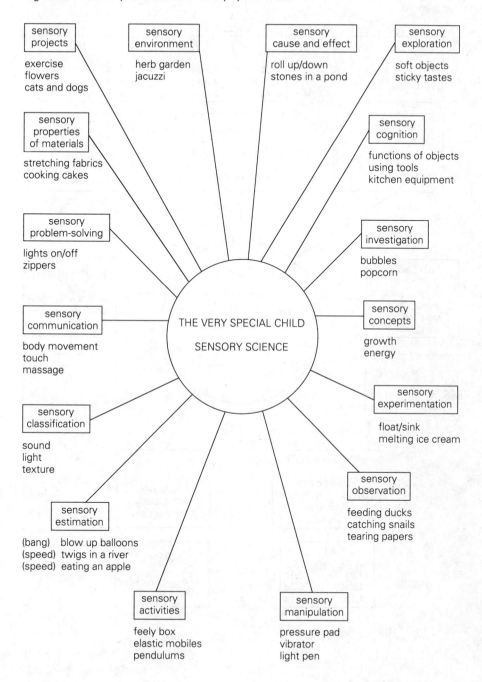

sensory
projects

exercise
flowers
cats and dogs

sensory
environment

herb garden
jacuzzi

sensory
cause and effect

roll up/down
stones in a pond

sensory
exploration

soft objects
sticky tastes

sensory
properties
of materials

stretching fabrics
cooking cakes

sensory
cognition

functions of objects
using tools
kitchen equipment

sensory
problem-solving

lights on/off
zippers

sensory
investigation

bubbles
popcorn

THE VERY SPECIAL CHILD

SENSORY SCIENCE

sensory
communication

body movement
touch
massage

sensory
concepts

growth
energy

sensory
classification

sound
light
texture

sensory
experimentation

float/sink
melting ice cream

sensory
estimation

(bang) blow up balloons
(speed) twigs in a river
(speed) eating an apple

sensory
observation

feeding ducks
catching snails
tearing papers

sensory
activities

feely box
elastic mobiles
pendulums

sensory
manipulation

pressure pad
vibrator
light pen

Figure 5.2: A web on the sense of touch, showing project work and the ATs being experienced

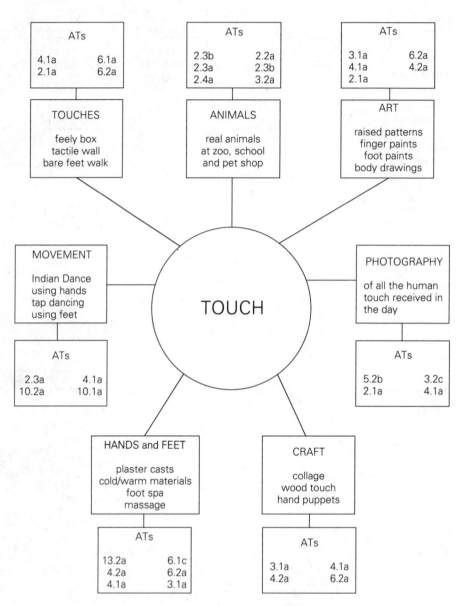

Here are three sample experiences of sensory Science through the resource bank:

1 Attainment Target 6.1a

Should be able to describe familiar and unfamiliar objects, for example, shape, colour, texture and describe how they behave when they are, for example, squashed and stretched; or, in sensory terms, by using the senses of touch, taste, smell, sound, vision and movement, will experience and experiment in describing familiar and unfamiliar objects.

Resources to be used from the sensory bank for AT 6.1a are from the 'Messy Materials' tray:

Materials	*Experience and Experimentation*
cornflakes	crunch wet dry soggy mix taste
breadcrumbs	mash taste shake wet dry pound
pasta	cook taste grind make float thread
gravel	pulverize smash rattle sieve touch
salt	wet dry sink blow taste pour dissolve
cornflour	stir cook smear spread taste cold
dough	pull push hot cold cook roll squash
bath salts	dissolve smell swish stir splash

2 Attainment Target 15.1b

To be able to discriminate between colours and match them or, where appropriate, demonstrate an understanding of colour in their environment; or, in sensory terms, by using vision, and associated senses, experience and experiment in discriminating between colours, matching them or, where appropriate, demonstrate an understanding of colour in their environment.

Resources from the visual bank for use in the dark room and other environments to experience AT 15.1b:

gold tray	concave/convex tray	mosaic tray
silver tray	fluorescent tray	colour paddles tray
coloured shiny tray	revolving wheels tray	kaleidoscopes
textured material	coloured lights tray	projector and slides
prism tray		

and a range of lighting to use with these trays.

3   Attainment Target 6.3b

To be able to list the similarities and differences in a variety of
everyday materials; or, in sensory terms, by using the senses of taste,
touch, smell, sound, vision and movement, will experiment and
experience the similarities and differences in a variety of everyday
materials.

Resources from the sensory bank for AT 6.3b:

Take any two trays of everyday materials and mix them for looking
and finding similarities and differences. Examples may be: glove tray
and sock tray; feather tray and sequin tray; polystyrene tray and silk
tray.

Delivery through the Language of Sensory Science

This approach is refreshingly different and can be used to avoid
repetition and stagnation of thematic ideas. Simply look at the language of sensory Science, take one word and build a range of situations around the word. Here are some sensory Science words to
activate and motivate a range of activities, generalizing actions in
many situations.

Sensory Science Language

bubbling	dissolving	handling	peeling	smelling
banging	dripping	heating	pushing	stroking
blowing	dangling	measuring	rubbing	sucking
beating	dropping	mashing	rolling	scratching
bouncing	eating	melting	rocking	tearing
bursting	examining	massaging	rattling	tapping
cracking	exploring	mixing	whisking	touching
chopping	freezing	noticing	washing	tasting
cutting	folding	opening	wetting	tracking
catching	floating	poking	sinking	tickling
creating	grinding	pulverizing	shaking	tipping
cooling	gripping	pinching	swishing	upturning
crunching	growing	punching	squeezing	vibrating
drying	hitting	pouring	spreading	etc.

An example of this approach may be:

Popping	fizzy drinks	cheeks
	pop corn	pea pods
	balloons	bubbles
	bags	polystyrene
Vibrating	footspa	rubber bands
	bed	throat
	hand massager	balloon
	guitar	metronome
	piano	big bass drum
Opening	can opener	windows
	cans and jars	parcels
	boxes	bags
	seeds	flowers
	doors	mouth

Assessment and Recording Sensory Science

A Whole School Approach to Recording

It is very important that the recording and assessment work devised by a school include the levels of the very special child. Staff should ensure that records show a positive and forward planning record for every child. It would be depressing for everyone if records showed only a stark comment, without revealing the wealth of sensory work being undertaken. Any professional would be truly impressed to see such ingenious, ongoing and lively sensory Science work, especially for the very special child. Be proud of the work undertaken and your record keeping.

Recording Sensory Science

The sensory curriculum recording in a school should be utilized for sensory Science. The minute observations and checks on a child's learning patterns and reactions to experiences are vital in planning the next steps.

The main aim for sensory Science should be clearly stated and it may state:

The main aim for sensory Science should be to present a wide and varied range of Science experiences and experimentation through a sensory approach. This aim complements the sensory curriculum and does not compete with it.

The main goals may include extending sensory learning, enhancement of the senses, exploration, experimentation, fun and enjoyment, stimulation, and experience of Attainment Targets. (ATs should be seen as a bonus if they are achieved or provoke a child into extending their sensory learning).

Remember the definition of 'know' is 'be aware of', 'acquainted with', and 'have information about' when planning goals and objectives.

Recording Experiences of Sensory Science through a Spider's Web

It is a simple matter to photocopy the spider's web drawn up at the beginning of a term, and place it on file for each child. As the term progresses each area completed can be shaded to suit the recording system of the school. (One school links it to the recording shading for the Derbyshire Language Scheme in school). At the end of term, there is a visual record showing the range and breadth of the activities undertaken. There are also the spaces where there was no work completed. This forestalls the danger of just one area of sensory pursuit to the detriment of others. The web reveals all. Figure 5.3 is a web completed over a term by one very special child. Families appreciate receiving such a record of what their child has achieved over a term.

The spider's web information can be easily transferred to a Core Curriculum 'overview checklist' (see Figure 5.4).

Records of Achievement

Records of Achievement may prove to be the most effective means of recording a very special child's progress through school and through sensory Science. They are not limited to written achievements but would include video, photography, information technology and tape recordings. The new technology of interactive video and computer graphics give a fascinating glimpse of Records of Achievement in the future. Information about Records of Achievement should be readily available at local secondary schools and they are usually very willing to share the technology they have devised. Sensory Science could form part of these Records of Achievement.

Figure 5.3: *Record of one term's experiences of sensory Science*

Date : Summer term, 1989   *Child* : (name)
Web project : 'trees'
Notes : Link to *Ginn Science* Project on Plant Growth

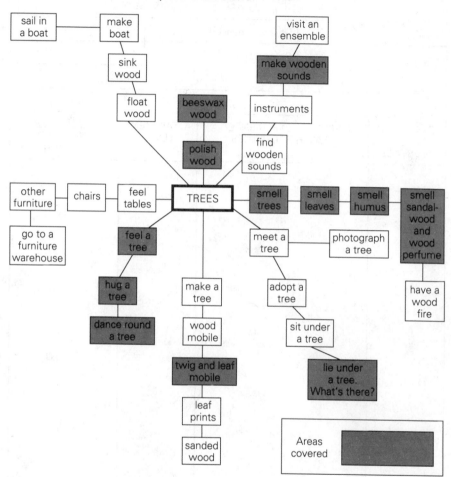

Project Work Collections:

Personal wooden
object box

wood necklace
piece of bark
wooden elephant
miniature wooden chair
bunch of twigs
clothes pegs
sandalwood powder

Wood smells
collected

bag of leaves
bark
wooden incense
charcoal
burnt wood

Next Steps

continue 'meet a tree'
  with adopted tree
visited and photographed
and 'met' each changing
  season

Figure 5.4: Sensory Science curriculum — overview checklist

St. John's School

Sensory Science Curriculum — Overview Checklist

Project / web:	Date commenced:	Class:
Focus:	Date completed:	Pupil:
		Teacher:

ATTAINMENT TARGET KEY STAGE	SENSORY EXPERIENCE/ EXAMPLE ACTIVITIES	ATTAINMENT LEVEL	RESOURCES IDENTIFIED AND USED

Environmental Sensory Science Records

The use of video, photography and tape recorders can provide a vivid and meaningful record of sensory Science. A simple written record of environmental learning should be included in the records of the very special child. This will highlight repetition or lack of study in certain areas. It can be as simple as the example shown in Figure 5.5.

Figure 5.5: Record of environmental learning

St John's School

Record of Environmental Learning

Pupil:	Date commenced:		Class:	Teacher:
Environmental work	Date	Place	Objectives (ATs, if applicable)	Comments

References

DES (1989) *Circular 6/89: ERA: The National Curriculum: Mathematics and Science Orders under Section 4*, London, HMSO.

DES AND WELSH OFFICE (1989) *Science in the National Curriculum*, London, HMSO.

Resources

1 Recommended monthly magazines which regularly add inspiration to staff on science project work: *Infant Project Work; Junior Project Work; Child Education*. Available from Scholastic Publications, Westfield Road, Southam, Leamington Spa.
2 *Ginn Science* packs. Details from Ginn & Co. Ltd, Prebendal House, Parsons Fee, Aylesbury, Bucks, HP20 2QZ.

3   Lots of animal and insect project work from Centre for Life Studies, Zoological Gardens, Regents Park, London, NW1 4RY.
4   Excellent poster packs and film strips from Phillip Green Educational, 1129, Alcaster Road, Studley, Warwicks, B80 7NR.
5   Excellent source books for the senses are the *Think About* series published by Franklin Watts.
6   Activity ideas from *Into Science* topic books, such as *Bouncing Balls, Weather, Earthworms* by Terry Jennings, published by Oxford University Press.
7   *Playing with Natural Materials* and *Early Explorations*, obtainable from TMRS, Russell House, 14, Dunstable Street, Ampthill, Beds.
8   *Bright Ideas* series published by Scholastic Publications: *Seasonal Activities* (author unnamed); *First Science Pack for Infants* by Terry Jennings (1990); *Project Teaching* by David Wray (1989); *Science Activities* by Max de Boo (1990).

Suggested Further Reading

CORNELL, J.B. (1979) *Sharing Nature with Children*, Exley Publications Ltd.
JONES, A. (1983) *Science for Handicapped People*, London, Souvenir Press, Human Horizons Series.
RICHARDS, R. (1987) *An Early Start to Science*, London, Macdonald.

6   Aspects of English

Judy van Oosterom

Introduction

Twenty years ago this chapter on literacy would not have been considered, for the idea that pupils with severe learning difficulties (SLD) might acquire reading and writing skills beyond a limited social sight vocabulary coupled with ability to write their name, would have been thought unrealistic. This attitude is reflected in Kirk's statement, 'In general, trainable pupils do not learn to read from even first grade books. Their ability is limited to reading and recognizing their names, isolated words, and phrases' (Kirk, 1972).

When the DES assumed responsibility for educating these pupils in 1971 great changes in both organization and resources were initiated. The emphasis moved from training to education, and it was recognized that the pupil with SLD differs only in degree from the so-called dull and backward pupil. Given a finely structured programme based on the needs of the individual, many of these pupils can acquire limited skills in both reading and writing. The question is whether the time and effort on the part of both teacher and pupil are worthwhile, or whether classroom time would be more profitably spent on attaining less academic skills.

If we assume that it is both desirable and possible for some pupils with SLD to read and write even to a limited extent, what is the purpose of the exercise?

Reading and writing are essential skills for full acceptance into our Western society. Any lack of them restricts independence and, of course, further academic learning. 'To join a group you have to possess most of the skills of the other members' (Gillham, 1987).

Even limited success in reading and writing increases self-respect and confidence and improves motivation. It also changes the attitude towards the pupil both at home and at school. 'You're really one of the family now' and 'I never knew he had it in him' are comments that have been heard by the writer.

Learning to read also encourages pupils with articulation difficulties to speak more clearly and the use of some form of visual code would seem to help the development of spoken language, for the written message remains available for re-inspection and repetition, whereas speech is a temporal activity.

Although an increasing amount of information comes to us through non-print media, such as television, films, video and audio cassettes and radio, written instructions, public notices, forms, captions, signs and labellings still require reading. The increasing emphasis on the integration of severely learning disabled people with their local community means that some ability to read and write at a functional level will certainly be needed if they are to achieve any degree of acceptance and independence.

A New Perspective

The Education Reform Act 1988 (ERA) and the establishment of a National Curriculum bring both opportunities and dangers for pupils with SLD. The opportunities presented by being considered as pupils able to follow the National Curriculum programme, with its attainment targeting providing a sequence of steps forward, are overshadowed by the danger of failure to recognize that the same 'curricular progression' is not appropriate for all. These pupils vary greatly in abilities and learning styles (Clements, 1987) and need a diversity of educational programmes to ensure individual progress. These reservations apply particularly where pupils with SLD are integrated into mainstream schools and inevitably will seem very backward when compared with their more able peers. In consequence much less may be expected of them. The personal educational programmes that are needed are demanding both in terms of structure and of implementation; without them these pupils may neither make the progress nor have the sense of achievement that is their due.

> Fundamental applied research may lead to more effective programmes or early intervention and education. Joint research and educational programmes may grasp the opportunity offered by integration to prevent handicap and to help positive

attitudes in mainstream pupils and their teachers. (Kiernan, 1989)

In *English Key Stage 1: Non-statutory Guidance* (NCC, 1989) it is stated in Section C. 8, paragraph 6.0, 'When we read something we make sense of it for ourselves, not just by decoding but by bringing our own experience and understanding to it. Teaching has to take account of the breadth of children's print experience', and in paragraph 6.2, 'Children entering the infant classroom may not be able to "read" but in their desire to order their lives they will have considerable and varied experience of responding to print in their environment...'. Both of these statements assume some breadth of print experience, and the ability to make use of it, and the second takes for granted the desire for order. Pupils with SLD will probably have a very narrow experience of print, and will need specific teaching to develop the skills to respond to what they read and to order their lives.

The second report of the National Curriculum English working group states, 'Pupils with learning difficulties with or without statements are likely to make only slow progress in reading and writing. For such pupils oral work should be given greater emphasis initially though the skills of reading and writing should not be neglected' (DES and Welsh Office, 1989a, Section 12.9). As was suggested earlier, some form of visual code often supports and encourages the developing oral skills of pupils with SLD. It may be that for some of them oracy and literacy should go hand-in-hand. In the Portsmouth Project (Buckley and Wood, 1983) eleven Down's Syndrome children under 2 years old, who were enrolled in a Portage home teaching project, participated in a systematic reading programme. Weekly targets were set and they progressed from visual discrimination and object recognition to matching, selecting and naming single words on flash cards. The weekly records when pooled showed that high levels of reading skill can be achieved with such children by the use of systematic preschool instruction, and suggested that their language development might be facilitated by teaching them to read; also, decline in developmental quotients might be prevented.

In the past twenty years there have been great advances in both knowledge and expertise leading to the development of programmes designed to help pupils with SLD achieve some degree of literacy. There is no way in which details of this work could be given a place in the report of the working group or in the resulting Statutory Orders for English (DES and Welsh Office 1989b). Considerable further research is required for effective development of educational programmes for these pupils (Kiernan, 1989). Let us examine what has been achieved over these years and consider ways in which the requirements resulting from the National Curriculum can provide the impetus for further progress.

Functional Reading

In the early 1970s only exceptional pupils with SLD learned to read and write in the accepted sense. Most of the more able were taught a basic protective and social vocabulary of words with any associated symbols. These social sight words are still taught to some pupils, and the modern photographic materials available for teaching these everyday socially useful signs and symbols take into consideration differences which may be found in lettering, size, situation and colouring, but unless they are taught in context they are unlikely to be functional, which is the object of the exercise. Difficulties occur when there are several variants of the same basic instructions, for example: 'Entrance', 'Way in', 'Entry', 'In', 'This way', and a visit to any supermarket reveals complex shopping choices. Also, the concepts involved in some warning notices may prove confusing, for instance: 'Open the other end', 'This side up', 'Entrance for staff only', 'Use the far door', 'Keep off the grass'. A little probing into the last instruction produced this exchange:

Teacher:	[Pointing to notice] What does this say?
Pupil:	Keep off the grass [reading the notice with ease].
Teacher:	Good. What does it mean?
Pupil:	You mustn't keep on.
Teacher:	Keep on what?
Pupil:	Keep on doing it.
Teacher:	Keep on doing what?
Pupil:	Keep on the grass ... Keep on ... going on the grass. Don't be so thick, Van.

Not so far wrong, but he has some confusion about 'keeping' (an emotive word) and 'on' and 'off', also frustration with his inability to convey what he meant.

Picture symbols are not without their mystery either. Which lavatory is appropriate for a female wearing trousers and not a skirt?

'Functional reading' is the ability to use words, phrases and sentences which have been memorized as a whole and to respond to their messages appropriately. Brown and Perlmutter (1971) defined functional reading as 'discrete and observable motor responses to printed stimuli'. It may be used to meet varied individual needs ranging from those arising from life in a sheltered environment to meeting the demanding requirements of a more independent life style. A core vocabulary may include detailed personal information, useful names and addresses, basic sight words, shopping, cooking and household words, quantitive and temporal words, local knowledge and simple direction finding, information such as street and road names and plans, alphabetical listings such as telephone directories, Yellow Pages, address books and simple dictionaries, and for very high fliers, high interest news such as sport and local events, and also television programme information, instructions and form filling. At this later stage the user would be bordering on functional literacy, the main difference being that the person who attains 'functional literacy' has the ability to read and write to the minimal standard commensurate with the need to cope with the everyday reading and writing demands of our society; and is not dependent on a remembered sight vocabulary although the content may not necessarily be so very different. In our complex modern society that is quite a challenge.

Functional Literacy

It has been considered that a reading age of around 9 or 10 years is needed for functional literacy. Research suggests that skills of a higher order in both reading and writing are required to cope with the more complex problems of form filling and to make use of instruction manuals for modern appliances, and repair and maintenance manuals for cars. At present insufficient research has been undertaken to say with any certainty what levels of literacy can be achieved by some pupils with SLD, for while rote learning or training does not encourage flexible responses to new situations, the present emphasis on meaningful reading and writing does so from the outset.

The approach outlined in the National Curriculum proposals for Attainment Targets for Reading at Levels 1 and 2 (DES and Welsh Office, 1989a) assumes possession of a broad knowledge of basic concepts and good receptive language. It encourages the application of what has been learned to new situations. It is to be hoped that this habit of active response will help many pupils with SLD to develop a higher level of literacy in adulthood than has previously been thought possible. 'Learning to read as opposed to acquiring a sight vocabulary is a complex cognitive task demanding a high level of integration and maturity of a wide variety of abilities and skills' (Moyle, 1972). It involves the transference of auditory signs for language signals to new visual signs for those same familiar signals. It is *not* the learning of language or language code, or new words and structures. These skills and this bank of knowledge must be present to some degree before reading is attempted. The learner must develop habitual response to specific written shapes, and in the beginning reading is the practice of this varied skill. Later, when this has become automatic, fluency develops. The response is no longer to actual graphic shapes, but more attention is paid to tone sequences, stresses and pauses. Material read now reflects the semantic ability and understanding of the written message.

The final stage when written language is used with the same ease and fluency as spoken language is unlikely to be achieved by many people with SLD, even adults. It should also be appreciated that 'mechanical reading' has a neurological basis and that therefore reading success is not possible unless a certain level of neurological development has been attained. Many pupils with SLD would seem to have some impairment affecting the central visual or auditory functions. Diagnosis at an early age, and specific learning programmes designed to ameliorate these problems, might make some success possible for those pupils who, while apparently capable of doing so, are not able to learn to read or write. Sight and hearing problems are also common in these pupils and early remediation is important to prevent additional learning difficulties developing. Against all the odds, we know that many severely impaired pupils can and do develop limited literacy skills. 'We do not know for certain how children learn to read and write, we know that different pupils learn in different ways ...' (Raban, 1988). There can be no best method.

Teaching Literacy Skills

There are three main approaches to teaching literacy skills: A 'language experience' approach with the emphasis placed on the pupil's immediate interests; 'developmental reading schemes' using a carefully controlled vocabulary and involving progression through a series of readers; 'phonic' or 'synthetic' programmes based on learning letter sounds and blends leading to word building or alternatively to breaking down whole words into components. They are not mutually exclusive and many teachers use something of all three. Less familiar perhaps are systems which make use of diacritical marks, extended alphabets or colour coding, and lastly, those which change the medium by the use of symbol accentuation (Jeffree and Skeffington, 1980) or by the use of pictorially based symbolic systems (rebuses) (Devereux and van Oosterom, 1984; Staff of Blythe School, 1986).

Whatever the approach, the principle of teaching in response to the observed needs of the individual is easier to follow in the context of a well structured and systematic programme which starts at the optimum level. Clear objectives and order of attack need to be decided, but the method of approach, pace of advance, amount of overlearning, length and frequency of teaching sessions must be flexible. Simple and regular recording of progress will indicate any need for programme adjustment, for response to message received is as important for the teacher as it is for the pupil.

The habits and skills which must be present before any structured reading and writing programme can be started, may be encouraged by the use of 'learning to learn' games. These should be based on simple adaptable materials which require the pupil's active participation and give immediate knowledge of results. Presented at the right level, these activities are motivating and pupils are encouraged to look, to listen, and to concentrate for increasingly long periods. Sorting, matching, ordering and classification activities and games played with others, can help to develop discriminatory skills, good working strategies and social skills leading to more confident and competent behaviour. These activities build up self-esteem which enables pupils to attempt the more exacting skills that are basic to reading and writing.

Alongside this work pupils may be encouraged to 'read' wordless picture books, and so begin to understand a sequence of events and try to predict what might happen next. Reviews on the use of wordless picture books and bibliographies are provided by Abrahamson (1981) and D'Angelo (1981). The use of wordless picture books paves the way for language-experience approaches to reading which use the pupil's own immediate related experiences. These are written down and illustrated, providing a meaningful text, and an association between the spoken and written word is established, for the more closely sentence structures resemble the pupil's own the greater his or her comprehension.

These personal stories are supplemented with a variety of activities including word and picture matching, and games which aim at teaching the association between words and objects or actions. Common objects in the room may be labelled first with a single word, and later with an appropriate phrase such as 'Here is the door', 'There is the cupboard'. Once the pupil is familiar with a basic vocabulary of words, sentence making may be introduced, and with the use of word cards and cardholders pupils can construct their own sentences. These are expressive activities; receptive activities include responding to written instructions (Gillham, 1987; Thatcher, 1984).

The 'shared-book experience' uses group teaching (Holdaway, 1979); the teacher uses a greatly enlarged 'Big Book' placed on an easel and runs her finger under the words as she reads. This method mainly utilizes nursery tales and predictable books for story content. The assumption is that pupils will learn to read if materials are based on well loved and familiar stories, or, in the case of predictable books, repetitious events. There is a clear association between the words on the page and the accompanying illustration, and after repeated readings pupils can be encouraged to join in with certain anticipated words and phrases and will eventually learn to read along with the teacher. Predictable books in particular are valuable in the early stages of reading. Pupils enjoy familiar stories and the repetitive patterns; they are also cumulative, and the events require more and more involvement and concentration. *The Great Big Enormous Turnip* by Tolstoy is an excellent example. Specific suggestions about books and teaching techniques to use with young, normal pupils are given by Rhodes (1981) and by Tomkins and Webeler (1983). Adaptation of techniques for use with young pupils with learning difficulties is a matter of adjustment in length, content and timing.

The advantage of using both language-experience type activities alongside the shared book approach is that while the language-experience materials rely on the pupils' own limited vocabulary and experiences, the shared book introduces a wide range of much richer materials from the world of pupils' literature. This gives pupils with SLD a common experience with their more able peers, and reading is seen as an enjoyable social skill. Paired reading in a simplified form can introduce the pupil with SLD to 'real' books and encourage independent reading for content. One-line-to-a-page story books are readily available. Story quality is a key factor in reading for meaning and in motivating a pupil to read (Gillham, 1987). Once more, the emphasis is on reading for content and confidence building. This semantic approach to reading makes pupils more willing to look for pictorial and 'closure' clues; this ability can be further encouraged by picture matching and missing word games.

Since this activity involves significant others it can be an enriching and extending experience for all concerned. 'It is not to arrive at a destination but to travel with a different view' (Peters, 1965). Parents have reported that paired reading has resulted not only in improved reading skills but also in greater self confidence, achievement satisfaction and enjoyment (Dickinson, 1987).

Language Through Reading (John Horniman School, 1985) is a structured reading scheme with a practical linguistic base, designed primarily for pupils with special language learning needs and based on David Crystal's LARSP (Crystal, Fletcher and Garman, 1976). It is presented at three levels of difficulty and teaches reading of the written symbol within developmental grammatical structures. Level 3 extends comprehension and expressive skills, and these books have the interests of the older readers in mind.

Basal reading schemes emphasize the acquisition of a minimum sight vocabulary ('look and say'). Since they are usually compiled with the 'average' pupil in mind, they will require both modification and the introduction of individualized supplementary materials if they are to be used effectively with slow or learning disabled pupils. The limited vocabulary restricts the story content, and since this is written for the young primary school pupil it may be inappropriate for the more mature but less able pupil of similar 'reading age'. However, the consistency in style, type face, and the concept of progression through the scheme may outweigh these reservations for some teachers and pupils. It is not generally easy to supplement one reading scheme with books at the same level from another, since there is little agreement between the authors on what constitutes an essential vocabulary. Differences in format and writing style, together with the need to learn names of new characters, shakes the confidence of pupils who are not accustomed to a more flexible approach to reading.

It must also be remembered that printed material has its own rules which are sometimes at variance with the concepts which the pupil has already developed. For example, in letters and words, orientation is significant; 'b' and 'd' and 'p' are different letters, whereas a flag is a flag whichever way up it is placed. Also 'A' and 'a' look different but mean the same, and 'o' and 'a' look similar, but are different. The words 'BIG' and 'big' look different, but mean the same, while 'hot' and 'hat' and 'saw' and 'was' look rather similar but are not. The experience of reading for content means that when pupils get such distinctions wrong, the resultant nonsense helps them to appreciate the importance of the crucial differences and to adjust their ideas accordingly.

Although methods already discussed establish reading as a pleasurable occupation, they will not by themselves lead to fluency. The ability to decode new words is essential if reading is to progress beyond a sight vocabulary. Phonics involves learning letter sounds and their various combinations. A structured programme with small enough steps to ensure success, and enough overlearning to stabilize what has been learnt, is a basic necessity.

'Only a well considered master-plan accompanied by meticulous recording can lead to structuring the learning situations for continuous individual progress' (Southgate and Roberts, 1970). The original *Distar Reading Program* (Engelmann and Bruner, 1969), now revised and incorported into SRA's Reading Mastery Series, is meticulously planned, and is an application of operant conditioning theory. Designed in three parts, Part 1 of the Distar Reading Program concentrates on teaching basic decoding skills, the sequence of skills is strictly controlled, active involvement and positive responses are required from each pupil. The great strength of this program lies in the systemized logical approach, which reduces teacher decision making to a minimum and so allows concentration on what is being presented, and full attention to pupil response. Emphasis on auditory skills may make the system less effective with the pupil who has problems with auditory processing; it must also be said that some teachers find the imposed structure and formal teaching unacceptable. *The Programmed Reading Kit* (Stott, 1970), now out of print, consists of a series of structured and motivating games by which basic phonic skills are built up and practised. The games, played alone or with a partner or group, are largely self corrective and carefully graded to ensure success.

Phonic blending using cassette tapes and workbooks, board and domino games, initial letter and picture matching materials are readily available. However, concentration on letter sounds and blends is not enough.

> There are good grounds for supposing that the sequencing of groups of letters in a word is a major source of information. It is probable that, as we gain experience in written language, we build up a memory bank of similarities and differences in the letter strings that make up individual words. (Gardner, 1986)

A Hand for Spelling (Cripps, 1988) teaches handwriting and spelling together. The photocopy masters provide a programme which starts with prewriting skills, letter formation and basic pattern making, and leads to joining letters together, enabling pupils to look at, and write words that share the same letter patterns. This system gives pupils the opportunity to experience how words feel to write as well as seeing how they look. It is in accord with Attainment Targets for spelling and handwriting at Levels 1–4 (see DES and Welsh Office, 1989b). The computer program *Hands on Spelling* (Cripps, 1990) enables pupils actually to see words being built around letter patterns. As well as words which have been pre-selected in groups, teachers can create their own groups of words to match individual needs.

Relevant Research on Reading

The acquisition of a basic sight vocabulary by pupils with SLD has been the focus of interesting new ideas. Using errorless discrimination or stimulus shaping (Terrace, 1963), the *Edmark Reading Program* (Edmark Associates, 1972) used words only, with no pictorial cueing, in this stimulus/response program. The teacher presented and said the word to be learned, requiring the pupil to point to it only. In subsequent presentations the target word appeared with other words or wordlike configurations which, although very dissimilar from it in the first place, became more similar with each presentation. In the final presentation the pupil was told to 'read this word', the target word being indicated by the teacher.

Dorry and Zeaman (1975) and Dorry (1976) based their approach on the attention theory of Zeaman and House (1963). They presented words together with matching pictures, gradually fading the pictures over a series of exposures until only the word remained. The pupils' task was to look at each stimulus card and say the word; this was thought to be learned more readily because the picture mediated a stronger attention response.

A comparative study of these two approaches by Walsh and Lamberts (1979), using covariance analysis on three measures (word identification, word recognition and picture-word matching) showed a 'highly significant' difference between the two methods. Pupils' performance was better after instruction with the errorless-discrimination method than after instruction using picture fading. While tempering the findings for a variety of reasons, they postulated that failure to shift control from the picture to the printed word might have been a causal factor in the less successful picture fading results.

One of the prerequisites for reading competence is immediate recognition of roughly 95 per cent of words encountered in a passage of prose. Only a small proportion of these words is nouns, which are easy to illustrate and generally the first to be recognized. *Keywords to Literacy* (McNally and Murray, 1962) gives suggestions for learning 200 keywords to improve reading fluency. However, memorizing words out of context, particularly since many 'key words' are non-information bearing, is not motivating for backward pupils, and seems in some ways to be in conflict with the emphasis on reading for meaning.

Research into teaching pupils with SLD to read using 'integrated picture cueing' by Worral and Singh (1983) compared a rebus programme with a picture cue method. It was found that the group using cued words was significantly superior in reading standard orthography both during and at the completion of the training period. This suggests that a form of picture-cueing, (embedded pictorial cues within a spelled word), is well worth further exploration. It is interesting to note that in common with the picture fading findings, the problem appears to be the shifting of the stimulus control from picture to word. This problem of attentional switching is likely to be greater for pupils with SLD than it would be for more able pupils. The practice of symbol accentuation has also been explored as a means of transfer from pictures to print (Jeffree and Skeffington, 1980). This technique involves incorporating the letters of a word to form a pictorial representation of it, the transition of it being accomplished by encouraging the pupil either to accept the written word, or by a gradual fading and transformation. Lastly, the approach to the reading and writing of traditional orthography through the initial use of a simple pictorial code has been used successfully with many slow and learning disabled pupils.

The Use of Rebuses

As language historians have observed, the earliest forms of written communication were pictorial in nature. It would therefore seem appropriate to use a modern version of such symbols to introduce simple literary skills, the more so since symbols, signs and signifiers (rebuses) are used to convey instructions and information in many situations today. Rebuses may be pictorial, relational or abstract; pictorial symbols are immediately recognizable, relational signs require explanation, while abstract signifiers require teaching. Since they are all easier to learn and to remember than spelled words, pupils are enabled to process more demanding information both in terms of amount and content, as they can devote their attention to meaning rather than to identification. 'All activities in which children engage to meet the teacher's objectives of developing concepts and language structure are a form of reading or writing because all, in essence, are responses to messages' (Devereux and van Oosterom, 1984).

The National Curriculum Statutory Orders for English (DES and Welsh Office, 1989b) require that at Level 1 of the reading component pupils should be able to 'Recognize that print is used to carry meaning in books and in other forms in the everyday world'. In the widest sense 'print' refers to any printed symbol, and it would seem that a system that enables pupils to understand and respond to a visual code is a step in the right direction. One such system, *The Peabody Rebus Reading Program (REBUS)* (Woodcock, Clark and Davies, 1969), resulted from research into rebuses as a medium for beginning reading. The four essential features of this program are: reading for content; decision making; immediate knowledge of results; and overlearning of graded material. This program provided the impetus for the development of rebus-based materials in this country (Devereux and van Oosterom, 1984). Since rebuses are in no way exclusive they may be used with or alongside other materials.

Blank folders from the *Breakthrough to Literacy* materials (Mackay, Thompson and Schaub, 1979) are useful to store and order rebus vocabulary cards. Using rebuses on one side and spelled words on the reverse, pupils are enabled to construct their own captions or sentences using the rebuses. The cards may then be reversed, read and written in traditional orthography. Even if pupils are unable to manage the writing themselves, watching their own message being written is more informative than merely reading it. *Breakthrough to Literacy* materials in modified form have been used at the Canterbury Social Education Centre for adults with SLD with the conclusion that these materials have considerable potential in such centres (Manley and Povey, 1985).

From Pictures to Words (Beste and Detheridge, 1990) comprises computer software for the BBC computer. Supplied on four discs, it offers a powerful set of language development activities for pupils in the primary school or older pupils with special educational needs. Using rebuses taken in the main from the *Learning with Rebuses Glossary* (van Oosterom and Devereux, 1985; 1988), this flexible program can be adapted for use with pupils with a wide range of abilities to support the language and literacy curriculum, relating in particular to Attainment Targets 2–5 in English in the National Curriculum. Since it is content free, teachers can decide which words and pictures to use from the Picture Library Disc. There is also the facility to create further pictures as required. Choice in text size, screen colour and the use (or not) of sound are further options. There are instructions for making overlays for the concept keyboard, the use of which is particularly appropriate to this program.

The proposals for English in the National Curriculum (DES and Welsh Office, 1989a) for Writing at Level 1 stipulate that pupils should be able to 'Use pictures, symbols or isolated letters, words or phrases to communicate meaning'. Making meaningful marks on paper, whether pictorially based or a form of scribble writing, helps to develop the skills needed for the more ordered activities leading to the formation of letter shapes and words. This in turn makes it possible for pupils to develop the more advanced skills of writing as a means of expression. Writing for meaning is a more advanced skill than reading for meaning, since the writer is responsible for the text and therefore must have matters to communicate as well as the ability and desire to do so.

Conclusion

It has been suggested that 'the nature of educational experience provided for children in special provision is often characterized by narrowness of opportunity' (Ainscow, 1989). Special educators have always been involved in modifying and adapting both curriculum content and approaches to learning. These skills will be given a new meaning and direction with the introduction of the National Curriculum. It will also make meaningful dialogue and exchange of ideas easier between special needs teachers and their mainstream colleagues. In the case of English in the National Curriculum, the common language of the Attainment Targets and levels within it, will make it easier to pinpoint a pupil's present knowledge and abilities, and to implement work at each level as is necessary for the individual, for 'access to the National Curriculum means carefully planned learning routes' (Archer, 1989).

Programme building within the structure of the Attainment Target will be all important since many pupils with SLD may remain at very early 'Levels' throughout their school lives, thus taking eleven years to accomplish what their more able peers achieve in less than two. Many of the ideas and materials that have been discussed in this chapter will form the basis for these learning routes, and since many of them have been developed for pupils with SLD they take the maturity factor into consideration. There are pupils with profound and multiple learning difficulties for whom the National Curriculum will require significant modification, which should be undertaken with vigour, for once entitlement is accepted the issue becomes one of access. Exclusion means isolation.

The educational environment must be constantly adapting to the needs of the individual. This requires flexible, knowledgeable and observant teaching and support staff, who have time to look, to listen and to respond to the pupils in their charge. This interactive perspective is the ideal for all pupils, but is essential for those with SLD if they are to be motivated and successful.

Finally, all the effort on the part of the staff, parents and pupils seems of worth when a group of older teenagers in a special school for pupils with SLD could express their thoughts and feelings so well when, on being asked 'What makes you feel sad?', they wrote variously:

I feel sad when ...
... Dad shouts at Mum,
... When I'm ill,
... When it's raining,
... When I don't like my present.

Further questioning about how it felt to be sad brought this response:

I feel heavy,
I feel tired,
It makes me cross,
Hide in my bed — cold,
Like sinking into the ground.

Not polished writing perhaps, but real expressive power.

The next day they were asked to write how they felt when they were happy. Their response was buoyant and so were they.

References

ABRAHAMSON, R. (1981) 'An update on wordless picture books with annotated bibliography', *The Reading Teacher*, 34, January, pp. 415–21.
AINSCOW, M. (Ed.) (1989) *Special Education in Change*, London, David Fulton Publishers in association with the Cambridge Institute of Education.
ARCHER, M. (1989) 'Targetting change', *Special Children*, 33, October, pp. 14–15.

BESTE, R. and DETHERIDGE, M. (1990) *From Pictures to Words*, Leamington Spa, Widgit Software.

BROWN, L. and PERLMUTTER, L. (1971) 'Teaching functional reading to trainable level retarded students', *Education and Training of the Mentally Retarded*, 6, pp. 74–84.

BUCKLEY, S. and WOOD, E. (1983) 'The Extent and Significance of Reading in Pre-School Children with Down's Syndrome', paper presented to BPS London Conference.

CARPENTER, B. (1987) 'A Formative Evaluation of a Symbols Based Reading Scheme', unpublished MPhil Thesis, University of Nottingham.

CLEMENTS, J. (1987) *Severe Learning Disability and Psychological Handicap*, Chichester, John Wiley & Sons.

CRIPPS, C. (1988) *A Hand for Spelling*, Wisbech, LDA.

CRIPPS, C. (1990) *Hands on Spelling*, Wisbech, LDA.

CRYSTAL, D., FLETCHER, P. and GARMAN, M. (1976) *The Grammatical Analysis of Language Disability*, London, Arnold.

D'ANGELO, K. (1981) 'Wordless picture books and the young language disabled child', *Teaching Exceptional Children*, September, 32, pp. 34–7.

DES AND WELSH OFFICE (1989a) *English for Ages 5 to 16*, London, HMSO.

DES AND WELSH OFFICE (1989b) *English in The National Curriculum*, London, HMSO.

DEVEREUX, K. and VAN OOSTEROM, J. (1984) *Learning with Rebuses: Read, Think and Do*, Stratford upon Avon, National Council for Special Education.

DICKINSON, D. (1987) 'Paired Reading: Its value with children with severe learning difficulties', *Mental Handicap*, 15, pp. 116–18.

DORRY, G.W. (1976) 'Attentional model for the effectiveness of fading in training reading vocabulary', *American Journal of Mental Deficiency*, 81, pp. 271–9.

DORRY, G.W. and ZEAMAN, D. (1975) 'Teaching a simple reading vocabulary to retarded children: Effectiveness of fading and non-fading procedures', *American Journal of Mental Deficiency*, 79, pp. 711–16.

EDMARK ASSOCIATES (1972) *Edmark Reading Program: Teacher's Guide*, Seattle, Edmark Associates.

ENGELMANN, S. and BRUNER, E.C. (1969) *DISTAR Reading: An Instructional System*, Chicago, Science Research Association.

GARDNER, K. (1986) *Reading in Today's Schools*, Edinburgh, Oliver & Boyd.

GILLHAM, B. (1987) *A Basic Attainments Programme for Young Mentally Handicapped Children*, Beckenham, Croom Helm.

HOLDAWAY, D. (1979) *The Foundations of Literacy*, Sydney, Ashton Scholastic.

JEFFREE, D. and SKEFFINGTON, M. (1980) *Let Me Read*, London, Souvenir Press.

JOHN HORNIMAN SCHOOL (1985) *Language Through Reading*, London, Invalid Children's Aid Nationwide.

KIERNAN, C. (1989) 'Research in the nineties', in BARNES, R. (Ed.) *Mental Handicap: Meeting the Challenge of Change*, Stratford upon Avon, National Council for Special Education.

KIRK, S.A. (1972) *Educating Exceptional Children*, 2nd Edition, Boston, Houghton Miffin.

MacKAY, D., THOMPSON, B. and SCHAUB, P. (1979) *Breakthrough to Literacy*, 2nd Edition, London, Longmans.

McNALLY, J. and MURRAY, W. (1962) *Keywords to Literacy*, London, Schoolmasters' Publishing Co.

MANLEY, R. and POVEY, R. (1985) '*Breakthrough to Literacy* — its use with adults who are mentally handicapped', *Mental Handicap*, 13, pp. 20–1.

MOYLE, D. (1972) *The Teaching of Reading*, London, Ward Lock Educational.

NCC (1989) *English Key Stage 1: Non-statutory Guidance*, York, National Curriculum Council.

PETERS, R.S. (1965) 'Education as Initiation', in ARCHAMBAULT, R.D. (Ed.) *Philosophical Analysis and Education*, London, Heinemann.

RABAN, B. (1988) *Literacy Learning — Planning a Programme for Early Development*, University of Reading, Reading and Language Information Centre.

RHODES, L.K. (1981) 'I can read: Predictable books as resources for reading and writing instruction', *The Reading Teacher*, 34, February, pp. 511–8.

SOUTHGATE, V. and ROBERTS, G.R. (1970) *Reading — Which Approach?*, London, University of London Press.

STAFF OF BLYTHE SCHOOL (1986) *Working with Makaton at Blythe School*, Camberley, Makaton Vocabulary Development Project.

STOTT, D.H. (1970) *The Programmed Reading Kit*, London, Holmes McDougall.

TERRACE, H.S. (1963) 'Discrimination learning with and without errors', *Journal of the Experimental Analysis of Behaviour*, 6, pp. 1–27.

THATCHER, J. (1984) *Teaching Reading to Mentally Handicapped Children*, Beckenham, Croom Helm.

TOMKINS, G. and WEBELER, M. (1983) 'What will happen next? Using predictable books with young children', *The Reading Teacher*, February, pp. 498–502.

VAN OOSTEROM, J. and DEVEREUX, K. (1985) *Learning with Rebuses Glossary*, Ely, EARO.

VAN OOSTEROM, J. and DEVEREUX, K. (1988) *Learning with Rebuses Glossary Supplement*, Ely, EARO.

WALSH, B.F. and LAMBERTS, F. (1979) 'Errorless discrimination and picture fading as techniques for teaching sight words to TMR students', *American Journal of Mental Deficiency*, 83, pp. 473–9.

WOODCOCK, R.W., CLARK, C.R. and DAVIES, C.O. (1969) *Teacher's Guide: Peabody Rebus Reading Program*, Circle Pines, Minnesota, American Guidance Service.

WORRAL, N. and SINGH, Y. (1983) 'Teaching TMR children to read using integrated picture cueing', *American Journal of Mental Deficiency*, 87, 4, pp. 422–9.

ZEAMAN, D. and HOUSE, B.J. (1963) 'The role of attention in retardate discrimination learning', in ELLIS, N.R. (Ed.) *Handbook of Mental Deficiency*, New York, McGraw Hill.

7 Meeting the Needs of Pupils within History and Geography

Judy Sebba and John Clarke

Introduction

In our discussion of History and Geography for pupils with severe learning difficulties (SLD) within the National Curriculum context we seek to observe three broad principles:

We shall, in the first instance, deal separately with History and Geography rather than look initially at possibilities for integrated work.

We hope to avoid tokenism. To this end we shall not be viewing current practice in schools for pupils with SLD and seek to make that fit the National Curriculum in History and Geography. Rather we shall examine existing National Curriculum documentation for these two areas and seek to demonstrate where National Curriculum History and Geography are relevant to the needs of pupils with SLD.

We hope to offer practical approaches which teachers and schools may use in, and out of, the classroom.

It has been the practice in many mainstream schools to teach History and Geography together in some form of Humanities programme, which might also include religious education and aspects of social science and related disciplines. As we address the issues involved in teaching History and Geography to pupils with SLD throughout this chapter, it will become clear that this continues to be a viable approach. The integrated curriculum is not ended by the National Curriculum. Indeed, as all the documentation comes on stream it should be possible to see links between different parts which, perhaps, have not been seen before.

However, the starting point in planning for the National Curriculum has to be its constituent parts and that is the approach taken here. Only through a detailed examination of each National Curriculum 'subject' can teachers gain the confidence to integrate them in the future. To approach the challenge in reverse is to run the risk of offering to children, in all schools, a curriculum which lacks rigour and is tokenist towards some of the constituent parts. This seems to explain some of the inadequate practice in many primary schools over the last twelve years. From the Primary Survey (DES, 1978) to *Aspects of Primary Education: The Teaching and Learning of History and Geography* (DES, 1989a), HMI have reported on gaps in the curriculum of many primary schools. Those gaps frequently involve History and Geography which have been served poorly in some schools by the integrated topic approach. The lack of confidence in teaching these curricular areas and the lack of appropriate training and a reliance on a topic approach have conspired to produce an inadequate curriculum: 'Many schools had great difficulty in making satisfactory provision for History and Geography within integrated work' (DES, 1989a).

The same dangers exist, as schools containing pupils with SLD begin to address National Curriculum History and Geography. Only through an examination of the documentation and a shared understanding between teachers in the same institution of what the specific contributions of History and Geography are to a pupil's total curricular experience, will the pitfalls which have affected many primary schools be avoided. The first principle adopted in this chapter, then, is to deal with History and Geography separately, but to illustrate examples of integration with each other and other curricular areas through the suggested practical activities.

The second principle adopted is to seek to ensure that in the exemplary material outlined every effort has been made to avoid the tokenist and to stress the notion of relevance. Pupils with SLD are entitled to the National Curriculum. At its heart the 1988 Education Reform Act (ERA) provides for a curriculum which is broad and balanced, promoting the moral, cultural, mental and physical development of pupils and prepares them for the opportunities, responsibilities and experiences of adult life. In a sense, the National Curriculum is a means towards achieving this end. It is incumbent upon all teachers to understand the degree to which this can feasibly happen; where the interests of the child are served poorly by the ten core and foundation subjects and RE, teachers will need in their deliberations to return to the purpose of the whole curriculum and the particular focuses which that may have for the child with whom they are most involved. For example, the proposed Programmes of Study for Key Stages 2, 3 and 4 in History are likely to have little relevance for the needs of the majority of pupils with SLD because of the degree of detailed, factual content prescribed. This is explained more fully below. Nevertheless, the Attainment Targets, which will be the assessment standards against which the performance of pupils will be judged, and the Programme of Study for Key Stage 1 in History have a part to play in a relevant education for all and it is, therefore, those on which most concentration will be placed in this chapter.

Nevertheless, teachers and schools need to explore thoroughly what the National Curriculum has to offer before making these decisions. Surveys of special schools conducted by HMI (DES, 1989b; 1989c; 1990a) have repeatedly highlighted the need to broaden the curriculum in these schools. Each subject area must be judged upon what it has to offer and should not be rejected on the grounds of prejudice. In this respect History and Geography could become casualties whereas, in fact, they both have much to offer pupils with SLD.

In order to tease out the specific contribution which National Curriculum History and Geography have to make to the education of pupils with SLD, we shall not be attempting to examine current practice in schools for pupils with SLD and make that practice appear to fit the National Curriculum. This is for two reasons. In the first place some practice which has never had its roots in positive educational philosophy can be legitimized by such an analysis; the exercise can be merely intellectual and lead not to development but to sterility. Secondly, there is a real danger that an activity of this nature reduces curriculum thinking to absurdity. The impossibility of accessing some of the targets within the National Curriculum to pupils with SLD needs to be recognized, and that point should not be lost in a series of time consuming, and ultimately time wasting, logic chopping curriculum planning sessions. The efforts of some schools, for example, to accommodate pupils with profound and multiple learning difficulties (PMLD) within every Science Attainment Target have demonstrated intellectual gymnastics which combine Einstein with Nadia Comenec but, in reality, still sound rather implausible. Moreover, many schools for pupils with SLD are not currently offering any activities in History or Geography, suggesting that starting from the current curriculum in these subjects would be unhelpful.

The third principle is simple and self explanatory. The emphasis is on practical activities which teachers and schools can undertake in order to satisfy, certainly in part, the likely demands of National Curriculum History and Geography. We have deliberately given a slightly greater emphasis to History than to Geography as it is History which appears to be presenting teachers in these schools with the greatest challenge.

History

At the time of writing, the documentation with which we have to work is The Draft Order (DES, 1991a). Although there is a potential for change in this document before the final orders for History are published, we believe that the essential thrust of the document will remain largely the same. This central thrust is that the learning of History is concerned with process factors, not with historical facts. Provided that this remains the case there is plenty which can be done within the context of the curriculum for pupils with SLD in History. Only if the National Curriculum for History resembles a shopping list of facts to be memorized will History cease to have any meaning for this population — in common, perhaps, with the total population. While it is process based there is something for everyone.

The Purposes of Teaching History to Pupils with Severe Learning Difficulties

The History Working Group whose proposals have been largely accepted in this document, tried to strike a balance between competing views of the purpose of teaching History in mainstream schools. In their proposed Attainment Targets and Programmes of Study they attempted to:

> ensure that the teaching of History in schools is not characterized by undisciplined use of the imagination, nor by exercises designed to develop skills in isolation from a solid foundation of historical information, nor by the mere acquisition of quantities of historical information that contribute little, if anything, to an enduring understanding of the past. (DES, 1990b, p. 1)

In this attempt, largely, they have been successful and this gives an opportunity for teachers working with pupils with SLD to teach History within the National Curriculum. Clearly, as is outlined below, these teachers will concentrate on particular aspects of the History curriculum with their pupils, but there is something there for them.

The History Working Group identified the purposes of teaching History. Some will appear daunting for those involved with pupils with SLD, for example: 'to train the mind by means of disciplined study. History relies heavily upon disciplined enquiry, systematic analysis and evaluation, argument, logical rigour and a search for the truth' (DES, 1990b, p. 1).

Nevertheless it is important to realize that these are aims for the whole course of study and, as such, and as with all aims, they are somewhat high flown and concern themselves with the final outcomes for some pupils of the study of History. The process of 'training the mind by means of disciplined study' begins at a very low level of sophistication. Moreover, some of the aims of studying History have a particular and very important focus in the teaching of pupils with SLD.

Firstly, 'to help understand the present in the context of the past. There is nothing in the present that cannot be better understood in the light of its historical context and origins' (DES,1990b, p. 1). For the high achieving GCSE candidate this might mean that she or he is able to understand better the situation in the Middle East in the 1990s because of an appreciation of the historical antecedents, for example, British policy in the area during the First World War and immediately after. For the pupil with SLD it might mean an appreciation of the routines of school or the notions of getting older and change. Equally, 'to help give pupils a sense of identity. Through History pupils can learn about the origins and story of their family and of other groups to which they belong, of their community and county and of institutions, beliefs, values, customs and underlying shared assumptions' (DES, 1990b, p. 1).

For many pupils with SLD much of this is far too ambitious, but the aim of giving pupils a sense of identity is central to the process of education. In all the strategies which teachers adopt to heighten their pupils' perceptions of their individual identities, they can remind themselves that not only are they attempting something which has always been a pre-eminent aim of the personal and social curriculum, but also that they are working within the framework of National Curriculum History.

Thirdly, 'to enrich other areas of the curriculum. History draws on the record of the entire human past; it is a subject of immense breadth which can both inform and draw upon other areas of the curriculum' (DES, 1990b, p. 1). Activities in History teaching can be very exciting and highly motivating for pupils. There are spin-offs which go beyond whatever may be gained in a strictly historical sense. The language and communication, for example, which can stem from an historical activity provide a further justification for teaching History. This is as true in a school for pupils with SLD as it is for mainstream schools.

Programmes of Study

General advice relating to the organization of the National Curriculum for implementation suggests that teachers should work from the Programmes of Study rather than from the Attainment Targets. To do otherwise is to risk a narrowing of the curriculum. In the case of History, certainly teachers should plan from the Programme of Study for Key Stage 1, for here the Attainment Targets are well matched with those things which pupils will be asked to do. Thereafter, however, it is highly unlikely, because of the mass of historical information required in the History Study Units that teachers of pupils with SLD will gain much by working from the Programmes of Study. In other subjects, the Programmes of Study for the Key Stages are developmentally sequenced, reflecting a logical progression. In History the Programmes of Study at each of Key Stages 2, 3 and 4 are applicable across the whole range of levels, as they prescribe content but do not imply a particular level of sophistication. Beyond Key Stage 1 it is therefore necessary to plan from the Attainment Targets for all pupils in History, while in other subjects it may remain more appropriate to plan from the Programmes of Study. In practice, almost by definition in developmental terms, it is highly unlikely that teachers working with pupils with SLD will be planning schemes of work beyond Key Stage 1, particularly since there has been no previous coverage of History in most of these schools.

Historical content is prescribed heavily in the Programmes of Study of all but Key Stage 1 where there is no prescribed content. The areas for study are organized into History Study Units, some of which are compulsory, some of which are optional and some of which are designed by the school. The level of prescription puts many of these History Study Units, in their entirety, beyond the compass of pupils with SLD.

However, two factors need to be borne in mind. In the first instance, the function of these History Study Units is to provide a context in which pupils may achieve against all the levels set out in the Attainment Targets. Activities will take place within schools for pupils with SLD with pupils over 7 years of age, which may meet the requirements of any or all three Attainment Targets but will be limited to the Programmes of Study for Key Stage 1, that is, not the Programmes of Study appropriate to the age of the pupils. This will not be an issue provided that the experiences offered to pupils continue to be relevant and stimulating. In the second place there is much in the Programme of Study for Key Stage 1 which is of relevance and is accessible and will still be appropriate for pupils with SLD as they get older. In Key Stage 1 'pupils should be given opportunities to develop an awareness of the past and of the ways in which it was different from the present. They should be introduced to historical sources of different types.' (DES, 1991a, p. 11). The Key elements in the Key Stage are given as: —

1.1 Pupils should be helped to develop an awareness of the past through stories from different periods and cultures, including:
   * well-known myths and legends;
   * stories about historical events;
   * eyewitness accounts of historical events;
   * fictional stories set in the past.
1.2 Pupils should have opportunities to learn about the past from a range of historical sources, including:
   * artefacts;
   * pictures and photographs;
   * music;
   * adults talking about their own past;
   * written sources;
   * buildings and sites.
1.3 Progressing from familiar situations to those more distant in time and place, pupils should be taught about the everyday life, work, leisure and culture of men, women and children in the past, *for example: clothes, houses, diet, shops, jobs, transport, entertainment.*
   They should have opportunities to investigate:
   * changes in their own lives and those of their family or adults around them;
   * changes in the way of life of British people since the Second World War;
   * the way of life of people in a period of the past beyond living memory.
1.4 Pupils should be taught about the lives of different kinds of famous men and women, *for example: rulers, saints, artists, engineers, explorers, inventors, pioneers.*
1.5 Pupils should be taught about past events of different types, including local and national events, events in other countries, and events which have been remembered and commemorated by succeeding generations, *for example: centenaries, religious festivals, anniversaries, the Gunpowder Plot, the Olympic Games.*

2. Links with attainment targets
   Pupils should have opportunities to develop knowledge, understanding and skills relevant to each of attainment targets 1, 2 and 3, in particular to:
   * use common words and phrases relating to the passing of time, *for example: old, new, before, after, long ago, days of the week, months, years;*
   * identify a sequence of events and talk about why they happened, *for example: changes in the life of a pupil's family;*
   * observe differences between ways of life at different times in the past, *for example: the clothes worn in different periods;*
   * develop awareness of different ways of representing past events, *for example: pictures, written accounts, films, television programmes, plays, songs, reproductions of objects, museum displays;*
   * distinguish between different versions of events, *for example: different accounts by pupils of events which happened in the school a week, month or year ago;*
   * find out about the past from different types of historical source, *for example: historic houses, objects in museums, paintings, coins, newspapers*

3. Historical enquiry and communication
   Pupils should be encouraged to ask questions about the past. They should have opportunities to communicate awareness and understanding of history orally, visually and in writing, *for example: act out an episode from the past through drama or dance; make models; use a word processor to write captions for objects; write about a past event.*

(DES, 1991a, pp. 11–13)

The fleshed out material which is offered in the draft order for Key Stage 1 can be worked with for pupils with SLD and, clearly, not merely in the 5–7 age range. There is much here which can be developed with pupils with SLD through the whole 5–16 age range. Moreover, there really is no issue of age appropriateness in studying this. As a pupil gets older his or her history gets wider, and in seeking techniques to make these things accessible to a wide range of pupils teachers are merely mirroring the experiences of everyone within and after their school years. People seek to interpret their own lives in terms of their own history and they seek to celebrate the 'rites of passage' as they live their lives. There is a very strong link in this work with aspects of RE. There is much of value which can be attempted with pupils with SLD in this context. Much of it merely requires some imagination and a willingness to understand that just because a particular pupil may never understand the development of modern Britain, nevertheless the work which he or she is doing is History.

Attainment Targets

An analysis of the Attainment Targets proposed demonstrates that there are plenty of opportunities for the teaching of History to pupils with SLD. The Secretary of State has proposed a change in the final report of the History working group and has reduced the number of Attainment Targets to three. The original report had four. The omitted Attainment Target was cross-curricular in nature and referred to 'organizing and communicating the results of historical study'. This aspect of studying History will now be spread among the other three Attainment Targets. The three remaining are:

1) *Knowledge and Understanding of History*
   concerned with: — the development of the ability to describe and explain historical change and cause and analyse different features of historical situations.
2) *Interpretations of History*
   concerned with: — the development of the ability to understand different interpretations of History.
3) *The Use of historical sources*
   concerned with: — the development of pupils' ability to acquire evidence from historical sources and form judgements about their reliability and value.

Again, written as they are in History-Teacher-Speak, these may seem daunting to the teacher of pupils with SLD who may be looking at History for the first time. When these three targets are expressed in terms of precise levels in Key Stage 1, for example, they become more accessible and more manageable:

LEVEL 1
AT 1 Place in sequence events in a story about the past.
AT 2 Distinguish between a fictional character and someone who actually lived in the past.
AT 3 Communicate information acquired from an historical source.

LEVEL 2
AT 1 Place familiar objects in chronological order.
      Identify differences between past and present.
AT 2 Show awareness that there can be more than one version of the past.
AT 3 Recognise that historical sources can help answer questions about the past.

LEVEL 3
AT 1 Describe changes over a period of time.
AT 2 Distinguish between a fact and a point of view.
AT 3 Make deductions from historical sources.

(Extracted from DES, 1991a, pp. 2–8).

Although the working group pointed out that the acquisition of historical knowledge is implicit in each of these Attainment Targets and what pupils actually *know* of History can be assessed through them, there is no precise prescribed content within the Attainment Targets. This is crucial because it gives the teacher of pupils with SLD the opportunity to construct meaningful activities in History without having to pay too much regard to the acquisition of facts. The Secretary of State has accepted, in the main, the points of the working group although intends to weight Attainment Target 1 more heavily than the other two for assessment purposes. This should make little difference for those involved with pupils with SLD.

Irrespective of the increasing levels of sophistication demanded by these targets, it is possible to see from them a way through the future History curriculum for pupils with SLD.

The rest of this section on planning begins to look at ideas for exciting and meaningful classroom (and out of classroom) activities related to the Programmes of Study, which would assist pupils to achieve against the levels within the Attainment Targets. Essentially, the activities fall into those which support Attainment Target 1 on developing a sense of time or Attainment Target 3 which addresses issues which involve gathering and evaluating historical evidence. In many cases the activity supports both Attainment Targets. Attainment Target 2 which deals with understanding points of view and inter-pretations of History is qualitatively different from the others and demands a higher sophistication than they do.

Practical History Activities for Pupils with Severe Learning Difficulties

There is currently very little, if any, activity that is undertaken in schools for pupils with SLD which the teachers themselves would label as History. The curricular auditing activities that have been undertaken by the National Curriculum Development Team (Severe Learning Difficulties) based at the Cambridge Institute of Education, have repeatedly demonstrated this to be the case, with little or no History or Geography being recorded by the teacher, over a one week period. This may reflect a 'real' lack of coverage of these subjects or may simply reflect unfamiliarity with the subjects leading to lack of recognition of their coverage within activities currently being labelled as other subject areas or activities. Either way, further consideration of appropriate activities is needed.

Ten activities are suggested and described briefly. All the activities are relevant to the Programmes of Study at Key Stage 1 and the Attainment Targets, in particular, Attainment Targets 1 and 3. They encourage an understanding of change, chronology and the use of evidence. These activities are suggested on the basis of a mixed group of pupils in a school for pupils with SLD and will need careful planning to differentiate the activity on the basis of teaching strategy or task to ensure all pupils are genuinely involved. For a fuller discussion of teaching strategies applicable to History for pupils with learning difficulties see Wilson (1985) and to History and Geography for pupils with special educational needs (SEN) see Clarke and Wrigley (1988).

Activity 1

Introduce work on the seasons which will enable records, in the form of natural objects, charts relating to the weather or clothes worn by the pupils to encourage contrast and comparison. Regular sessions will be needed to compensate for the possible problems created by the overall timescale. Take the pupils outside to experience weather (without limiting this experience by overprotective clothing!). The emphasis should be on using evidence, for example, it is autumn because the leaves are brown and crunchy, and on the passing of time, for example, yesterday the leaves were wet but today they are dry. Use wall display as much as possible. This activity is highly relevant to Geography and Science and will inevitably involve Maths and English.

Activity 2

Use any local building work as an opportunity to study change over time. Visit regularly, look at, smell (cement, tarmac), or, if possible, feel (stone foundations) the changes. Keep a photographic record of the progress. This is particularly relevant where a new building is being constructed from drains to completion or some new building is taking place on the school site.

Activity 3

Use historical artefacts close to the pupils' experiences to contrast 'old' and 'new' or 'now' and 'before'. It is helpful to use items familiar to the pupils such as toys, games or clothes rather than the more traditional approach using museum items which are likely to be meaningless to them.

Activity 4

Use historical artefacts related to activities rather than objects as in *Activity 3*. For example, compare washing clothes without and with a machine, using flat or modern irons, non-electrical or electrical floor cleaners. An older person could be invited into school to demonstrate use of an artefact which has been superseded by modern technology.

Activity 5

Take photographs of significant people in the life of the pupils, for example, taxi driver, midday supervisor, swimming instructor, riding instructor. Keep a photographic, and perhaps audiotaped, record of these people and repeat each time a personnel change occurs. This might provide the basis for a book or display.

Activity 6

Some teachers who have been involved in special schools long enough will recall the work of Dorothy Heathcote, a pioneer in the use of drama techniques with pupils with SLD and may have seen the video of her work entitled *Albert* (Mental Health Film Council, 1973) about a tramp who is discovered in the corner of the school hall. Albert is in fact a less well known member of staff dressed suitably for the occasion and asleep under a pile of newspapers in the corner of the hall. The pupils are brought into the hall for a 'movement' session and discover Albert. He says little or nothing and, led by Dorothy Heathcote's carefully selected questions, the pupils are encouraged to use the evidence available in order to find out what they can about Albert. The skills demonstrated by this group of pupils covered almost every area of the National Curriculum but, above all else, it is an excellent example of teaching pupils with SLD the basic historical skill of using evidence. In addition, it could be used to explore the distinction between fantasy and reality, referred to in the Attainment Targets at level 1.

Activity 7

A range of other activities is available within common current activities in schools for pupils with SLD that provide appropriate opportunities for developing the skills of using evidence. Many schools encourage their older pupils to prepare their own meals. There is no reason, provided normal hygiene rules are adhered to, why the next group to use the kitchen, or even the same class the following day, could not go through the rubbish bin in order to identify what had been consumed.

Activity 8

A more sophisticated version of a similar activity might involve presenting the group with a handbag, briefcase or shopping bag and saying, 'I wonder whose this is?'. The items inside would have been previously selected by the teacher to enable those particular pupils to recognize some, while remaining uncertain about others and to be able to suggest to whom it might belong. A bus ticket, for example, might tell us something about where the person lives, or make-up *might* suggest a female. This activity, like *Albert* and the rubbish bin, encourages development of the skills involved in using evidence.

Activity 9

The importance of developing the pupils' sense of chronology and of their own history is highlighted in the Programmes of Study. Interesting activities are being undertaken in a number of schools which relate to these skills. The use of tape recorded talk from members of the pupil's family, and matching these to photographs, is an activity that has been successfully developed with pupils with PMLD. Taking this a step further, these family members could be sequenced by age on the tape and in the book, to see if any understanding of oldest to youngest could be developed. Simple family trees could be constructed.

Activity 10

David Banes from the National Curriculum Development Team (Severe Learning Difficulties) has been using pieces of video made for the purposes of illustrating school activities at annual reviews. He has sequenced the sections of video of each pupil from the current year back through previous years, as far as video material is available. He has shown these sequences to the pupils as part of a teaching session in which they were encouraged to consider such questions as 'Who is this?', 'Are you older here?', 'Do you look the same now?', 'What toy was that you had?', 'Who is that teacher?'. This has produced some fascinating responses including the recognition of a previous member of staff that the teacher doing the session had not been able to identify.

Wilson (1990) noted the value of teaching History backwards, from the known to the unknown. This activity starts with the pupils as they are now, the situation with which they are likely to be most familiar. In addition to introducing the historical aspects of chronology and personal history, this work relates to the current developments in Personal and Social Education, for example, developing self-esteem in pupils with SLD.

Items of importance at every stage of the pupil's life can be kept as a running record, for example, favourite clothes or toys. This would appear to constitute a 'real object' dimension to Records of Achievement and might be enhanced by photographs of the pupil with the item at each age which could then be sequenced by the pupil.

Both this activity and the annual review videos can be considered as attempts to create time capsules.

Geography

The Purposes of Teaching Geography to Pupils with Severe Learning Difficulties

As with History, a central purpose of Geography in the context of pupils with SLD is concerned with identity. In 1986, HMI identified several objectives for Geography in the early primary years. They form an interesting starting point for a discussion of what Geography might look like for pupils with SLD:

The curriculum for the early years should provide pupils with learning experiences that will enable them to

extend their awareness of, and develop an interest in, their surroundings;

observe accurately and develop skills of enquiry;

identify and explore features of the local environment;

distinguish between the variety of ways in which land is used and the variety of purposes for which buildings are constructed;

recognize and investigate changes taking place in the local area;

relate different types of human activity to specific places within the area;

develop concepts which enable them to recognize the relative position and spatial attributes within their own environment;

understand some of the ways in which the local environment affects people's lives;

develop an awareness of the seasonal changes of weather and of the effects which weather conditions have on the growth of plants, on the lives of animals and on their own and other people's activities;

gain some understanding of the different contributions which a variety of individuals and services make to the local community;

begin to develop an interest in people and places beyond their immediate experience;

develop an awareness of cultural and ethnic diversity
within our society while recognizing the similarity of
activities, interests and aspirations of different people;

extend and refine their vocabulary and develop language
skills;

develop mathematical concepts and number skills;

develop their competence to communicate in a variety of
forms including pictures, drawings, simple diagrams
and maps. (DES, 1986, pp. 5–6)

This is an interesting list if for no other reason than it challenges
popular perceptions of what Geography in schools is about. It
contains, though not expressed in this way, human and economic
geography, physical geography and environmental geography. It contains geographic skills and skills which are from other areas but are
used extensively in Geography. It talks about the beginnings of an
'enquiry process' through which geographers study their subject. It
does not list a series of capes, bays and rivers the location of which
young children should know. Neither does it give lists of settlements
for pupils to learn and be able to place on a map.

Programmes of Study

Finding a way through the Geography curriculum as set out in the
Draft Order, (DES 1991b) presents no difficulties. The Programmes
of Study are little more than reiterations of the statements with the
levels of the Attainment Targets. For example, the Programme of
Study of Key Stage 1 has forty six things which teachers ought to be
helping pupils to do. All of these activities can be easily cross-referenced
to the Attainment Targets and experience suggests that teachers of
pupils with SLD have no problems in identifying curricular activities
which cover many of these things in an appropriate and relevant
manner for their pupils.

The Programmes of Study are divided into two sections: geographical skills and places and themes. Within geographical skills,
pupils need to use the skills of observation, using senses, identifying
similarities and differences, describing and discussing experiences, and
collecting, interpreting and reporting information. This Programme
of Study focuses mainly on early mapwork skills, for example,
directions, and simple maps and plans. The section on places and
themes stresses the importance of the school and home areas, al-

though includes increasing pupils' awareness of other places and comparisons of these to home and school area. This Programme of Study includes identification of features and occupations in the vicinity, the pupil's own address, weather, environmental features such as different forms of water, landscapes, use of buildings and looking after the environment.

Attainment Targets

Substantially, The Draft Order for Geography (DES, 1991b) follows the approach identified by HMI and described above. The main difference is concerned with the issue of content prescription. The Draft Order has five Attainment Targets. Three of these are concerned with geographical content, in terms of locational knowledge, that is, places and specific features which children should know and be able to identify or place on a map. In terms of the response of geographers and Geography teachers, it is this aspect which has engendered most debate.

Although it is impossible to prescribe precise knowledge relating to the local region, for obvious reasons, in terms of national and international locational knowledge, no such flexibility exists. For example, in order to attain Level 3 in terms of their knowledge of the United Kingdom and Europe, pupils will have to be able to:

'identify on globes or maps the following points of reference detailed on the map in the Draft Order, namely: — the British Isles, Ireland, the United Kingdom — Northern Ireland, Scotland, England and Wales, Dublin, Belfast, Edinburgh, Cardiff, London, the North Sea, the Irish Sea, the English channel, the River Trent, the River Thames, the River Severn, the Pennines, the Lake District, the Southern Uplands, and the Grampian Mountains' (DES, 1991b, p. 37 and Map A).

It is doubtful that these statement of attainments are appropriate for pupils with SLD. Nevertheless, this is no reason to abandon the whole of the proposed geographical curriculum. There is plenty within Geography which deserves to be an entitlement for all pupils.

In the first place, the prescribed lists of content do not begin until Level 3 and there are statements within earlier levels which can be approached by some pupils with SLD. More importantly there are four Attainment Targets, which do not have prescribed content which should be accessible to all pupils. They are AT 1 — Geographical Skills; AT 3 — Physical Geography; AT 4 — Human Geography; AT 5 — Environmental Geography.

Arguably, some National Curriculum Geography is already being covered in the visits which, for example, older pupils with SLD might make to the shops. On these trips some pupils might be 'following directions' (AT 1, Level 1). Some might be 'identifying activities carried out by people in the local area', or 'naming features of the local area with which they are familiar' (AT 2, Level 1).

During the course of a series of visits to the shops, if the teacher were aware that these were appropriate curricular objectives, they might be able to 'recognize that buildings are used for different purposes' and 'recognize that adults do different kinds of work' (AT 4, Level 1). Moreover, in the nature of school trips of all types it is often difficult to stop pupils from 'expressing their personal likes and dislikes about features of their environment' (AT 5, Level 1).

This is a simple example but does demonstrate what Geography in the National Curriculum is about at its least sophisticated and how accessible it is for many pupils with SLD. It also demonstrates how in line many of the early statements are with the personal and social curriculum which can be found in most schools for these pupils.

There is nothing daunting about Key Stage 1 of the Geography curriculum. Teachers find that a number of statements within the Programme of Study are being covered already but were never before perceived to be Geography and, more excitingly, find in many cases their imagination fired into designing new activities which can meet some of the other statements *and* the needs of their children.

Moreover, the work of the Geography group has been a genuine attempt to serve the needs of all pupils. Although there are serious doubts as to whether success in this was achieved in terms of pupils with SEN in mainstream schools (Clarke, 1990), in terms of pupils with SLD there in no reason to assume failure. In Chapter 8 of the final report, which deals with 'Geography for All', the group stated:

> 'it was often difficult to find language for the statements of attainment and the programmes of study which fully reflected our desire not to exclude pupils unnecessarily. We trust that teachers and those who design any assessment tasks will have regard to the spirit of our recommendations rather than just the letter.' (DES, 1990c, p. 79)

This is an invitation for teachers of pupils with SLD to take the documentation and make the best use of it for their own pupils. There is much in this curriculum which should be of benefit to their pupils and there is certainly nothing in Geography to make these teachers run away with the forlorn cry that the National Curriculum is not for them.

The final part of this section begins to look at ideas for exciting and meaningful activities related to the Programmes of Study, which would assist pupils to achieve against the levels within the Attainment Targets. The activities focus predominantly on the school and home area in order to stress relevance and work based on pupils' own experiences. However, a further problem for special schools is that their catchment areas are larger than mainstream schools and that work on 'home areas' is likely to include a substantial part of the Local Education Authority. Many of the activities involve extensive work outside the school building. However, the suggestions here require prior identification of individual needs, careful planning of differentiated activities and systematic recording of outcomes, rather than simply 'a trip out in the minibus'.

Practical Geography Activities for Pupils with Severe Learning Difficulties

Many activities currently undertaken in schools for pupils with SLD cover geographical skills but are not recognized specifically as doing so. For example, every school makes some attempt to teach pupils their home addresses (AT 2, Level 1) and many record the weather on simple charts (AT 3, Level 2 and Science AT 9, Level 1). There are, however, areas of National Curriculum Geography that could be extended, and certainly teachers need to increase their confidence in identifying and recording activities as Geography. Simple mapwork, use of buildings and the work done by people in the vicinity could be further developed.

Many special schools are currently developing their Science curriculum and it is worth noting that projects on the weather, recycling, water or movement are likely to cover both Geography and Science. The *Collins Primary Science* pack (Howe, 1990) and the Humberside LEA (1990) Science document both provide excellent examples of appropriate activities in these areas. Geography activities for pupils with SEN (for example, the use of three dimensional maps) are also described in Clarke and Wrigley (1988). Within the Geography final report itself (DES, 1990c) there are some useful pointers under the description of what constitutes good practice in primary schools, for example, use of large scale maps and inviting into school a visitor from another area. There is also an example of a Unit of work on 'Moving' (*ibid*, pp. 106–7) which suggests many good ideas appropriate to some pupils with SLD. Examples of methods of assessing and recording activities in History and Geography are described in Blyth (1990).

Activity 1

Alison Peters (1990) designed a Maths game that provides a most useful approach to teaching basic grid work. The board is divided into twelve squares, three by four. The three rows are labelled A, B and C and the four columns 1, 2, 3 and 4. In each square there is a picture of an animal and a set of matching cards of the same pictures are available. The pupil selects the animal he or she wants and asks for it using the grid reference. It is designed for two players who can help one another. For pupils with limited communication, it could be adapted to a lotto game, using two home made dice, one with the three letters on it and one with the four numbers on it. Different versions could be sequenced in levels of difficulty, by increasing or decreasing the number of squares (and with corresponding sets of dice).

Activity 2

Simple mapwork might be done by setting out with a blank piece of paper and starting to mark down places in relation to each other, for example, the shop in relation to the school, or the dining room in relation to the classroom. This could then be transferred to the concept keyboard on the computer using 'Touch Explorer' in order to construct a map of the school or the immediate area around the school. Pupils from other classes could be invited to try to use the map to locate a place or object and give some feedback on any problems. This would encourage self evaluation of the activity and would cover a significant amount of Technology work as well as Geography. Some Maths and English would inevitably be covered as well. Pupils with sensory or multiple difficulties could begin by using a tactile path, for example, felt tiles, or a strip of corrugated paper on the wall, to locate places in school.

Activity 3

One of the schools, with whom the National Curriculum Development-ment Team (Severe Learning Difficulties) has been working, visits a local agricultural college as part of their early work experience. During one day at the college, they observed people carrying out different tasks; they were involved in horticulture sessions, landscaping indoor plants, use of compost, and use of greenhouse and outdoor beds. A substantial part of the Programme of Study for Geography at Key Stage 1 was covered by the activities during the day, including making use of senses, observation, using directions, identifying activities carried out by people locally, observing different use of buildings and land and ways of improving the environment. These activities were discussed, recorded and followed up through other activities at school. Parts of all three core subject areas were covered in addition to Geography and Technology. The follow-up work at school might be likely to include charting changes in plants or waste over time which would contribute to historical work suggested above.

Activity 4

Another school with whom the team has been working had a topic on 'The School Garden'. This involved planning food crops, planting for succession, discussion of preferences, keeping a garden diary with pictures, words and video, charting the weather, making a garden map to plan what to grow where, collecting compost, use and care of tools, going to the garden centre to buy the seeds, plants and tools and the physical gardening skills (digging, raking). This covered work in all the National Curriculum subjects, but geographical skills were particularly well developed by this project, in a school in which teachers felt they had not been tackling this area. Detailed and sys-tematic recording was needed to ensure precise monitoring of the activity. It is important to relate this type of 'topic' approach to the needs of individual pupils in other areas of the curriculum. How, for example, could the gardening skills be allocated to enhance physiotherapy activities identified elsewhere to meet the needs of individual pupils? These issues, illustrated more fully through this particular example, are discussed in Byers (1990).

Activity 5

A very successful project on recycling was undertaken by Jean Dalby while completing her Advanced Diploma at Bristol Polytechnic. She was teaching a senior group in a school for pupils with SLD but this particular class was sited in the grounds of a large secondary school.

Working with eight students she introduced a project on recycling. First, they were introduced very simply to different types of waste and waste disposal and this was related to looking after the environment through avoiding leaving litter and collecting items for recycling.

The pupils went out in small groups with refuse bags to each class in the secondary school and collected the rubbish at the end of the day. Each bag was labelled for one class. They used a very simple bar chart to record how much rubbish each class had in its bag. The group then sorted the rubbish into paper, plastic, metal, and so on. They recorded the types of rubbish on a simple chart, and kept separate what could be recycled. The pupils brought in rubbish from home and it was sorted into the same categories.

The class prepared a simple map of the school and a plan of the surrounding area. They marked the sites of the litter bins on the maps and also noted shops. The worst areas for litter were noted and discussed. They considered: Are there enough litter bins?; Are they in the best places?; What does most rubbish consist of?; Can these be recycled?.

The class discussed how they could let other people know about what they found out. Interviews were conducted by the pupils with the headteacher of the secondary school and some of the pupils from the school. They were asked what type of rubbish they throw away, where most of it comes from (for example the tuck shop), what they think about the rubbish around the school and about recycling. The interviews were taped and provided the basis for further discussion.

Other related activities undertaken included making posters about litter, recycling and the environment, drama about rubbish and role plays to practise interviewing skills, visits to a supermarket (to find out what they do with their waste), Friends of the Earth and the Waste Disposal Plant. They made videos of the school before and after the project in an attempt to observe any changes in the rubbish, and designed T-shirts. Throughout this project, the microcomputer was used to access activities to pupils who could not otherwise be involved and to make charts, write letters and record results. The classroom display was relevant and helpful as well as very active, changing daily as a result of pupil interaction with it. Self-recording was developed and the work was used in each pupil's Record of Achievement.

Described in this way, this project sounds easy to carry out. Discussion with the teacher revealed that it had not all run so smoothly. However, a very uncooperative pupil had become observably more involved and the class as a whole had completed a great deal of useful and relevant work across every subject area, but particularly Geography. It could be that the project was so successful because the best possible practice had been incorporated at every stage. For example, the project was carefully planned and each activity differentiated by task or task presentation to ensure every pupil was involved. Excellent use was made of the classroom assistant's time. The purpose of the activities was clearly explained at the start of each session. Planning and preparation by the teacher ensured pupils were meaningfully occupied (that is, for example, not endlessly colouring). Displays were done by the pupils and regularly added to by the pupils. Above all else, activities were systematically recorded by pupils and teacher.

Conclusion

It would seem appropriate to end this chapter on a positive note. The recycling project was not created by an academic in a training institution. It was successfully completed by a teacher with a class of pupils with SLD. By successful completion it is not being implied that every pupil attained each of the targets described. Rather, that a group of pupils were undertaking an 'Integrated Scheme of Work' (as it has been referred to elsewhere, Byers, 1990) which promotes the best features of traditional 'topic' work combined with the rigour, systematic recording, planning for individual needs and analysis of tasks in which teachers of pupils with SLD have considerable experience.

In both History and Geography the use of the local area which builds on pupils' direct experience cannot be overemphasized. Planning work within the National Curriculum may require special schools to reconsider current activities to see if the potential historical and geographical opportunities have been utilized. For example, when a colour table is set up, are there any old objects included, those which belonged to a pupil's grandparent? Could visitors be shown around the school by pupils using maps or plans they have constructed? Does the language used in school deliberately emphasize historical and geographical aspects, such as before, now, yesterday, tomorrow, last week, and left, right, up, down, cold, hot, windy, here, there, shop-keeper, baker, bus driver, hill, flat?

There is much discussion among teachers of pupils with SLD about the relevance of History and Geography to their pupils. Part of this concern relates to misconceptions about what is involved in these subjects, arising from their own school experiences and a lack of understanding about how much these subjects, like others, have developed. The first step is for teachers to familiarize themselves with the subject documents. This could be quite a reassuring process provided realism prevails.

History and Geography offer much to the pupil with SLD in his or her educational pursuit of a greater understanding of the world in which he or she lives. The National Curriculum in these subjects does offer a realistic starting point for these pupils. However, it is important to keep the needs of individual pupils at the forefront of planning and not fall foul of tokenistic gestures. The latter make a mockery of the subjects, teachers and the pupils themselves.

This chapter has attempted to introduce the subject areas of History and Geography from the perspective of the teacher of pupils with SLD. Brief descriptions and comments on the National Curriculum subject documents have been offered and some suggested activities that other teachers have found useful have been described. The success or otherwise of delivering the National Curriculum to pupils with SLD lies mainly with the teacher in curriculum implementation. This requires differentiation by task, presentation, and any other means, not just by outcome and it is this which will contribute most to successful teaching with any group of pupils in any subject area. History and Geography and pupils with SLD are no different in this respect.

References

BLYTH, A. (1990) *Making the Grade for Primary Humanities*, Milton Keynes, Open University Press.

BYERS, R. (1990) 'Integrated schemes of work: "Topics" in schools for pupils with severe learning difficulties', *British Journal of Special Education*, 17, 3.

CLARKE, J. (1990) 'Other times, other places: Geography in the National Curriculum', *British Journal of Special Education*, 17, 3.

CLARKE, J. and WRIGLEY, K. (1988) *Humanities for All: Teaching Humanities in the Secondary School*, Special Needs in Ordinary Schools Series, London, Cassell.

DES (1978) *Primary Education in England: A Survey by HM Inspectors of Schools*, London, HMSO.

DES (1986) *Geography from 5 to 16: Curriculum Matters 7*, London, HMSO.

DES (1988) *History from 5 to 16: Curriculum Matters 11*, London, HMSO.

DES (1989a) *Teaching and Learning of History and Geography: Aspects of Primary Education*, London, HMSO.

DES (1989b) *A Survey of Provisions for Pupils with Emotional/Behavioural Difficulties in Maintained Special Schools and Units: A Report by HM Inspectors*, London, HMSO.

DES (1989c) *Educating Physically Disabled Pupils: Report by HM Inspectors*, London, HMSO.

DES (1990a) *Special Needs Issues: A Survey by HMI*, Education Observed Series, London, HMSO.

DES (1990b) *History for Ages 5 to 16*, London, HMSO.

DES (1990c) *Geography for Ages 5 to 16*, London, HMSO.

DES (1991a) *National Curriculum: Draft Order for History*, London, HMSO.

DES (1991b) *National Curriculum: Draft Order for Geography*, London, HMSO.

HOWE, L. (1990) *Collins Primary Science*, Glasgow, Collins.

HUMBERSIDE LOCAL EDUCATION AUTHORITY (1990) 'Science for Special Educational Needs', unpublished manuscript.

MENTAL HEALTH FILM COUNCIL (1973) *Albert*, Video available from Concord Film Council, Ipswich.

NCC (1990a) *History Consultation Report*, York, NCC.

NCC (1990b) *Geography Consultation Report*, York, NCC.

PETERS, A. (1990) 'Mathematical routes to National Curriculum Level 1', unpublished manuscript, submitted as part of Advanced Diploma, Cambridge Institute of Education.

WILSON, M.D. (1985) *History for Pupils with Learning Difficulties*, London, Hodder and Stoughton.

WILSON, M.D. (1990) 'History: Issues to resolve', *British Journal of Special Education*, 17, 2, pp. 69–72.

8 Mathematics for All

Brian Robbins

Introduction

The teacher had decided to work with several of her pupils on one-to-one correspondence. She had drawn three circles on a card, each the correct size and shape to take the base of a cotton reel.

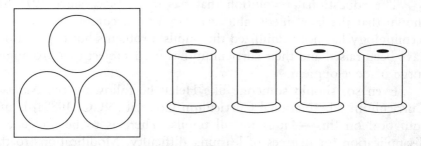

Helen, who was nine, had been given four cotton reels and was asked to put them on the card. The teacher had demonstrated the task with one of the reels. Helen was a renowned chatterbox and frequently verbalized her responses to tasks. True to form, on taking the first reel she said, 'This one has got somewhere to sit,' and duly placed it on one of the circles. She picked up the next one — 'And this one has got somewhere to sit'. Similarly with the third one, but on lifting the fourth one she noted sadly that it had nowhere to sit.

Her method of solving the problem in 1972 preceded by ten years the Cockcroft Report (DES, 1982) with its emphasis on mathematical experiences being presented in three modes: practical, oral and written. She was certainly having a practical experience, she was being encouraged to use her oral skills (and we hope the teacher was encouraging and extending her attempts to verbalize the task). She may not have been able to express in written form: 1 + 1 + 1 = 3, or

$4 - 1 = 3$, but she could colour in on a worksheet to show what she had just done. She might have been able to demonstrate it with magnetized cut-out shapes on a magnet-board had one been available. This would have shown that she could perform the given task and understand what she had done sufficiently well to reconstruct it in a different form and in another context.

Entitlement

Helen, who had Down's Syndrome, was in a school for pupils labelled severely educationally subnormal (ESN(S)). Three years previously, in 1969, she would still have been legally classed as ineducable. This categorization was based on a blanket assumption that pupils like her would not benefit from the kind of education suitable for other pupils. It was assumed that they would not be able to acquire more than very basic communication and self-help skills. The emphasis was on activities to occupy them and make them sociable.

The educational revolution that has taken place since 1971 has shown that the label ineducable was far from accurate. A change in terminology has not minimized the pupils' problems but expectations have been raised and their curriculum has been subject to a prolonged surge of development.

Even so, should someone like Helen be following the *National Curriculum*? The National Curriculum Council (NCC, 1989a) is unequivocal on this — it is for all pupils. There is to be no general disapplication for degrees of learning difficulty. Modifications to the Programmes of Study for individual pupils will be specified in their Statements of Special Educational Needs.

The task for teachers is twofold: firstly, to turn the principle of entitlement into practical teaching strategies that meet the current needs of all pupils and equip them for adult life; secondly, to describe these strategies in terms that make them recognizable within the context of the Statements of Attainment and Programmes of Study laid down in the statutory orders for Mathematics (DES and Welsh Office, 1989).

What Helen achieved in the cotton reels task would be accomplished by most children at an earlier age. We should, however, take note of the comment by the Secretaries of State in their response to the report of the Mathematics Working Group. They referred to each of the ten levels representing a 'unique standard of achievement regardless of a child's age'. Their remarks referred admittedly to another issue but, as an expression of principle, this phrase should be the springboard into the National Curriculum for all pupils with learning difficulties (DES and Welsh Office, 1988).

Access

The word 'access' is used here to refer to a cognitive preparedness for work related to the first Key Stage of the Mathematics National Curriculum rather than to facilities to overcome physical or sensory disabilities.

The NCC (1989a) says 'that for progress to be monitored and achievements acknowledged, there will be a need for ... careful pacing of work and activities which are both finely-graded developmentally and appropriately age-related'. Level 1 isn't the beginning — it encompasses a wealth of learning that cannot be taken for granted.

The Mathsteps materials (Robbins, 1988) are the result of an endeavour to plan a sequence of learning activities to take pupils from those very early, pre-concept stages to a point where they can cope with the kind of experiences provided for 5, 6 and 7 year olds in mainstream education — what we would today call Key Stage 1. (Other complementary materials are described by Ashdown and Devereux, 1990).

When Mathsteps was first begun there was a widely-held belief, based on the work of Piaget, that children passed through a stage of 'number readiness' and that before they reached that stage they would not be able to grasp the basic concepts. A series of Piagetian-based tests had been devised for use in a school for pupils with moderate learning difficulties (MLD). These sampled, among other things, their ability to count, match and put rods of different sizes in serial order. It became apparent that many of the younger pupils could not complete these tasks successfully. This finding was even more marked when the tasks were tried with pupils in Helen's school.

Piaget's view was that the development of these concepts could not be hastened but could only grow through exposure to rich learning experiences. Yet the classrooms were well-stocked with the kind of apparatus that would be found in number readiness activities: formboards, sorting materials, coloured wooden cubes, cotton reels and so on. The pupils used this material frequently but it was in a repetitive way. The same activity would be repeated day after day.

More able youngsters may well have explored and sought new ways of using it and by doing so extended their own learning through experience. Pupils with severe learning difficulties (SLD), and many with MLD, appear to lack this facility.

The Learning Process

There seemed to be two main hurdles. One was poor manipulative skills which made it difficult for them to handle the apparatus. The second seemed to be a cognitive one. It is not intended to go into a detailed account here of the link between concept development and language, but these pupils undoubtedly had problems in both areas. Whatever the cause, the result was that they were unlikely to make progress in the way suggested by Piaget, and a more deliberate approach was required. The chosen method was learning through activity in a meaningful context rather than the direct teaching of isolated skills.

The approach adopted was to seek ways of leading the pupils towards the necessary skills and concepts through a series of small learning steps (Robbins, 1978). This was done by devising a set of activities based on the skills that underlie a great deal of 'infant maths'. For example, the ability to fit together constructional unit blocks such as Unifix or Multilink is essential and needs to be taught deliberately. Observation showed that many of the pupils did not have the manipulative skills that would be expected of infants and that many had not mastered the fine motor skills of joining blocks together. Previous steps of learning appeared to be missing.

The STYCAR schedules of child development, (Sheridan, 1973) chart the growth of these skills in a sequential manner. Certain items bore a close relationship to the responses of the pupils to the materials. This can be illustrated by the sequence of handling cubes: at 9 months a baby grasps a wooden cube and manipulates it with interest; at 12 months it holds two cubes, one in each hand. This could be considered as a significant stage in the development of the concept of one-to-one correspondence and of the relative values of one and two. We would not expect the appropriate vocabulary to be understood by a child at that age but it does demonstrate what children need to master in order to acquire particular skills.

Taking the process further, at 18 months a child can build a tower of three cubes and at 2 years one of six or seven cubes. At 3 years it can build one of nine cubes and can copy a model of a bridge built from cubes. This indicates the merging of manipulative and perceptual skills to perform a task to specified requirements. This kind of information was used to build up an observation schedule.

The responses of the pupils in Helen's school to different sets of materials were noted and used to enlarge and refine the items on the schedule. A series of activities was devised that led progressively through the acquisition of each skill. In the example given above, later stages involved the materials being used to compare the numerical value of two sets of cubes.

We now had targets that would for most pupils be the beginnings of Maths teaching. They are significant steps along the road to learning and show what has to be learned before our pupils can achieve the Statements of Attainment at Level 1 in the National Curriculum.

O'Toole and O'Toole (1989) found that the vast majority of 7 year old pupils with SLD are not likely to have achieved any of the Statements of Attainment in the Level 1 Programme of Study. This demonstrates the need to go back to these very early foundations of learning to plot a path to lead them towards any recognizable standard of achievement in National Curriculum terms. Ausubel (1968) made the point that 'the most important single factor influencing learning is what the learner already knows. Ascertain this and teach him accordingly'.

Learning in Context

Whilst a fine gradation of steps is necessary to make learning more accessible, several other factors need to be taken into account (Reason, 1989). The context within which learning is to take place has to be relevant to the learner. No two people learn in quite the same way and we must appreciate individual learning strategies.

We may need to give alternative instructions. For example, these words are commonly used mathematical terms: add, subtract, divide, partition and sets. But we may need to use more familiar words, such as put together, take away, share, some and lot.

We must consider the process of learning as well as the outcomes. It is not enough to follow the National Curriculum Statements of Attainment at each level. These do not have the precision nor do they adequately describe the context. We need to look at the Programmes of Study and work from those.

Appropriateness

The progression within the National Curriculum is towards higher Mathematics. How can this be reconciled with the need to teach skills that will be useful to Helen in adulthood?

Schools have to produce a policy statement for each of the core and foundation subjects and the NCC has produced *Non-Statutory Guidance* (NCC, 1989b) to help schools in this task. A section at the end of this chapter gives further guidance on relating this advice to the particular needs of pupils with learning difficulties.

Before writing their policy document schools should identify the short-term and long-term needs of their pupils. The Cockcroft Report sets out a list of foundation skills. We can recognize these (money, calculations, measuring distance, time and quantity, percentages, a basic understanding of statistics) as the kind of mathematics we use in our daily life. Such a list, however basic it may appear to teachers in mainstream education, presents a formidable hurdle to the majority of pupils being considered here. 'Children with a range of learning difficulties, and adolescents with severe learning difficulties, will need more time and specially-planned activities to develop the knowledge and understanding required to work within Level 1' (NCC, 1989a, p. 24).

Inservice Training

The detail required has to be developed by teachers and it has to be both relevant and appropriate for their pupils. This should be done in association with colleagues, especially when some teachers admit to lack of confidence with Mathematics.

School-based inservice workshops are an effective way of developing a consistent and coherent approach within a staff. The *Working Together* INSET pack (Open University, 1989) has a number of suggested activities for school-based professional development in Mathematics. There is considerable emphasis on discussion and the booklet sets out strategies that group leaders will find useful. It suggests that every session should consist of three parts; a pre-set activity, a talking point leading to discussion and then time for reflection. The content is aimed at mainstream teaching but the principles can be applied in special education. For example, the following format could be followed with a group of teachers of pupils with SLD.

Session One

Activity

What Maths have you used in getting here this morning? Working in pairs write down all the mathematical skills you used in: getting up, having breakfast, travelling to the school/conference.

You may wish to give a few prompts such as Time, Volume, Capacity, Estimation, Number.

Talking point

What use is Maths — what Maths is useful?

Reflection

In groups of four to six discuss whether the initial activity brought out information that could be useful to you as a class teacher.

Session Two

Activity

As a full group or, if numbers warrant it, several groups each with a leader or facilitator:

Identify the mathematical skills that your pupils use in their activities at school and at home. It is important that the group understands that this activity requires them to consider the whole curriculum — language development, home economics, PE, swimming, technology, social skills, day and residential visits — and not limit their thoughts to 'Mathematics'. The list of curriculum areas you use should be modified according to the headings used on your own school timetable.

Talking point

In groups list the Maths used in the 'whole curriculum'. Each group to discuss in detail the teaching implications in one of the areas you have listed.

Reflection

What links across the timetable can you identify? How does Maths underpin the rest of the curriculum?

Session Three

Activity
In groups analyze the mathematical content of a real-life activity, such as preparing a meal, highlighting the particular mathematical skills being used.

You will probably identify some of the ones given in brackets:

Planning the meal:

How many people are coming? (number)

How much food will we need? (quantity)

List the ingredients and make sure you have enough money (budgetting)

Travel to and from the shops (number, money, time)

Shopping (money, shape, measure, number).

Cooking the meal:

What time do we need to begin cooking? (time, subtraction)

What size utensils? (shape, volume)

What temperature? (symbols, measure, numerals)

Laying the table:

How many places? (number, one-to-one correspondence)

Talking point
Relate the skills identified to the Level 1 Programme of Study and Statements of Attainment.

Reflection
In what way is Maths relevant for pupils with SLD?

Session Four

Activity
You are planning a visit to a café. Make a list of the mathematical experiences that can you draw out of:

the journey to the café, whether on foot or by bus;

the visit to the café;

the follow-up discussion back at school.

Talking point

Which experiences that you have noted down relate to one of the Statements of Attainment at Level 1 or at Level 2? Have some pupils acquired the specified skills but others not?

Any response from a pupil that indicates a partial grasp of the mathematical skills inherent in the task, however broadly interpreted, should be regarded as evidence that he or she is working towards gaining them.

Reflection

After taking your pupils on a visit to a café, note which of the skills you had identified were actually used by the pupils and were there any others that you had not thought of?

Session Five

Activity

Explore further teaching possibilities that could arise from this topic — for example, during the journey you may work on the spatial skills that underpin measuring:

Can they recall landmarks on the journey?

Can they discriminate between somewhere being 'near' or 'far'?

Can they appreciate the usage of time as a measurement of distance?

Talking point

We might say it takes a 'long time' to get to the town centre. Phrases like 'a short time', 'soon', 'later' are commonly-used estimates of time with which they should be familiar. When might it be appropriate to take a stop-clock on the journey as a means of introducing them to standard measurement of time?

Reflection

Is it reasonable to consider these as steps towards achieving Attainment Target 8?

The next stage is to relate the activities and skills you have listed to the Programmes of Study for Levels 1 and 2 (DES and Welsh Office, 1989, pp. 49–50).

Further sessions can follow a similar format and can lead into consideration of the best way to deliver Maths in your school. It is possible that you may decide not to identify Maths as a separate timetable component. If you do decide to take a cross-curricular approach you should note this in your curriculum audit and make an estimate of the proportion of Mathematics-related activity the pupils are undertaking. You should also consider whether some specific teaching of mathematical skills, probably at a very early level, should be included in each pupil's programme.

Good at Maths?

Another probable outcome of the inservice activity described above is the recognition that on any staff there will be some more competent in teaching Maths than others. Many teachers have negative feelings about Maths as a result of bad experiences in their own schooldays. Undue emphasis on right and wrong leads to a lack of confidence in those who had more crosses than ticks!

Varying degrees of competence and confidence in Maths should be seen as a potential strength for a school. The person who is uncomfortable with Maths can have a great deal of empathy with the pupils. The colleague who enjoys the subject can inspire others to 'have a go' by showing the fun that can be had in an active Maths task. Teachers may decide to work together with several classes in a Maths activity session. By teaching collaboratively they can each use their interests and specialisms for devising interesting and varied ways of approaching particular learning goals. It can also give both teachers the opportunity to take some time out of direct involvement to observe how the pupils are responding. The author has been involved in this kind of teaching where the headteacher, outreach teacher, class teachers and teachers' assistants all worked together with two classes in a 'Maths afternoon'. The staff and pupils have all enjoyed and benefited from the variety of ideas that have been generated. In this kind of setting everyone's contribution, staff and pupils, can be acknowledged and valued.

Progression, Continuity and Differentiation

The National Curriculum is intended to achieve higher standards by requiring the curriculum of all schools to conform to these basic principles.

The NCC non-statutory guidance for Mathematics (NCC, 1989b) concentrates on progression and continuity. It sets out different ways of teaching towards the fourteen Attainment Targets in the Mathematics National Curriculum (DES and Welsh Office, 1989). Regular assessment and schemes of work based on the Programmes of Study at each of the ten levels will inform teachers of what pupils have previously learned and experienced. The Statements of Attainment indicate what pupils should be working towards at each level.

This should not appear revolutionary to teachers in special education. They are used to achieving progression by breaking down the steps of learning so that their pupils can be seen to be making progress at a suitable pace. Continuity is essential and the record keeping is often more detailed than that carried out by their mainstream colleagues. Many special schools have programmes running through giving a built-in vehicle for progression and enabling teachers to plan and evaluate their work within a whole school context. Information passed on from one class to the next is in a common format. The teacher in the new class is able to continue from the pupil's current level of attainment in all areas of learning rather than take up time assessing what the pupil has already achieved. An ongoing record-keeping system will give an immediate indication throughout the year of progress being made and whether the learning activities need to be modified.

Differentiation

Differentiation can be achieved in a number of ways, many of which are familiar in the methodology of special education.

Differentiation of input
We could set out with quite different aims, though this would contradict the assertion of the Warnock Committee that the aims of education are the same for all pupils.

The content of the Maths curriculum could be modified. Activities aimed at infants could be redesigned so that the tasks would be appropriate for older pupils. For example, an exercise in an infants Maths scheme to develop the pupils' ability to match similar objects might be built around toys. We would probably want to present it in a life-skills context such as selecting tins of beans of the same size and price from a supermarket shelf. In doing this we would have also modified the learning context from a desk-bound activity to one that involved using educational experiences in the world outside school.

Some of the best Maths lessons take place in the gym or the playground. Spatial awareness is fundamental to an understanding of both shape and measurement and terms such as bigger, smaller, under, over, around, can all be practised in physical education activities.

Stories, rhymes and photographs can all make Maths come alive. *Talking Maths* (Gallagher, 1990) is a set of photographs with guidance for teachers on how they can be used to develop the vocabulary associated with basic mathematical concepts.

The personal attention of the teacher is one of the most effective ways of ensuring that a pupil can understand and work through a task, but other types of input should be used as well. Television presents quite difficult ideas in ways that are more readily understood. Some TV programmes may contain too much information for the pupil with SLD to absorb all at once, but they can be recorded and played back in manageable chunks. Computer programs are constantly developed and many are now very straightforward to operate. They have the advantage of encouraging the pupil to work independently or in cooperation with another pupil and thus reduce their dependence on the teacher.

Adapting the pace at which tasks are presented and the depth to which they are investigated are other ways of differentiating the Programmes of Study. We may take care in the terminology we use so that the pupil is not overloaded with a mass of unfamiliar vocabulary.

We must decide whether we are going to encourage active learning or whether we will use a highly-structured direct teaching approach.

Between the 1970 Education Act and the Education Reform Act 1988 (ERA) there was considerable emphasis on the definition of specific behavioural objectives. We should question whether teaching should aim solely at achieving set objectives or take account of the process of learning, which may not follow quite such a strictly hierarchical pattern as the framework of the National Curriculum might lead us to believe.

Learning is an interaction between the pupil, the teacher, the materials available and the context within which they are being used. In this respect every learning experience is unique. There are, however, certain elements that set the context and elicit particular responses from the pupil. None of these need be static and there is an

infinite number of ways in which Maths teaching can be made interesting and enjoyable.

We have already noted how childhood experiences can affect
attitudes towards Maths in adult life. We must be aware that even
pupils with SLD might make a sudden leap in understanding. A
positive ethos that values their response and encourages them to go
further at a pace that is challenging yet achievable is likely to be
reflected in their absorption in the task.

Differentiation of outcome

So far we have considered differentiation of the input but it is also
possible to set the same task for a group of pupils with widely-varying
levels of attainment. In this instance we would be looking for ways in
which all pupils could be seen to be achieving even if at different
levels.

There are a number of ways of grouping pupils and a variety
of arrangements can be made at different times of the day or week.
These range from working individually, working in groups according
to age, ability or interest to being in fully mixed ability groups. Peer
tutoring could involve pupils in working together, paired Mathematics could be one pupil helping another and in the process
reinforcing his or her own learning.

If there is more than one adult in the classroom this increases
the range of grouping permutations that can be achieved. The collaborative teaching approach described earlier increases the range of
possibilities and can be useful for extending the higher achiever and
supporting those who are struggling with the task.

Methods of teaching go in and out of fashion but it is worth
varying the approach if the pupil does not seem to grasp what you
might think he or she is capable of understanding. It is important to stress
that the scenario of the teacher presenting material and the pupil being
expected to absorb it has limitations.

Assessment

A view of Mathematics teaching that is broader than a desk-bound
approach has profound implications for assessment. A criterion-based
approach will need to be flexible enough to take note of the unpredict-
able and the unmeasurable. It is vital that assessment is seen as part of
the teaching process and not as a separate activity.

There is a relationship between the materials used for teaching
and learning and the methods employed by the teacher. Published
materials are restrictive and inflexible by their very nature. They

should be used sparingly and as reinforcement, not for initial teaching. No scheme should prevent a teacher seizing opportunities that arise such as a pupil coming to school with news of the arrival of four kittens at home. An interesting discussion which could range across several of the statutory subject areas could be followed up at a later date. Pupils could be asked a week later to calculate how old the kittens now were. Teachers might feel unable to give an objective measurement of how each pupil has progressed as a result of the experience built around the arrival of the kittens. But it would be possible to make and record a sound professional judgment of the extent to which each pupil was involved in the discussion and whether it awakened some interest that the pupil had not shown previously.

Assessment should not be a meaningless chore — it should be part of the process by which teachers judge the effectiveness of the resources they have as well as the methods they use. Dynamic assessment shows whether teaching materials are appropriate and whether the current objectives are relevant to the needs, learning skills and interests of the pupils.

School Mathematics Policy

What should be in the school policy statement? Section B of the *Non-Statutory Guidance* issued by the NCC (NCC, 1989b) gives eleven headings to help schools develop their Mathematics policies. These notes are intended to relate the NCC guidance to the needs of pupils with learning difficulties. They should be regarded as a starting point for staff discussion rather than as a definitive list.

1 The Nature of Mathematics

Maths is hierarchical in the sense that concepts are built upon what has been learned previously. That is not necessarily the way children learn Maths, but it does provide a useful framework for gauging pupils' progress. The Statements of Attainment at Level 1 in the National Curriculum statutory order do not give sufficient acknowledgment of what has been learned previously. For many pupils these are a major achievement, not a starting point.

The steps of learning Mathematics need to be broken down and all staff must appreciate that mathematical knowledge is called upon in other areas of the curriculum. How does Maths support and underpin the skills required for pupils to succeed in other curriculum areas? Is task analysis one way of identifying these skills?

2 *School Policy and the National Curriculum*

Are all pupils working towards the National Curriculum? If a structured approach is used, are teachers aware of the opportunities for undertaking open-ended investigation?

3 *Pupils' Mathematical Experiences*

Is there a range and balance — not just sums? Does learning take place in a variety of settings, for example, individual and group work, teacher led 1–1, groups or individuals with classroom, using support staff? Is there practical, oral and written work? Are microcomputers used and for what purpose? What is the policy on the use of calculators?

4 *Pupils' Mathematical Activities*

Is there a structured framework for teacher guidance and to inform progression, continuity and differentiation? What is the framework based on?

5 *Pupils' Records of Work*

Pupils can find motivation from recording their own progress.

6 *Cross-curricular Issues*

Maths is a means of quantifying our environment — it makes our world understandable and presents information in a way that the human mind can grasp. It should simplify the difficult — not the reverse. It gives access to other areas of the curriculum.

Maths is also an art form and the source of considerable pleasure to some people. How imaginatively are spatial words and the vocabulary of comparison taught in your school? What data collected by the pupils is on display?

7 Assessment

Assessment should tell us what the pupil knows, not how many worksheets or books he or she has completed.

8 Recording Pupils' Progress

Records should be comprehensive, accurate and up-to-date. They should ideally be understandable to both teachers and parents and, wherever possible, to the pupil. One approach is to use a grid profile, which gives an immediate visual indication of progress, with extension sheets to be used when required. Specify which teacher has responsibility for ensuring that each pupil's records are kept and who on the staff can give specialist help and advice.

9 Evaluation

How, when and by whom will this policy be reviewed? Has the Maths Adviser been invited to support the school?

10 Staffing and Resources

Are the Maths materials in the school appropriate for the pupils? Are they being used effectively?

All teachers utilize a pupil's mathematical knowledge. Some of these ways are more obvious than others, for instance, Home Economics, Design and Technology. Should there be a core Maths programme to be taught by one person and a breakdown (topic webs) of the Maths taught in other areas? Would it be beneficial to timetable opportunities for collaborative teaching?

Have you planned next year's expenditure on the basis of identified gaps in your materials and developments you have agreed should take place? Have you recognized the inservice training implications of the new resources and planned your professional development programme accordingly?

11 Classroom Management

All pupils should be actively involved in their own learning and should be presented with work that challenges but does not demoralize. All should be free to progress at their own pace, without undue distraction. All should have a reasonable amount of the teacher's time and support.

Summary

The Programmes of Study set out for Mathematics in the National Curriculum should be the means of demonstrating the validity of the curriculum for pupils with SLD and the justification for gaining the resources to give them broad, relevant and challenging mathematical experiences.

Schools may not have Mathematics on their timetable but they should include mathematical experiences within the curriculum. These experiences will be part of their overall Programmes of Study and they should be able to demonstrate the progress being made by each pupil in developing mathematical knowledge, skills and understanding at whatever level. Many pupils with SLD will spend a considerable amount of their school life on activities which come within the range of experiences leading towards Level 1.

References

Ashdown, R.W. and Devereux, K. (1990) 'Teaching Mathematics to pupils with severe learning difficulties', in Baker, D. and Bovair, K. (Eds) *Making the Special Schools Ordinary*? Volume 2, London, Falmer Press.

Ausubel, D. (1968) *Educational Psychology — A Cognitive View*, New York, Holt, Rinehart and Winston.

DES (1970) *The Education (Handicapped Children) Act 1970*, London, HMSO.

DES (1982) *Mathematics Counts*, (The Cockcroft Report), London, HMSO.

DES (1988) *The Education Reform Act 1988*, London, HMSO.

DES and Welsh Office (1988) *Mathematics for Ages 5 to 16: Proposals for the Mathematics National Curriculum*, London, HMSO.

DES AND WELSH OFFICE (1989) *Mathematics in the National Curriculum*, London, HMSO.

GALLAGHER, C. (1990) *Talking Maths*, Wisbech, Learning Development Aids.

NCC (1989a) *Curriculum Guidance Two: A Curriculum for All*, York, National Curriculum Council.

NCC (1989b) *Mathematics — Non-Statutory Guidance*, York, National Curriculum Council.

OPEN UNIVERSITY (1989) *Working Together — School-based Professional Development in Mathematics*, Milton Keynes, The Open University.

O'TOOLE, B. and O'TOOLE, P. (1989) 'How accessible is Level 1 Maths?', *British Journal of Special Education*, 16, 3, pp. 115–18.

REASON, R. (1989) 'Evidence of progress?', *British Journal of Special Education*, 16, 4, pp. 149–52.

ROBBINS, B. (1978) *Step by Small Step*, Wisbech, Learning Development Aids.

ROBBINS, B. (1988) *Mathsteps*, Wisbech, Learning Development Aids.

SHERIDAN, M. (1973) *Children's Developmental Progress — The STYCAR Sequences*, Slough, NFER.

9 Dimensions of Design and Technology

Andy Tearle

The Nature of Design and Technology

What is Technology? Most activities in school can be related to Technology. Technology in the National Curriculum, as described in the statutory order (DES and Welsh Office, 1990), is a new subject which requires pupils to apply knowledge and skills to solve practical problems. The subject is divided into the two profile components of Design and Technology Capability and Information Technology Capability. It is Design and Technology which is the focus of this chapter. The non-statutory guidance for Design and Technology capability (NCC, 1990) states that the reference to 'capability' is intended to emphasize the fact that the subject is concerned with practical action, drawing on knowledge and understanding from a wide range of curricular areas. It is all about identifying needs, generating ideas, planning, making and testing to find the best solutions.

How can schools approach this subject? Is it to be fitted in, adopted wholesale, tackled by themes or ignored? The stance taken here is that teachers have to be honest and put the direct needs of the young people first. Schools for pupils with SLD have attempted to do this for years and the result is a practical, relevant and realistic approach to the pupils, which best equips them to cope with themselves, others and life. There is no reason to ignore or change this approach in the light of Technology in the National Curriculum since it deals in reality.

At the heart of Design and Technology lies a 'process' of designing and making. There are four Attainment Targets which are process-based rather than knowledge-based. Teachers do not have to teach pupils to achieve an AT but to use all four together in most activities. All four ATs must be considered as activities and used in a flexible way throughout a process of designing and making.

The statutory order makes provision for pupils with disabilities in various ways. For instance, if a pupil is unable to undertake a practical activity required by the Programmes of Study because of a disability, the pupil is permitted to do an alternative activity which closely matches that activity but which is not so demanding. Obviously, the onus is upon teachers of pupils with SLD to structure tasks so that they can achieve success and to ensure that the work is challenging but achievable. In fact, the Programmes of Study may be followed by many pupils without significant modification as long as appropriate adaptations are made to equipment and materials and ways of presenting problems.

Curriculum Guidance Two: A Curriculum for All (NCC, 1989) identifies several characteristics of good practice. Certain principles are worth highlighting: learners should be allowed to become active learners in their own programmes; a supportive environment should enhance self confidence and a positive self concept; and pupils should be encouraged to evaluate their own learning. There is a need for an essentially positive approach emphasizing the importance of process and the Programmes of Study rather than the achievement of Attainment Targets alone.

Even a simple task like setting a table for a meal is not just responding to the need to eat but also involves designing an answer to the need within a socially acceptable limit. The four Attainment Targets in the statutory orders can be related to this example. AT 1 is 'Identifying needs and opportunities', in this case the need to eat. AT 2 is 'Generating a design' or designing an answer to the need; here it is planning the cooking of a meal and setting the table. AT 3 is 'Planning and making' and, obviously, entails preparing the food and laying the table. AT 4 covers 'Evaluation'; was the food hot enough, for example. The example may seem trivial but the non-statutory guidance (NCC, 1990) recommends that pupils should begin by working in familiar contexts and progress to less familiar ones. Furthermore, it comments that in Key Stage 1 most work will be in the contexts of home, school and familiar aspects of the pupil's local community such as shops.

A 'Mind Map'

My own views, as a teacher with responsibility for 'craft' among other things, have developed and changed over the years. Originally,

I stressed the social skills and work skills which could be fostered by the subject of craft. This was influenced later by a more behaviouristic and task-orientated approach, including checklists of skills. Next, came recognition of the implications within craft for gross motor skills and fine motor skills. Finally, I moved further into model making, design and creativity. I now feel that my work actually helps to develop the self concept of the students, as will be discussed below.

Pupils setting out to 'design' anything should be trying to meet a 'need' that they have identified. In fact, when I have tried to list what my students 'need' or 'learn' through my craft sessions, three key words emerge — *need, relevance* and *priority*. The 'mind map' in Figure 9.1 is an attempt to encapsulate some of my ideas about this. Jameson (1974) says that the teacher should be in charge of the whole process. The 'mind map' implies that there are many integral processes within Design and Technology related to the needs of young people.

What is the relevance of a craft-based approach? In fact, it is not until Level 3 of AT 3 'Planning and making' that hand tools are mentioned and the hands-on style of working familiar in craft and woodwork as such. The craft label has been removed from the statutory order and Design and Technology are now the key words. The 'mind map' is intended to highlight two things: process and cross-curricular education. It provides a physical basis to an expanding involvement in this area and shows how it links to other curriculum areas, such as language (English), Mathematics and Science. In effect, it is a 'design' response to the need, mine, of having to write about Technology.

In Figure 9.1 there are thirteen identifiable strands, some of which are more closely linked than others to the craft model. The range from Gross Motor Skills to Decision Making and Creativity plus the direct cross-curricular links are viewed as especially important. For any person to respond to the environment they need to develop their own position towards it. In 1974 the Schools Council, commenting upon 'normal' children's growth through creative experience, noted the impulse to explore and examine the environment by way of the materials it contains, and went on to talk about the value in children being able to express ideas and deal with real materials. The report sums up by saying that this creates a bridge between the individual and the world around him or her (Schools Council, 1974). In this sense Design and Technology is no more than a response to the environment through concrete or abstract media. To explore and examine the world demands increasing physical interaction with it and, therefore, development.

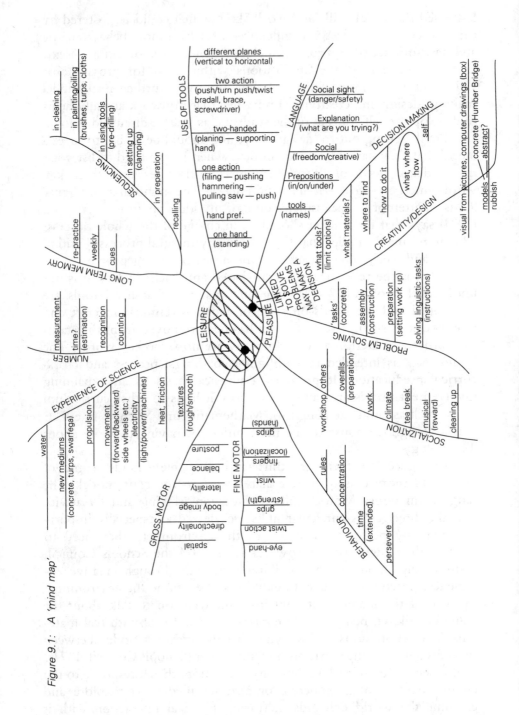

Figure 9.1: A 'mind map'

Within the Art/Craft session there are many opportunities to teach motor skills. Examples include standing/sitting in a position to work, sweeping the floor (a complex task) or hammering a nail. However, many situations also incorporate a creative theme which effects some environmental impact. Therefore, important though they are, the physical skills are only part of the picture. As stated in the Schools Council report, first sensory experiences provide the foundation for learning. Indeed the 'Learning to See' research project had its basis in developing awareness and feelings of response to the environment. This project was commissioned in 1988 by the Art and Architecture Education Trust set up by the Royal Fine Art Commission. Eileen Adams, one of the project team, comments upon it in the April 1990 edition of the project's magazine *Streetwise*. The principles elucidated were: work must be experiential; it must be based on pupils' previous experience; and pupils must have needs, skills and opportunities to confront these areas. This joint art/architecture venture has greatly influenced modern thinking, notably in Technology and Environmental Education, and the magazine has some excellent teaching ideas.

If Technology is a response to the environment or situation, through design, then it must include an element of problem solving. Someone cannot build a bridge without overcoming many problems of how to build one. Within an example like that there must be thousands of problems. Mainwairing and Shouse (1983) say that seldom in any area does one see pupils as deeply involved in their work as in the construction area. Construction can involve many media but the finished building is not as important as the process of resolving the many design problems inherent within that building.

Is there a link between problem solving and learning? Costa (1990) has developed the ideas of Feurstein and Sternberg on 'effective thinking' and 'intelligent behaviour'. Costa drew up a list of twelve characteristics of intelligent behaviour. The first is *persistence* which he describes as the ability to analyze a problem, develop a system, structure or strategy of problem attack, evaluate it, reconsider and try again. A relevant example here would be that of a young girl with SLD who will not sit down, runs around the classroom and climbs on anything. She wanted to get a doll from the top of a steel cupboard and she tried standing on first a box, then a chair, a table and, eventually, a Wendy House until she was able to climb up and collect the doll. How many times a day do pupils face and persist with similar problems? Returning to Mainwairing and Shouse's comment on construction work, it may be argued that this is only a more closely monitored way of observing problem solving which could be happening all the time and in meaningful contexts. It relates to the statutory order in that construction is full of references to systems, structures and mechanisms.

Technology in the National Curriculum will be perceived more positively when it is seen to be only a name for a range of existing subjects and when its integral parts are compared to everyday activities. There seems to be a tendency for teachers of pupils with SLD to perceive at first the relevance of only AT 3 'Planning and making'. This is to ignore the need to involve all four ATs in pupils' work and the significance of the inherent processes within the Programmes of Study. Is this due to the fact that schools for pupils with SLD have traditionally worked with behavioural objectives, recordable tasks and teachable objectives? In other words, they are oriented to the content in all subjects, that is, the Attainment Targets rather than the Programmes of Study, whereas the emphasis here must be on process.

One final comment on the 'mind map' in Figure 9.1 should be made. Decision making by pupils is now inherent in modern educational thinking as, for instance, with the 'self advocacy' movement. There would seem to be plenty of scope within Design and Technology to explore this. Since it is based in reality then decisions made daily can be worked through to see if they are wrong or justified. Seemingly, this places more emphasis on the consequences of such processes than a prescriptive, behaviourist approach which entails, for example, continual manipulation by the teacher of antecedents to achieve errorless learning, and sees consequences only in terms of potential reinforcers. Errors and their consequences may in fact be an important part of learning. Costa's seventh characteristic of intelligent behaviour is that of *questioning and problem posing* for oneself (Costa, 1990).

Some Basic Principles

Williams and Jinks (1985) argue that Design Technology has no factual content although it is possible to identify a range of concepts, skills and attitudes appropriate to the process. Like the statutory order, they list four parts to the process: identification of a need; proposal of a solution(s); realizing the design (making); evaluation and testing.

No doubt this sounds familiar. Williams and Jinks say that the process is about 'learning to learn'. They emphasize a need for problem solving, thinking skills and a move away from biased sex stereotypes. Taking the notion of 'process' further, Williams and Jinks argue that Technology has to be integral within primary schools. Indeed, the Bullock and Cockcroft Reports commented upon the integrated primary curriculum that links subjects together. The models presented had Technology as the core subject with Language, Mathematics, Physical Education, Social Studies and Science all surrounding the core and linked to each other. Perhaps that is one reason for Technology's high priority in the National Curriculum. This approach has been criticized on the grounds that certain subjects need to be taught separately to ensure that Programmes of Study are covered. However, a thematic approach would seem an appealing way to teach young people who are responding better to the environment but who find generalization difficult. The non-statutory guidance makes it plain that teachers in primary schools should use both approaches and the same should be considered by teachers of pupils with SLD.

Williams and Jinks highlight the role of good interaction, decision making, problem solving, self concept, spatial development and the use of the community. Their overall perspective emphasizes cross-curricular themes. However, their ideas are based on research in primary schools and are intended for primary schools and pupils in that chronological age range. The problem with their model is simply that primary schools generally do not have many pupils who have special needs for physiotherapy, occupational therapy, speech therapy, behavioural management strategies and other physical, medical or sensory requirements. The special needs of young people with SLD may be, indeed, more important than the obvious curricular ones specified by various statutory orders. However, I have already noted the relationship between the person and environment which is the basis for sensory development. Teachers need to be aware of the processes within the therapeutic support and previously indirect environmental learning.

It would be sad indeed if schools and departments uncritically adopted projects, themes, or aspects of the new curricula to the detriment of personal and social development, such as the behaviour emphasized in self-care, practical and community independence programmes. Students need more opportunities to 'learn to see' and, as Costa (1990) says, teachers should engage students in the real problems facing them in order to encourage thinking skills in the context of realistic situations. Life is full of real problems and many young people with SLD may only need to be given the opportunity to face them.

A major point has to be made concerning the language used in the statutory order. This relates to the fact that words like 'describe' are used throughout. This immediately creates a difficulty because of the poor or non-existent speech skills of many youngsters with SLD. In this context, there are several points to note; the statutory order does offer other avenues for expression, such as drawing, role play and Information Technology. A note to each Attainment Target states that pupils who are unable to communicate by speech, writing or drawing may use other means including the use of technology and symbols. Statements which require pupils to 'ask' or 'discuss' can be satisfied by pupils who can only communicate by, for instance, signing (see Carpenter, 1990). Moreover, teachers should not ignore the pupil's non-verbal communication and should actively interpret the pupil's behaviour. The emphasis is on the process of Design and Technology rather than linguistic skills in expressing it. Finally, creativity in the use of media may be seen as a personal quality and not needing description.

There are two further points to be considered concerning teaching: the level of work in comparison to chronological age; and the encouragement of creativity. Age relevant work is important in that it can assist the pupils in their own self perception; it involves respect, dignity and social maturity. This has to be balanced so that work is at a level where the pupils can achieve by themselves. This match breeds success and, hopefully, will lead to an improving 'self concept' because learning progress during the process may become 'self' enhancing. If the level of the task is carefully matched to the pupil, the media, approaches, methods, attempts and strategies are in the individual's hands.

A strong argument has been made that young people with SLD think or operate only at a concrete level. Thus, the argument goes, all ideas or stimuli must be presented with similarly concrete manner and media. However, this view tends to discount any emotional input and imagery within the translation of what they see or intend into their eventual action. The Schools Council report (Schools Council, 1974) argues that it is through creative work that pupils explore ways of expressing feeling, thinking and imagining and it is precisely because it is to do with their ideas, sensitivity and perception that this cannot be standardized or measured. Therefore, teachers should accept the pupils' interpretation of their work and encourage more of it and not simply judge it against their own perceptions.

Practical Activities

Ideas from the Environment and from Pictures

An initial starting point for my own work on Design and Technology has been to base it in reality, that is, relate it to visible concrete objects around the school. These have included swings, trees, cookery, the playground, plants and a beam pump. Even closer to home have been topics like bodies, faces and people. Indeed there are numerous physical starting points. A simple example, albeit environmental, was to collect rubbish from around the school; this involved problems like where to find it, how to collect it and who would collect the most. We then worked through what was metal, plastic, wood and sorted the rubbish into groups. Then, the students were asked to attach any rubbish they liked to a backboard (problems again!) and, finally, devise a way to finish off their work by splattering paint, spraying, and so on. The result was a multi-media picture from rubbish.

Another simple topic was to represent their body — feet, legs, body, head, arms, nose, ears, hair. Working in groups, the students located their lowest body part, their feet, and found among old rubbish something to represent it. Together we slowly built up their model getting into various problems, such as matching size, shape, and position, joining materials, achieving balance — a whole catalogue of processes.

I have used many Science inspired ideas as starting points, from 'water' to 'working mechanisms'. Williams and Jinks (1985) concluded a section of their work with twelve starting points in Technology which are well worth considering. A simple one is to get or make anything that could lift an object from the floor onto a table.

One of our more recent environmental efforts is to build or design a simple putting golf course on an area of grass. There are many ways to tackle this from just cutting a hole or putting a marker down anywhere to drafting a plan view of the area which demands a more complex spatial skill.

Pictorial stimuli, such as magazines, books, computer images, pictures, photographs, films or television, offer chances for students to identify a 'need' or area to work from. There are many media to work through once a need has been identified. Media we have used include plastic, rubbish, canvas, papier-mâché, broken crockery, wood, tiles and grout, and stones. Projects that we have started in this way are models of cars, ambulances, aeroplanes, plants, flowers, people, boats, helicopters, dogs and so on. Taking the example of the ambulance, three were made, differing somewhat in shape and all unique in methods of movement, that is, the wheels and the attachment of them. The students used cotton reels, wood or plastic tops for wheels. At difficult points, they could refer back to reality, in this case a roller skate. As required by AT 4 on evaluation, they could measure the effectiveness of the wheels by seeing if they moved and how far the vehicles rolled when run down a slope.

It could be argued that these needs were contrived, but, as noted earlier, teachers must look at the everyday tasks and situations. Moreover, craft sessions can be more easily monitored in terms of processes. Also, hopefully, students will eventually offer their own ideas more confidently as they experience success.

Here are some more examples illustrative of the potential range of ideas. One young man designed a display of pictures on a free standing panel. He suggested using it and, within its confines, he designed, planned and effected an answer to his need of wanting to display some work. There are many processes within that. Another young lady made a model flower. However, she then had to experiment with many containers until finding one that supported the plant. In the end she filled it with soil. Again relative to AT 4, she had to evaluate her design proposal. Even more simple is getting the students to set up patio tables and chairs outside. The need to sit down outside can instigate what may appear to be chaos but when observed is a simple design plan.

The 'Design Line'

I have explored the possibilities of students following a stimulus through various stages or media, what Williams and Jinks (1985) called the 'design line'. For example, one young lady found an image of an aeroplane on the computer; it was built up body, wings and tail. I asked her to draw the aeroplane; interestingly, the three parts were all coloured differently by her. She then made a three part model of an aeroplane with scrap rubbish, made another in wood and, finally, after many attempts made one in paper that flew. Many skills and processes were inherent within these activities.

In a situation, more obviously linked to 'real life', a young lady who walked with a rollator worked out, through her basic need, an effective method of entry into a swimming pool and from the bottom of the stairs into the changing areas. These are examples of students being active in their own learning. Another example is during showering/dressing sessions; it can be said that they are actively involved in working through many problems and eventually solving them.

A Creative Environment

Returning to Costa's (1990) article again, his prescription for enhancing his twelve intelligent behaviours revolved around creating a safe, risk-taking environment. The Schools Council report (Schools Council, 1974) also picked up on this by suggesting opportunities for creating, inventing and originating. It is reasonable to assume that students work better when they feel comfortable or secure enough to have a go; that is when they are not inhibited by rules or fearful of error which are part and parcel of evaluation. The pupil must be provided with opportunities to attempt to solve problems (Linderman and Linderman, 1985).

This point can be illustrated by two examples of craft-based activity in my experience which were enhanced by the environment. The first example involved a young man who found an image of a jumping man on the computer. I asked him if he could find anything in the workshop that 'jumped' or 'went up'. After an eternity of exploring the room, cupboards and boxes, he came up with using a ruler to waft up a piece of paper from the edge of a table (he received some prompting here). I then asked him to find things for sliding or moving across a surface. He started pushing tops (tubs) around a table with sticks. I joined him in this activity and we hit them to one another; ten minutes later he had constructed two goals out of containers with a crosspiece between them and a game was born. The second example was provided by a young lady who travelled twice a day across the Humber Bridge. I showed her a picture of it, we discussed it and I left her to make it. After thirty minutes she had produced nothing: then, all of sudden, she began and completed in a short time an eight-foot model which showed the roadway, towers and cables.

Several points emerge from these examples. As highlighted by the Lindermans, time, patience and understanding made possible the development of the two designs. The students were not pressured to produce rapid work and so were left to make their own decisions. Although the 'need' was somewhat manufactured in both cases, they planned and designed, made and, in the case of the game, evaluated. Integral to both examples were processes including mechanisms, structures and strategies.

To encourage an environment where students feel comfortable enough to 'have a go' eventually, I have over the years constructed a twenty-job woodwork programme with the help and practical advice of Joe Waller, a lecturer at Humberside Polytechnic. It is heavily task-oriented with progressively more difficult motor and tool usage skills. The 'mind map' in Figure 9.1 shows it in its basic format. The programme includes a comprehensive checklist per student and job sheets. These emphasize observable behaviour and limit creativity but the programme does create problem solving opportunities and allows students to test out approaches, tools, equipment and so gain confidence in moving around and tackling problems. It does not meet all of the demands implicit in Costa's (1990) statement about suitable environments, but in its time has served as the starting point for work that students tackle now.

The need for this creative environment is not restricted to craft activities; it must benefit pupils with SLD in all sorts of activities. Arguably, they are not give sufficient opportunities to take risks or are given too many cues at home, at school and in the community in general and, as a result, the development of a positive self concept of many pupils is not encouraged. Jameson (1974) has a valid point when he says that a teacher should be poised between intervention and skilled non-intervention.

Drawing

Drawing is, or can be, visual thinking. Adults' perceptions of pupils' drawings are nothing to do with theirs. Olson sums this up nicely as follows:

> No drawing is an automatic point out of some perceptual world. What is seen or intended must be translated into the action of drawing and what we need to understand more fully is the nature of the translation and of the action. (Olson, 1970)

Teachers must accept the students' view of the picture and ask for their interpretation. This encourages imagery and sequencing which are integral processes of their developing awareness of situations around them. Goodnow (1977) reports studies of children's drawings. Personal drawing is somewhat different from drawing for design but it is another medium to initiate a process. I emphasize that students should draw on a sloped drawing board and have a variety of pencils, crayons and rulers. I have noted that plan drawings are often produced by students, for instance, a football pitch or a garden. But these have potential when it comes to adding to or designing from the drawings.

Music

Music is creative, impulsive and spontaneous, varying according to moods and situations. When a 'need' is identified, it follows the 'design line' and is full of experimentation and testing of machines (that is, the musical instruments). There is a full range of possible actions: banging together, moving across, rattling, shaking, two moving parts colliding. Thus far the chapter has tended to concentrate on visual problem solving but here lies the auditory aspect. My students have created music to pictures, to moods produced by pictures and stories, when making up stories and when experimenting; they are the designers.

One development was to build up a percussion-based sound as musical backing for a student who could play a passable version of the *Eastenders* tune on the piano. We recorded this step by step at a recording studio; each musician laying down their bit onto the increasingly chaotic sound. The students really enjoyed the whole process, especially using the earphones.

Drama

Drama is another means of enhancing design and technology. A good Drama teacher can create an environment in which students feel confident enough to work. The teacher can use their ideas and allow them to 'work them through', solving problems, planning attacks on problems, making and creating from their images. The statutory order and the non-statutory guidance both emphasize the value of working in imaginary contexts where there are few constraints, and of using role play.

171

PE

Aspects of PE can be used to encourage problem solving. Such situations can arise in Drama but PE permits the creation of more structured situations. The activities are non-competitive and involve teamwork. Instructions are issued via a captain for the teams to try to resolve problems, for example, carrying hoops, mats and other items over obstacles. This more structured activity lends itself better to providing verbal reward and, like the structured woodwork programmes, can act as a catalyst for the development of enhanced 'self concept' and, hopefully, the day-to-day problem solving strategies they employ, often unremarked by adults. The teacher can control the language and systematically observe decision making within teams and by individuals. But also the responsibility for control of the situation can be placed squarely on the students' shoulders. The teacher may act as a stimulus for what is regularly noted is Costa's (1990) eleventh characteristic of intelligent behaviour, *ingenuity*.

Photography

Photography is another potential area for fostering Design and Technology capability. I have tended to work more with camcorders and videorecording equipment. For instance, I have encouraged groups to design and produce a short film; nothing like *Ben Hur*, rather simple and based on their environment. One example was of things and activities inside and outside the nearby school to show what went on and where it was. The film was rooted in discussion of the school and surrounding areas and what to include. The students drew up a list and converted it to their own storyboards made up in sequence with a beginning and an end. The process included negotiation with school staff for 'filming rights', times to film and what they wanted. Some still photos were taken to enhance the storyboards. In terms of planning and design it was superb. Even if they point the camcorder the wrong way, talk too much or move it too quickly, it can be seen graphically on playback. Use of the tripod is recommended, though; camcorders are non-bounceable.

With regard to stills photography, there are some very simple cameras available. I often use a Polaroid Instamatic, particularly with a more highly dependent group for faster feedback on activities, such as a walk in the locality, although this is expensive.

Both stills photographs and videos have been used by me as a stimulus for work on figure-ground relationships. This involves taking a flat, two-dimensional picture and bringing it to life in a three-dimensional form. One example was a beach scene with two palm trees, beach, sea and sky. The student drew a backcloth herself, put the beach on a table and made palm trees out of rolled newspaper to stand in the foreground.

Domestic and Practical Skills

Activities traditionally used to foster domestic and home management skills entail innumerable sequences, machines, tools and combinations of these. There is no more influential 'need' than that of food and drink: designing activity is involved in planning a meal, snack, sandwich, drink or dessert; then there is making the delicacy; and there can be no finer evaluation than tasting the result. As noted earlier, this is one of many problems faced every day in a meaningful context by young people; it is commonly known as survival.

Conclusion

Teachers should aim to create in other curricular areas the opportunities which occur in the more effective real-life situations for developing Design and Technology capability. The students' own interests should be used to lead them to create their own 'needs' for which they have to design solutions. This is closely allied to another of Costa's named characteristics of intelligent behaviour which is *inquisitiveness and curiosity* (Costa, 1990). Clearly, there are many curriculum areas which can contribute to Technology. There are direct, structured approaches and more subliminal approaches to developing Design and Technology capability. It may be easier to monitor the direct situations and to reward and encourage technological thinking along the 'design line'. But, in terms of generalization, pupils with SLD need to be able to utilize their problem solving, decision making skills in real life. Therein lies the justification for reality-based situations for providing the stimulus for the initiation of processes. The most effective areas are those with a 'climate' for processes which are inherently self-enhancing and positive.

The experience from primary schools offers curricular ideas for teachers which must be adapted to make them age-appropriate, relevant and practical, as has been done in special schools for years for other subjects. The integrated primary curriculum cannot be applied without modification to schools for pupils with SLD.

Success in introducing Design and Technology depends a great deal upon teachers' attitudes. Through their relationships with their pupils, through skilful non-intervention and thought, staff can assist them to develop their capability. Costa (1990) is convinced that with time and proper support pupils can show amazing growth in intelligent behaviour. He argues that we must have faith in all our students' ability to think. Similarly, Williams and Jinks (1985) believe that the majority of teachers, by careful thought and planning, can place the individual child or children in problem solving situations. As has been shown here, teachers can observe pupils with SLD solving problems directly related to their exclusive needs and can create situations where they have to do so. Technology is all around us all. Teachers must learn to see it, use it and allow pupils to deal with it in their own ways. Teachers must learn to look and listen, then intervene.

References

CARPENTER, B. (1990) 'Unlocking the door', paper presented at a conference on Interactive Approaches to the Core Subjects at Westhill College, Birmingham. (The proceedings are due to be published).

COSTA, A.L. (1990) 'What human beings do when they behave intelligently and how they can become more so', *Curriculum*, 11, 1, pp. 31–7.

DES AND WELSH OFFICE (1990) *Technology in the National Curriculum*, London, HMSO.

GOODNOW, J. (1977) *Children's Drawing*, London, Fontana Press.

JAMESON, K. (1974) *Pre-School and Infant Art*, 2nd edition, London, Cassell and Collier MacMillan.

LINDERMAN, E.W. and LINDERMAN, M. (1985) *Art and Crafts for the Classroom*, London, Collier MacMillan.

MAINWAIRING, S. and SHOUSE, C. (1983) *Learning Through Construction*, Ypsilanti, Michigan, High Scope Educational Research Foundation.

NCC (1989) *Curriculum Guidance Two: A Curriculum for All*, York, National Curriculum Council.

NCC (1990) *Non-statutory Guidance: Design and Technology Capability*, York, National Curriculum Council.

OLSON, D.R. (1970) *Cognitive Development: The Child's Acquisition of Diagonality*, London, Academic Press.

SCHOOLS COUNCIL (1974) *Art and Craft Education 8 to 13*, London, van Nostrand Rheinhold.

WILLIAMS, P. and JINKS, D. (1985) *Design Technology: 5–12*, London, Falmer Press.

10 Cross-curricular Approaches to Information Technology

Paul Roberts

Background

In the beginning, roughly 1983, there was no Information Technology (IT) in schools for pupils with severe or profound learning difficulties, only the computer. This, in most cases, arrived suddenly under a Department of Trade and Industry initiative. So, into a relatively young branch of the education system came a precocious and demanding newcomer accompanied by problems that are not yet fully resolved.

The first BBC computers came without disk drives or peripherals to cater for the majority of pupils who were unable to use the keyboards. There was a similar lack of software and the early titles, usually borrowed from Infant or Junior Schools, often lacked curricular relevance or age appropriateness. Inservice training (INSET), when available, was often misdirected in attempting to train teachers to write programs.

The supply of hardware and dissemination of software improved under the coordinating influence of regional Special Educational Micro Electronic Resource Centres (SEMERCs) and the National Micro Electronic Support Unit (MESU) now known as the National Council for Educational Technology (NCET). The rigid drill style and closed content of early software was gradually superseded by open-ended framework programs, whose content could be created flexibly by teachers and whose links with the curriculum were clearly documented. Other bodies such as the Research Centre for the Visually Handicapped (RCEVH) and a number of individuals developed more specialized applications of IT to meet more specific or profound types of need. The quality of INSET was raised initially through regional

SEMERC courses which created networks of coordinators and in recent years, by the appointment within LEAs of advisory teachers for special needs IT who have supported coordinators and provided IN-SET within individual schools.

These developments have had a widespread influence on classroom practice, demonstrating to many the power and flexibility of IT as a curricular tool. However, recent developments cast serious doubts over continued progress. Due to withdrawal of DES support of SEMERCs, less than half of all LEAs now enjoy the support of a regional centre. Added to this, the rapid phasing out of Education Support Grant funding for IT has severely curtailed the number of advisory teachers for special needs IT. In this uncertain climate the National Curriculum represents a welcome positive development for the reasons which are discussed below.

Some Characteristics of the National Curriculum and their Implications

The Statutory Order for Technology (DES and Welsh Office, 1990) lays down the Attainment Targets and Programmes of Study for IT. The Non-statutory Guidance for IT states 'All pupils have an entitlement to develop IT capability. Pupils who are unable to communicate conventionally because of physical or sensory impairment, may have access to the curriculum only through information technology' (NCC, 1990, para. 4.1).

This statement asserts two key principles. First, the principle of entitlement pertains for pupils with learning difficulties across all the published subjects of the National Curriculum. The second principle, the principle of curricular access, recognizes that IT has a key role in translating entitlement into meaningful participation. The non-statutory guidance goes on to cite the example of communication aids as a means of curricular access, and these are also referred to in the statutory orders for English (DES and Welsh Office, 1989c). Several other examples of IT as a means of access to the curriculum spring to mind. Concept keyboard based wordprocessors put reporting and creative writing within the grasp of some pupils who lack the otherwise necessary handwriting skills. Switches can open up new horizons for many pupils with profound and multiple learning difficulties (PMLD) in exploring and controlling their environment.

The principles of entitlement and access are complemented by other aspects of the National Curriculum. The framework it provides is a common one for the education of all pupils against which the achievements of pupils with learning difficulties can be reported in a way that makes sense to all. This common framework offers a remedy for the tendency of developments in IT to outstrip detailed consideration of their curricular role. Software and hardware developers will now be able to refine their products in the light of Programmes of Study and spot areas of potential where IT could be usefully employed. Similarly teachers should be helped in evaluating the learning goals of software.

The statutory orders and non-statutory guidance for IT and the three core subjects give useful illustrations of the way that IT should be used in the classroom. They recommend that applications for IT be used in concert with other approaches; for example, writing a rough draft of a story and polishing it using a wordprocessor, or using a calculator to check the reasonableness of one's mental arithmetic. A requirement at Level 3 of the Attainment Targets for IT is that pupils should be able to describe their use of IT and compare it with other methods, implying that they develop an awareness of where it is best used or set aside. Instead of saying what can we do with the computer we should ask what can the computer best do for us. The non-statutory guidance for the core subjects also see IT used within a process approach; for example, using a simple database to record and compare the results of a scientific investigation.

A wider implication of the National Curriculum may be to encourage teachers of pupils with learning difficulties to take advantage of relevant INSET opportunities offered by their LEA to groups largely composed of mainstream teachers. Perhaps most significantly, given the current financial climate, the National Curriculum should allow teachers to demonstrate clearly the types of need that they are seeking to address when requesting resources and to cite the principles of entitlement and access. Some encouragement for this can be found in the fact that the Statements of Attainment for IT go much further than the previous draft proposals in stating that computers and other electronic devices should be used within Level 1.

By forming a bridge between practice in mainstream and special schools the National Curriculum points to the use of IT in integrated settings. At Blythe School, which has a background of initiatives in integration (Moore *et al.*, 1987; Carpenter *et al.*, 1988; and, with reference to IT, Carpenter and Lewis, 1989), such a project has been running since September 1988. Word and symbol processors and the 'Our Facts' database have been used to support practical investigations, providing a focus for discussion and problem solving and increasing pupil interaction. The National Curriculum themes of process and communication have encouraged varying roles for pupils within a shared activity. Thus, whilst pupils with severe learning difficulties (SLD) have tended to concentrate on deciding between presented options, gathering and entering information, their mainstream peers have been involved in forming and testing hypotheses and representing results in ways which make sense to their peers with SLD.

Teachers of pupils with learning difficulties should feel liberated by the breadth of applications of IT to be found in the statutory orders and non-statutory guidance for IT and other subjects. This invites them to look far beyond the scope of microcomputers to the potential of devices such as electronic communication aids, switches and the growing range of sensory stimulation media. Such breadth promises to greatly enrich the use of IT in providing access to the curriculum. It is particularly significant for those pupils with PMLD in stimulating the use of electronics in creating sensory environments over which they can exercise control through switching.

Information Technology Capability

The non-statutory guidance for IT sets out in its opening paragraphs the five aims of developing Information Technology capability in pupils and of using IT to enhance and extend teaching across the curriculum. Teachers of pupils with SLD and PMLD have understandably been less concerned with the development of IT capability than with using IT to enhance curriculum delivery and provide curricular access. Nevertheless, the idea of IT capability is a useful one which can be subdivided into its main constituents, which in turn can be used to suggest how IT can usefully be applied across the curriculum. The constituent areas can also be used to audit the use of IT in a school and highlight any gaps.

The need to address IT capability also arises from the impact that IT is having upon all of our lives. The experience of home visits suggests that most youngsters with SLD can operate the play facilities of a video recorder or hi-fi system. Might they not also learn to make regular transactions using an automatic cash dispenser or, in the future, make purchases which are debited electronically from their bank accounts?

The non-statutory guidance for IT identifies five strands of progression within the development of IT capability which will be used here as a framework for discussion:

Information handling — the ability to use IT to gather, organize, store, retrieve, modify and present information;

Developing ideas and communication information — using a variety of forms such as text, numbers, pictures, sound;

Measurement and control — the ability to use IT to measure physical quantities and to control movement and other effects;

Modelling — using IT to model real or imaginary situations and to explore and develop such models;

Applications and effects — the ability to make informed judgments about applications of IT and about their importance to the economy and the quality of life.

Information Handling

This is probably the most familiar of the five areas to teachers of pupils with SLD. Simple wordprocessors such as 'Prompt Writer' or 'Folio' allow pupils to sequence whole words or phrases at a touch of the concept keyboard. Those pupils with little or no knowledge of text can meaningfully parallel this work using symbols or symbols and words. Accounts of the use of symbol systems can be found in *Learning with Rebuses: Read, Think and Do* (Devereux and van Oosterom, 1984), *Symbols for Makaton* (Walker, 1985) and *Working with Makaton at Blythe School* (Staff of Blythe School, 1986). *Using Symbols* (Beste and Detheridge, 1990) is an excellent piece of symbol processing software with its own symbol library and symbol design facilities. The National Curriculum suggests that we fully explore the use of such software tools through a planned sequence of processes in which pupils are involved in gathering, storing, retrieving and modifying information as well as simply entering it.

The Programmes of Study and Statements of Attainment for the core subjects suggest a range of opportunities for this, for example, in gathering and recording results during a scientific investigation or involving a small group in writing successive drafts of a story or an account of a visit.

Other powerful benefits of word and symbol wordprocessors lie in their ability to present options via overlays and to produce high standards of presentation. These attributes are valuable to pupils in producing records of their own work or deciding on future areas of study. By providing access to these activities they are enabling Blythe School pupils to participate fully in the Warwickshire Records of Achievement scheme.

Databases offer pupils a powerful tool for exploring the significance of information by categorizing and interrogating it as well as representing it in tabular or graphic form. Traditionally, we have spent much time asking pupils with SLD to categorize information in ways which are closed by our questions or the materials themselves. The Mathematics and Science Programmes of Study and Attainment Targets (DES and Welsh Office, 1989a; 1989b) challenge us to move forward from this and invite pupils to make their own sense of information (see Mathematics statutory order, DES and Welsh Office, 1989a, pp. 49–51 — Programme of Study for Levels 1, 2 and 3, 'Using and Applying Mathematics and Handling Data' [ATs 1, 9, 12 and 13]; Science statutory order, DES and Welsh Office, 1989b, p. 65 — Programme of Study for Key Stage 1, 'Explanation of Science' [detailed provisions, ATs 1 and 12]).

Processes, such as selecting criteria, formulating questions prior to integration and seeing relationships or significant factors within tables or graphs, may seem abstract or beyond the reach of pupils with SLD. However, the skills and concepts involved arise from concrete activities, such as pupils classifying by their own criteria or noting similarities and differences between people and objects in the context of direct experience and immediate oral or signed reporting. Unfortunately, as yet, even simple databases like 'Our Facts' require text handling but, hopefully, software writers will see the niche for a database which allows pupils to enter, for example, personal information using a choice of categories or fields which appear and are entered in symbolic or pictographic form.

Video provides an exciting and motivating medium through which pupils can objectively learn to handle information. The increasingly widespread availability of camcorders makes it possible for staff and, wherever possible, the pupils themselves to record work in other settings, for example, during integration at mainstream schools, special events or role plays which can then form the basis for discussion within a class group. The use of video and other media, such as tape recordings and television, is stated in the detailed provisions of the English Programme of Study for Speaking and Listening (DES and Welsh Office, 1989c). The use of these media links with most pupils' home experiences and, hopefully, engenders greater awareness and control of them. The use of recordings of pupils' own experience offers additional advantages in helping pupils with SLD to reflect and draw upon them. Information gathered through video and other media may make up a significant part of the Record of Achievement of a pupil with SLD or a pupil with PMLD, presenting evidence of their capabilities more immediately and accurately than words.

The range of IT devices which allow pupils with SLD to handle information continues to grow and to merge into everyday life. Electronic calculators are described in the Mathematics non-statutory guidance (NCC, 1989) as a powerful and useful tool for pupils to use, both in their development of the understanding of number and for doing calculations, which should be used within a balanced approach involving paper and pencil methods and mental calculations in learning to calculate. Providing pupils understand the concept involved in a calculation and are able to check whether an answer is sensible, electronic calculators can prove a versatile means of supporting number skills, for example, reckoning up, or spending on a shopping expedition.

IT and sensory learning for pupils with PMLD
It is unlikely that the IT applications which have been discussed so far would be relevant to the needs of pupils with PMLD. For such pupils the priority lies not in the development of IT capability but in the use of broadly based IT applications as a means of access to and enhancement of the curriculum. This curriculum has come to emphasize such pupils learning to interact more effectively and pleasurably with their environment through carefully planned and recorded sensory experiences, and is echoed particularly in the National Curriculum for Science.

Many pupils with PMLD have needs which lie in learning to recognize objects and events in their environment. The Statement of Attainment of Science AT 1 Level 1 is that 'pupils should observe familiar materials and events in their immediate environment, at first hand, using their senses' (DES and Welsh Office, 1989b); this is resonant of the kind of sensory curriculum which many of these pupils follow. IT offers various means by which sensory information can be presented with added advantages of consistency and flexibility.

These are apparent in visual stimulation software of which the suites of programs from TGW and Alan Bickerstaff and currently the leading examples. TGW have also produced an excellent book, *Computer Assisted Development for Children with Profound and Multiple*

Learning Difficulties. Both suites of software allow teachers to select variables such as colour, sound and duration, and provide a graded series of experiences requiring increasingly complex visual recognition skills. Together, they provide a vast flexible resource of visual experience which can be delivered consistently in terms of the variables mentioned. The TGW publication also highlights other pertinent factors in the environment such as distance and angle from screen, lighting and time of day, which need to be taken into account. The ability to control the learning environment provides a good basis for assessment over a large number of trials through a long period. Then having achieved a baseline of visual functioning the environment can be carefully modified to provide transfer and lead to more complex visual tasks. Both TGW and Alan Bickerstaff also produce software for aural stimulation and learning.

IT provides several other tools for recognition learning for pupils with PMLD. Visual information can also be presented using a cassette wheel projector which is more portable than a computer and which can be used in conjunction with sensory mini-environments. Devices, such as the bubble tube which sends bubbles up a column of liquid which changes colour, have proved attractive to pupils who show little observable response to computer based visual material. This and similar devices combine visual stimulation with sound and vibration and lend themselves to active exploration. Similarly, the digital delay line, which can be used to echo, distort or layer sounds by a pupil and others, can be used to enhance aural information for purposes of recognition or active experimentation. Together, these media allow pupils with PMLD meaningfully to explore light and sound as described in Science Attainment Targets 14 and 15 at Level 1 and in the Programmes of Study for Levels 1 and 2 (DES and Welsh Office, 1989b).

IT can also be used to provide associative cues for pupils with PMLD. These are valuable for pupils who are unable to use existing situational ones to anticipate routine events. Alan Bickerstaff has pioneered the use of musical and sound effects tapes to provide enhanced cues, for instance, sounds of traffic played just before the arrival of transport at the end of the day. Such cues can help pupils with severe memory defects to find stability in their surroundings by making predictions based on experience. This ability to predict is one of the basic characteristics of Mathematics and is given as a Statement of Attainment in Level 1 of 'Using and Applying Mathematics' (DES and Welsh Office, 1989a).

Developing Ideas and Communicating Information

Using IT to handle information ties in closely with another of the identified areas of IT capability — its use to communicate and develop ideas. Here again IT used in conjunction with other media provides vehicles of curricular access across the PMLD/SLD spectrum of needs.

To date, communication by pupils with PMLD through IT has typically been indirect through the recording of observable responses. For example, in the visual training software discussed earlier, an observer might record instances and duration of visual focusing and contact and turning towards a stimulus. By compiling such records and inferring trends as different components of a stimulus are varied, an observer may gain some insight into a pupil's level of response to one stimulus as compared with another. However, such an approach requires careful structuring of the environments, several repeats of each set of conditions for habituation purposes and precise recording techniques.

IT may be able to speed up and simplify this process by providing more direct measures of pupil response. Currently, there is considerable excitement about the possibility of using galvanic skin response — the kind of electrical skin activity employed in a lie detector as a measure of arousal. Such an approach is currently being pioneered by Alan Bickerstaff. These kinds of devices used in conjunction with a broad and balanced sensory education could help to establish the preferences of pupils with the most profound learning difficulties, which, if interpreted sensitively, could give them some indirect control of their environment. Galvanic skin response can also provide printouts of measured responses which can then used as evidence of a child's reaction to an experience.

More direct communication is possible for those pupils whose physical learning difficulties prevent them from using vocalization and signing but who have emerging understanding of cause and effect and are able to operate some form of switch. The work of regional communication centres highlights the potential of IT based devices in this area used in conjunction with any other available means of communication such as gross gesture or eye pointing. On the simplest level, pressing a switch linked to a simple tape recorder can produce a call for attention. As the number and proximity of the switches increase, so can the number and complexity of requests or other ideas available to the child. The devices used are portable enough to travel between home and school, facilitating communication throughout the pupil's day and opening out those areas of the National Curriculum which require discussion or communication of results. Other devices such as the 'Microwriter' provide similar portable access to communication via text. Hopefully, the National Curriculum will help teachers and parents to demonstrate the necessity of this kind of provision for some children.

Speech synthesis can be produced via a computer by means of software or a peripheral device. This reduces pupils' dependence upon decoding text and promotes exploration and discussion through software such as 'Touch Explorer Plus'. Using this, pupils could, for example, help create an overlay showing a plan of their school which when explored might reveal equipment, peers or staff in given areas.

Using word and symbol processors to communicate and develop ideas gives access for many pupils to creative writing and the reporting of results in Mathematics and Science. Their flexibility lends them to the writing of rough drafts and the production of text over a number of sessions. Some pupils with SLD may be able to write short stories or contribute to a school magazine; many more could create messages for Christmas or birthday cards.

Software such as 'Moving In' and the other 'Scenario' programs enable pupils to produce sentences of text via the concept keyboard and combine them with graphic effects in a way which pupils find highly motivating. Even greater potential lies in the use of computers to transmit and receive electronic mail through which pupils can communicate with schools on a local, national or international basis. To realize this potential, electronic mail would need to be used in the context of interests common to the centres employing it, and access remains a problem whilst it is solely reliant upon text as a medium.

Measurement and Control

A third important area of IT capability is that of measurement and control. A number of IT based measuring devices exist which can support practical investigations. In this context pupils should learn to use a stop watch and various digital instruments such as scales. However, it is in the area of control where the greater potential is apparent for pupils with PMLD. For these pupils control occurs at a fundamental level through learning to control effects in the environment by means of switches of various kinds. Such pupils spend virtually all of their time as the passive recipients of experiences, and we can only guess at the delight they may feel in realizing that they are making things happen. Switches which are now available in a wide variety of forms can work off pressure, proximity sound or movement to produce effects via a microcomputer or in the wider environment. A wide repertoire of software is available for switch users with PMLD including much of the TGW suite, much of Derek Harrison's 'Compact' series and 'Switch On' by Brilliant Computing. Details of a wider range is available in the NCET Briefing Leaflets. Much of this software promotes attention control and understanding of cause and effect. Direct control of devices can be achieved by adapting battery operated toys for switch use. A range of adapted toys and switches is available from 'Toys for the Handicapped'. For some pupils battery operated toys are less appealing and age appropriate than electrical devices, such as tape recorders, lights, radios or TVs. These too can be brought under the control of a pupil with PMLD by means of an environmental control unit and a choice of switch, which allows control of any device which is plugged into it.

Taken together, these simple control applications open new horizons of exploration, autonomy and choice for youngsters with PMLD. In terms of the National Curriculum they also contain elements of prediction (Mathematics AT 1: Level 1 in DES and Welsh Office, 1989a) and scientific exploration in terms of 'What will happen if I ...?' described in Science AT 1 (DES and Welsh Office, 1989b). Given that a pupil with PMLD has a functional understanding of cause and effect, he or she can also be said to be communicating a preference if he or she consistently presses one of two switches.

Control projects provide an exciting medium for integrated investigations involving youngsters with PMLD and their peers with SLD, moderate learning difficulties or in mainstream. This could involve pupils either designing and producing and/or assessing a switch for the use of their peer. Younger children might tape-record songs or stories to be assessed via a switch and then observe and record the responses and infer preferences. Older pupils might carry out a more complex process of switch design and assessment considering significant variables and designing a fair test. In either type of activity, in all IT applications, these activities would be based on the moral and social values which pertain to working sensitively with pupils with learning difficulties. Such values would be strengthened by the way in which the pupil with PMLD would be an active participant in the kinds of project that have been described.

For the pupil with SLD, control can take on more abstract spatial characteristics. This may be with using a joystick to move an image around a monitor and, eventually, follow spatial instructions. This in turn could lead into work with a 'Roamer' or 'Floor Turtle' on giving instructions for moving through space or producing shapes or designs. Such work could parallel more open-ended exploration of similar concepts through the wide variety of graphic art packages which are already available, and which can be assessed via concept keyboard or more commonly a 'mouse'. Such packages enjoy similar advantages to those of wordprocessors in terms of storage, flexibility and enhancement of produce. Work in this field has obvious aesthetic curricular applications and also relates closely to mathematical concepts of shape and space addressed in Mathematics ATs 1 and 10 (DES and Welsh Office, 1989a).

Modelling

The area of IT capability termed modelling is defined as the ability to use IT to model real or imaginary situations and to explore and develop such models. For pupils with SLD/PMLD the emphasis will lie in the concrete exploration of models which have already been developed.

For pupils with PMLD great potential lies in the use of IT to enhance sensory environments by means of lighting, sound, vibration and even smell or movement. The example of 'Snoezelen' suggests that we may soon be able to offer these pupils exciting yet safe simulations of environments which they would otherwise be unable to encounter through a combination of such effects. A resource of this type is currently being planned in this country. On a more manageable scale, IT resources, such as an effects wheel projector and or a digital sampler/delay line, may be used with pupils with PMLD and pupils with SLD to create visual and auditory environments to accompany language, drama or movement work.

Adventure games and simulations provide excellent opportunities for pupils to enter and explore imaginary situations. They provide a natural focus for group work involving discussion, problem solving, hypothesis testing and data handling in ways which cross key areas of the three core subjects. Used properly, they also provide a stimulus for a range of cross-curricular investigations and activities. 'Albert's House' is an excellent example of an adventure game which meets all these criteria whilst making minimal requirements on understanding text and keyboard skills. A range of other adventure games and simulations, many of which are appropriate for youngsters with SLD, appear in NCET's Briefing Leaflet 27, *A Core Library — Adventure Programs and Simulations.*

The principles of modelling can also be applied to life-like settings in providing controlled rehearsals of social skills. A number of pieces of simulation software exist which allow youngsters to use a cash dispenser, detect and rectify dangers in the home, control a budget, and so on. In addition, content free software such as 'Touch Explorer' allows teachers to design their own simple simulations, which can be explored through the concept keyboard, for example, locating items in a supermarket which could correspond in layout to that used by pupils on a shopping expedition. Such software, as well as providing trial and error learning in a risk free setting, also encourages discussion and the formulation and testing of simple hypotheses and can involve cross-curricular problem solving.

Applications and Effects

For pupils with SLD and those with PMLD the area of IT capability termed 'applications and effects' which deals with knowledge and judgments about IT applications, would be dealt with within a cross-curricular approach encompassing the previously reviewed areas of IT capability. However, the area does have implications for the way in which IT is delivered. Pupils should come to see IT applications as tools which help them to carry out a piece of work. As their awareness grows they should carry out as much of the operation of a piece of IT as possible, and learn through practical decision making which software or hardware to use for varying purposes. They should also learn to decide between IT or other methods, such as pencil and paper, as mentioned in the Level 3 Statement of Attainment for IT, basing their decision on factors such as standard of presentation and time taken.

An equally important facet of applications and effects concerns uses of IT in society. Pupils need to be able to use such media as video recorders, camcorders, teletext and answering machines as they become more prevalent in their homes. The teaching of social skills should also take account of the use and understanding of cash points and direct debit cards and it seems likely that other IT applications will continue to arise rapidly in the years ahead and the curriculum will need to keep pace with these developments.

Conclusion

This chapter has demonstrated the relevance of IT in helping to meet some of the needs of pupils with SLD and pupils with PMLD. The National Curriculum establishes two complementary roles for IT: the development of an IT capability to equip pupils for modern society and the enhancement of the delivery of curriculum as a whole. For pupils with learning difficulties it goes beyond this in establishing the principles of entitlement and of curricular access. The latter is becoming highly significant as we realize the power of IT to redefine or dispense with hitherto prerequisite skills, with speech and pen control being two obvious examples.

The orders and non statutory guidance for IT and indeed the whole National Curriculum can be likened to a powerful framework program, which is broad in its conception, universal in its application and flexible in its approach. Like any piece of good framework software, there is room for the teacher to exercise imagination and creativity in developing content or, in this case, specific applications, which link to the rest of the curriculum and relate to pupils' needs. These applications probably already far outstrip those that have been touched on here as people involved in the education of pupils with learning difficulties respond to this challenge. It is to be hoped that regional and local networks and centres will receive the support they need to ensure that these develop.

References

ARCHER, M. (1990) 'Redeeming recreation', *Special Children*, 42, p. 24.

CARPENTER, B. and LEWIS, A. (1989) 'Searching for solutions: Approaches to planning the curriculum for integration of SLD and PMLD children', in BAKER, D. and BOVAIR, K. (Eds) *Making the Special Schools Ordinary?*, Volume 1, London, Falmer Press.

CARPENTER, B., FATHERS, J., LEWIS, A. and PRIVETT, R. (1988) 'Integration: The Coleshill experience', *British Journal of Special Education*, 15, pp. 119–21.

DES AND WELSH OFFICE (1989a) *Mathematics in the National Curriculum*, London, HMSO.

DES AND WELSH OFFICE (1989b) *Science in the National Curriculum*, London, HMSO.

DES AND WELSH OFFICE (1989c) *English in the National Curriculum*, London, HMSO.

Paul Roberts

DES AND WELSH OFFICE (1990) *Technology in the National Curriculum*, London, HMSO.
DEVEREUX, K. and VAN OOSTEROM, J. (1984) *Learning with Rebuses: Read, Think and Do*, Stratford upon Avon; National Council for Special Education.
MOORE, J., CARPENTER, B. and LEWIS, A. (1987) '"He can do it really" — Integration in a First School', *Education 3–13*, 15, 2, pp. 37–43.
NCC (1989) *Mathematics: Non-statutory Guidance*, York, National Curriculum Council.
NCC (1990) *Technology: Non-statutory Guidance For Information Technology*, York, National Curriculum Council.
O'GRADY, C. (1989) 'Jolly mixture', *Times Educational Supplement*, 24 November, p. 62.
STAFF OF BLYTHE SCHOOL (1986) *Working with Makaton at Blythe School*, Camberley, Makaton Vocabulary Development Project.
WALKER, M. (1985) *Symbols for Makaton*, Camberley, Makaton Vocabulary Development Project.

Notes on Resources

Software

Wordprocessing
'Prompt/Writer' — NCET, £3
'Folio' — Tedimen Software, PO Box 23, Southampton, SO9 7BD, £15, or less if licenced by your LEA

Symbol processing
'Using Symbols' — Widget Software, 102 Radford Road, Leamington Spa, Warwickshire, CV31 1LF, £25.00.

Information handling
'Our Facts' in 'Information Handling Pack' by NCET, £5
'Touch Explorer Plus' — NCET, £12.50

Adventure games
'Albert's House' — Resource, Exeter Road, Doncaster, DN2 4PX, £14.15
'Moving in', 'Elstree Farm', etc. — NCET, £3 each

A much wider range of software in these categories can be found in NCET Briefing Sheets.

189

Cause/Effect and Concept Formation

'Compact' — NCET suite of 10 disks

'Switch On' — Brilliant Computing, PO Box 142, Bradford, BD3 0JN

TGW — Kinder School, Bassetlaw Hospital, Worksop, Notts. A suite of over 10 disks of visual stimulation and cause/effect software plus an excellent 100-page book describing use of visual stimulation software with PMLD pupils, £30

'Vision Box', 'Audio Box' — large graded suites of PMLD software and sensors and software for bio feedback. By Alan Bickerstaffe, Hilltop School, Larch Road, Maltby, S. Yorks. S66 8AZ.

Switches and Communication Aids

Extensive information in *Communication* from 'Equipment for the Disabled', Mary Marlborough Lodge, Nuffield Orthopaedic Centre, Headington, Oxford, OX3 7LD.

'Toys for the Handicapped', 76 Barracks Road, Sandy Lane Industrial Estate, Stourport on Severn, Worcs. DY13 9QB. This company supplies a wide range of switches, battery adapted toys, etc.

'Liteworks', 66A Yorkshire Street, Morecambe, Lancs. LA3 1QF. This company supplies modular and hardware switching systems and various sensory stimulation devices, including effects wheel projectors, bubble tubes, fibre optic displays, light/sound, walls, tracking tubes, smell machines, etc.

'Snoezelen' (derived from the Dutch for 'sniff' and 'doze') originated in Holland over a decade ago. It combines soft play equipment with controlled light, sound, smell and other devices to create a range of sensory experiences from which pupils with even the most profound learning difficulties may benefit. 'Snoezelen' has led to the growth of sensory curricula for pupils with PMLD in this country (see Chapter 5, this volume) and to the creation in many special schools of multi-sensory rooms using a variety of technology, such as light projectors, bubble tubes, fibre optic displays, audio-feedback systems, aroma machines, etc. Equipment is available through specialist suppliers, e.g. Liteworks, Rompa, etc.

Section Three

Further Implications of the Challenge

11   Access to the National Curriculum for Parents

Philippa Russell

Parents as Partners

The Warnock Report (DES, 1978) heralded a new era for 'parents as partners' in special educational procedures. The concept of parent participation was written into the Education Act 1981 (DES, 1981), with its emphasis on collaboration and informed consent. If the rhetoric has not always matched the reality, the failure has been not in lack of intent but rather in the timescale of acknowledging that both voluntary and statutory services must work together to provide parents with the advice, training, support and respect needed in order to become full partners. The work of Sheila Wolfendale (1989), Robert Cameron (1989) and others, who have developed new strategies for helping parents to use their expertise and observational skills during assessment, has reflected what Warnock forecast as a 'sea change' in attitudes and expectations, not just about disability and special needs, but about the feasibility of families contributing directly to the assessment process. The new partnership goes wider than assessment. The Education (No. 2) Act 1986 and the Education Reform Act 1988 (ERA) have been hailed as 'empowering' parents in other directions. Research from Plowden onwards has shown the importance of bringing parents into schools.

But there are threats as well as opportunities in some of the new procedures. Norman Tomlinson (1988), writing about parental power and the National Curriculum, reflected that 'parents now may be asked to adopt the role of inquisitor and monitor of teachers and schools, and to use the new complaints procedures all in the exercise of consumer sovereignty'. *Circular 22/89: Assessments and Statements* (DES, 1989b) clearly states the need to develop a new 'frankness and openness' between parents and professionals.

The same circular notes that 'close cooperation' between parents and the statutory services will be needed, 'with a thorough understanding by each of the participants of the part which they and others play in the procedures. Authorities may need to give thought to arrangements which assist families and maintain effectiveness in relationships with the various services' (*ibid*). In effect, schools will need to give careful consideration to the *conditions* for effective partnership, and to ensure that parents are supported in exercising their new powers, if the Tomlinson fears of 'inquisitorial monitoring' are to be avoided.

The outlook, despite parental concerns about the implications of the National Curriculum, open enrolment, local management of schools and declining resources, is not all negative. The DES White Paper, *Better Schools* (DES, 1985) emphasized that quality in education must be everyone's business. But the 'business' is more complex than it has been for many years. The tension between centrally directed education policy and devolution to individual schools (which may be less benevolent and harder to challenge on policy issues than LEAs) must have repercussions for parents, whether or not they are exercising their own personal powers under the 1981 Act and the ERA. Many parent organizations wonder whether parents of pupils with special educational needs (SEN) will have the time or energy to assume new responsibilities as governors and managers of schools, where the partnership may assume the new role of a quasi-business enterprise. Most importantly, the ability of the LEA to advise and orchestrate a range of complex support and advisory services may be greatly limited. Attainment Targets, Programmes of Study and assessment are intended to offer parents, schools, LEAs and the government clearer and comparable information about the achievements of pupils and schools in a way which can improve performance individually and collectively. However, the assessment arrangements of the ERA are essentially 'in school' and many parents of pupils with severe learning difficulties (SLD) are critically aware of the significance of the need for multiprofessional assessment, the joint endeavour, which is needed to ensure their children develop to their full potential.

Despite criticisms from the House of Commons Select Committee (1987) and the University of London Institute of Education's DES funded research into the implementation of the 1981 Act (Goacher *et al.*, 1988), most parents would agree that things *have* got better. The 'effective relationships with the various services' endorsed by

Circular 22/89 (DES, 1989b) are being improved. Parents are playing a more active role and there is growing commitment to actively seeking their views. Many parents have commented on the greater specificity of the USA's 'individual educational programmes' with their clear curricular statements. A parental campaign to have such a curricular component in the 1981 Act's Statement of Special Educational Needs was rejected as the Bill went through Parliament. The ERA restores this balance, with statements having a clear curriculum relevance and with any modifications or exemptions to be clearly specified. Now, however, many parents fear that the curriculum content of the Statement may be over-cautious, and that (despite Government reassurances) the inherent flexibility of the National Curriculum may not be tested. The new arrangements may seem particularly threatening to pupils who are in full or part-time mainstream placements. Schools which are preoccupied with the new curriculum (and their governors) may be less sympathetic to pupils with very specific learning difficulties. Scarce resources may not be stretched to include such pupils, who may be seen as lowering overall academic achievements at a particular school. Governors (unless well trained in special educational needs) may resist accepting pupils with any special needs unless the financial resourcing and the teaching implications are full explored.

Seamus Hegarty (1988), reviewing part-time integration schemes in schools, found that 'incremental integration', with pupils sharing mainstream and special school placements, was growing rapidly and frequently represented a new partnership between special schools and their community equivalent. However, he noted that most of such schemes operated on what he described as a 'happenstance' basis. He went on to say that 'whilst there is wisdom in flexibility when there are no absolute truths ... diversity permits experiment and can encourage creative responses to individual needs'; there could be problems for parents and schools when arrangements needed to become more formalized. In effect, private informal arrangements could be at risk and many parents are already seeking reassurance that their children with special needs will not be discriminated against in the supposedly 'best interest' of the wider group of pupils for whom the National Curriculum poses no special threat. Parents will therefore need reassurance from school and LEA that

> the 1988 Act aims to raise expectations of all pupils, including those with statements. Built into that Act are provisions to ensure that these expectations are appropriate, so that all children including those with SEN can benefit to the best of their

ability. Irrespective of the type of school placement, appropriateness and quality of provisions are vital. (DES, 1989b)

'It's Not a Doggy, It's a Cow!' The Learning Process and Access to the Curriculum from the Parent's Point of View

From the time they are born, young children learn through their spontaneous interactions with their environment and with people around them. The quality of these interactions will inevitably vary and will determine whether a child feels encouraged to express his or her natural curiosity or feel discouraged. For example, the child who points excitedly to the first cow she sees and shouts 'look, big doggy', may elicit any number of responses from an adult. She may be ignored, in which case she may eventually learn not to share her discoveries with that adult, or the adult may answer abruptly 'it's not a doggy, it's a cow' and carry on walking, giving the child no time at all to internalize the differences. On the other hand the adult may stop and encourage the child to look closely and think about the differences between the cow in the field and dogs they have seen and to verbalize the similarities and differences ... attitudes and behaviour patterns established during the first seven years of life provide the foundation for future education and social developments. (Lally *et al.*, 1989)

The Early Years Curriculum Group strongly argues for an acknowledgment of the links which need to be made between the principles and practice of early years education, and the parents' relationship with their children and what happens subsequently with the National Curriculum. Access to the National Curriculum, with a full understanding of Attainment Targets, Programmes of Study and arrangements for assessment and testing, will probably not be seen by most parents in terms of 'it's not a doggy, it's a cow'. Yet the majority of parents *are* teaching their children all the time. From the day they are born young children learn through their own spontaneous interactions with their environment and the people around them. The attitudes and behaviour patterns established during these early years provide the foundation for future educational and social development. The success of Portage and other home-based learning programmes is based on the ability of parents to stimulate, record and build upon these interactions with children whose developmental delay or learning difficulties might make spontaneous progression difficult. The DES booklet for parents, *Our Changing Schools* (DES, 1989a), endorses the fact that '*you* (the parent) are your child's first teacher', and goes on to say 'you don't need to take on this responsibility on your own'. For many parents, indeed, the prospect of being their child's teacher is daunting. But parents familiar with Portage and early intervention programmes will be confident of sharing in such a role. For some other families, the options and models for involvement need to be further explored.

The National Curriculum is certainly not the *whole* curriculum. *Curriculum Guidance Three: The Whole Curriculum* (NCC, 1990) from the National Curriculum Council reminds everyone of the *whole* curriculum context. Parents need to be reminded of Section 4 of the earlier NCC *Circular No. 6* which states that

> the whole curriculum goes far beyond the formal timetable. It involves a range of policies and practices to promote the personal and social development of pupils, to accommodate different teaching and learning styles, to develop positive attitudes and values and to forge an effective partnership with parents and the local community. (NCC, 1989a, Section 4)

The circular and curriculum guidance emphasize the importance of promoting the personal and social development of pupils, which will include what pupils learn out of school as well as in other parts of the curriculum. If cross-curricular strategies are to 'bond the bricks' of the new National Curriculum into a cohesive structure, then new ways must be found to enable parents to understand the importance of their contribution to their child's education, and to record such activities in ways which are relevant to work in school.

All children need periods of 'free time', as well as more structured activities, in order to actively explore their own environment, set their own challenges and make their own discoveries. They need opportunities to work collaboratively with other children and they need adults who will respond to their interest and questions. Learning through play is as important for children with SLD as for their more able peers.

For example, the National Curriculum Council's *Curriculum Guidance Two: A Curriculum for All* (NCC, 1989b) suggests a number of positive activities to be carried out as part of Attainment Target 1, which could be shared with and replicated by parents working at home. Step 1 (learning through undirected play) suggests that a range of materials such as dough, sand, water, containers and leaves are shown to pupils, who are encouraged to explore them, identify simple differences and use their powers of observation. The importance of *play* will be self evident to some parents, but may be less so to other families who perceive schools as primarily concerned with formal education, and may need encouragement to understand the importance of some informal and undirected activities. For example, Mathematics may seem a subject far removed from the day-to-day life of a young child with SLD. But many children's games develop sorting and matching skills. Others begin to build upon awareness of number or the use of money. The NCC has suggested that some 'mathematical games' can be used without *any* need for language, for example, with two and three dimensional 'shapes' or with recognizing and matching shapes such as rectangles, circles, triangles and other mathematical shapes, to begin to perceive their similarities and differences. Parent workshops are a useful way of building parental (and teacher) confidence and ensuring that similar approaches are used at home and at school. They also continuously reinforce new skills and increase positive expectations for the future.

Developing a Whole School Policy

Parental involvement as described by Sheila Wolfendale (1989) and others will be ineffective unless there is clarity about the role and contribution of parents. *Curriculum Guidance Two* (NCC, 1989b) envisages an 'atmosphere of encouragement, acceptance, respect for achievements and sensitivity to individual needs' occurring only if there is 'continuous communication with parents and mutual parent-teacher support'. The same document looks to '*home-school partnerships* which enable families to support the teaching programmes for the child with special educational needs'. To achieve such partnerships it will be essential:

> To ensure that the governors of the school support the principle of partnership and full communication with parents. The willingness to fund parent workshops and other collaborative ventures should be one outcome of such a positive relationship;
> For parents and teachers to understand and share the same clear school-wide procedures on recording, reviewing and evaluating pupils' progress. In this context parents need to understand

the distinction between assessment arrangements with regard to the 1981 Act and the ERA and other more informal methods of continuous review. Pupil Profiles or Records of Achievement give parents (and pupils) incentives to share success stories and demonstrate the possibility of progress;

That arrangements for the 'whole curriculum' ensure that cross-curricular links are made — and that parents understand what they are. The use of 'parent profiles' as developed by Sheila Wolfendale (1989) is one example of simple tools for parents to use and to share knowledge of a child;

For schools to acknowledge the inherent stress for parents within a more tightly structured and specific curriculum approach. Although parents will in general welcome greater specificity and clarity about what is being taught, when and why, comparisons *between* pupils may become invidious. Any proposals for temporary exemptions will need careful explanations;

To recognize that the successful implementation of a coherent curriculum policy will not depend only upon the skills of teachers. Access to a range of other professionals, including the school psychological service, speech and physiotherapy, child health and social services may all be necessary. At a time of scarce professional resources, *parents* may be the more effective 'case-managers' and they should be encouraged to share other professionals' (and voluntary organizations') experience of their children.

Parents as Educators — Lessons from Early Intervention Programmes

A major consequence of the initiatives in the education of pupils from disadvantaged backgrounds has been the strong relationship between home background and early learning. Corresponding research into the impact of the birth of a disabled child upon family lifestyles and expectations and parental involvement in early educational strategies has shown the need to acknowledge family stress; to provide a counselling element in all professional services and to develop parental competence and confidence in bringing up a child who is 'different'.

Robert Cameron (1989), considering 'teaching parents to teach children', has noted the importance of acknowledging that parents have *two* primary educational roles when a child has a disability or special education need. Firstly, parents need to understand how to teach a child everyday life skills. Secondly, they need help in managing difficult or disruptive behaviour which the child may acquire. Since the mid 1970s, the Portage home teaching model has become increasingly popular and it has been estimated (Cameron, 1989), that there are now over 300 schemes in the United Kingdom. Portage is characterized by focusing upon helping *parents* to teach children with special needs within their own homes and by involving families in selecting their own education goals. The strength of Portage and other home-based learning programmes is that they:

> involve the strengths and knowledge which parents already hold;
> involve a trained home visitor who is able to link back to a wider
>   network of professionals;
> provide an essentially private service, inasmuch as they can take
>   place in a venue chosen by the parent;
> enable parents to select their own priorities not only in terms of
>   cognitive development but in seeking practical solutions for
>   difficult behaviour;
> match the actual level of parental involvement to individual fami-
>   ly dynamics. Home-based learning programmes such as Port-
>   age can be combined with other forms of provision such as
>   nursery or school classes, day care arrangements or members of
>   the extended family.

Successful home teaching programmes, like Portage, have sometimes been criticized as offering highly structured cookbook approaches to meeting individual needs. In practice Portage is a process, not a single solution. As Cameron (1989) and others have emphasized, the central feature of Portage is the home teaching process which has three key features, namely:

> using contact people (especially parents) to teach the child;
> using an individualized teaching programme which is based upon
>   a realistic assessment of the child's existing skills;
> providing *positive* monitoring and recording procedures.

One of the major successes of a good Portage scheme is that it permits information to travel *between* parents and professionals, and provides a detailed data base on a child which can be utilized by subsequent service providers. A major criticism of current early intervention programmes is that they frequently fail to manage the *transfer* of relevant information between families and different networks of professionals. Portage additionally provides a 'key worker' approach in offering support to parents through a familiar individual.

There has been considerable debate on the effectiveness of a range of early intervention programmes. Evaluations of Portage show encouraging development in children using Portage and in parents' positive feelings about their child. There are also a number of initiatives to utilize Portage strategies with *school age* children and parents and to continue early years partnerships in the wider school situation.

Parent Involvement in Assessment

'There is very general support for the comprehensiveness of the assessment procedures set out in the 1981 Act, particularly their multi-professional nature and the participation of parents' (House of Commons, 1987). The Select Committee on the implementation of the 1981 Act endorsed the genuine attempts to introduce a new collaborative approach to assessment of special educational needs. However, the Committee also acknowledged certain barriers to effective parent participation in the new procedures. These include:

> inadequate or unclear information about the Local Education Authority's assessment procedures and the range of special educational provision available;
> insufficient help in supporting parents during assessment;
> a lack of weight being given to their views during the assessment process;
> a lack of real choice about provision;
> failure to implement the role of a 'named person' or parent adviser;
> insufficient use of the resources (in particular counselling skills) of the voluntary sector.

Concerns expressed by parents about assessment under the 1981 Education Act should be seen as 'early warning signs' of similar difficulties under the ERA procedures. There is now substantial documentation on what parents feel about assessment. A review of special educational provision and parent views in Derbyshire (Kramer, 1985) found that parents particularly wished for more time for discussion about the purpose and nature of assessment; they wished for clear information about policies on resources, and fewer delays in implementing any provision recommended in the Statement. Like parents consulted by the Fish Committee (ILEA, 1985), many emphasized the strong emotional and personal feelings surrounding assessment, and the need to have a counselling element implicit in any procedures used during assessment. A review of parental feelings about special educational provision in the London Borough of Haringey (Berridge and Russell, 1987) similarly endorsed the ambivalence felt by parents who *wished* their children's difficulties to be fully investigated, but who at the same time felt considerable grief and loss in a process which often seemed to be deficit laden and to have uncertain outcomes.

However, the conclusions of these consumer surveys have not been all negative. The Fish Committee (ILEA, 1985) emphasized the positive contribution of a 'named person' or individual parent adviser during assessment. The Welsh SNAP (Special Needs Advisory Project) has effectively recruited and trained volunteer parent advisers, with considerable success, to provide support as well as information during assessment. SNAP demonstrated the value of training parents, and the problems often caused by parents failing fully to understand the information they were given. Concern to make statutory rights more 'user friendly' has become widespread, and Sheila Wolfendale's 'parent profiles' have provided important examples of parents being given a framework within which to record their own observations of their child. Parents in the Haringey survey (Berridge and Russell, 1987) were particularly concerned that their children might miss out on the wider curriculum, when social and independence training skills had to be seen as core components of the school programme for a pupil with SLD. Sheila Wolfendale's new parent profile, *All About Me* (Wolfendale, 1989) has been extensively piloted, and includes a series of questions under eight headings — language, playing and learning, doing things for myself, my physical development, my health and habits, other people, how I behave, my moods and feelings. The emphasis on the 'my' gives the profile personal relevance, and older pupils can join in answering the questions. The profile has been used in one primary school, Moordown St. John's School in Bournemouth. The head teacher, Hugh Waller (quoted in *The Times Educational Supplement*, 17 November, 1989) comments that the demands of the National Curriculum are forcing infant head teachers to find new ways of determining children's skills on entry, making it essential to find the baseline at which children start. Information about the pupil's early experiences (which only parents can know) are essential in giving a clear picture of the pupil's current ability and future progress. New assessment tools like *All About Me* can complement the more formal assessment procedures by helping parents to reflect on their child's development and to give a positive picture. As one parent said to the present writer, 'I often forget the real progress my child has made because the progress is slow, and I'm living with him every day'. Like Portage, *All About Me* is an enabling device to help parents work with professionals, and not to feel deskilled in the process.

Parent involvement, and parent advocacy, will never be easy. *Circular 22/89* (DES, 1989b), in Section 20, stresses the need 'for parents to have written guidelines to assist them in their contribution to assessment'. It emphasizes that such information should be in 'straightforward plain language' and that parents should have a right to bring 'an adviser or friend and translators for support at meetings' if they so wish. The assessment procedures to be introduced by the ERA with regard to the National Curriculum will similarly need to acknowledge the personal anxieties and concerns of parents, and to acknowledge that links to the child's wider home and social environment will be crucial in achieving progress. The ERA is intended to provide 'a balanced and broadly based curriculum which promotes the spiritual, moral, cultural, mental and physical development of pupils at the school and in society, and to prepare pupils for the opportunities, responsibilities and experiences of adult life' (DES, 1988). These objectives can only be achieved for pupils with SLD if some of the lessons of the 1981 Act are acknowledged and effectively built upon in the new procedures.

In 1986 a group of parents organized a conference for professionals on assessment and the 1981 Act. All the professionals were required to go through 'The Maze', which introduced them to a parents' eye view of assessment, its pitfalls and its problems. 'The Maze' has now been published by Camden Elfrida Rathbone as a resource to be used during the assessment process. The project clearly demonstrates the importance of acknowledging that assessment is not

> just about the allocation of scarce resources. The Maze is concerned with another dimension.... There is nothing really frightening about listening to parents talk about their children, hearing what they want for them and acting on what they have to say. Doing that will make it possible to design services sensitive to the needs of young people and their families. (Nelson, 1989)

Listening to parents is, in effect, the most important access point to both the 1981 Act and the ERA.

The Changing Role of Parent Organizations

The effectiveness of the implementation of the USA's Public Law 94:142 (the equivalent of the UK's 1981 Education Act) has to a considerable extent been attributed to the contribution of parent and voluntary organizations. The parent coalitions and the parent counsellors (directly funded by federal money) have enabled *parents* to have a collective as well as an individual voice in the development of special education systems. Equally importantly, parents have been assured of the availability of the 'named person', a concept of parent advocacy developed in the Warnock Report (DES, 1978) and endorsed by the Fish Committee (ILEA, 1985), but seldom implemented in practice.

The voluntary sector has always been a rich and creative resource for consumer groups in the UK. The major national 'voluntaries' like MENCAP and the Spastics Society have always played an educational advisory role for parents with young children with special needs. But an emerging trend in the 1980s has been that of 'coalition' groups (for instance, Parents in Partnership, KIDS, Contact a Family and Action 81) which are non-denominational in terms of specific disabilities and which work with parents of all special needs children. An evaluation of Contact a Family's parent groups in Wandsworth (Hatch and Hinton, 1987) clearly found that parent joiners were more confident and optimistic. They were more likely to make good use of all available services and they felt able to negotiate on their own behalf with professionals. Many parent groups will offer practical advice as well as ongoing support. They all offer solidarity and friendship when families feel at their most vulnerable.

In practice, changes in official policy and legislation have been insufficiently utilized to promote partnership with parents through the use of parent groups. Section 10 of the 1981 Act requires health authorities to notify parents of any voluntary organizations likely to be able to help them. In practice, (as a survey from the National Deaf Children's Society found in 1987), few make such referrals. Although health authorities and social services departments have used joint finance money (often with voluntary organizations) to support parent-led activities, there has been too little participation by education authorities. However, there have been some notable exceptions. The three South Wales Education Departments have collaborated with the Spastics Society, MENCAP in Wales and the Wales Council for the Disabled to establish SNAP (the Special Needs Advisory Project) which has clearly demonstrated the effectiveness of recruiting, training and supporting parents and other volunteers as parent advisers and advocates during assessment. The ILEA/Elfrida Rathbone Parent Advocacy Project in Camden similarly showed the need for many parents to have *independent* advice and counselling during assessment.

One important asset in any parent organization is the ability to *listen*. An evaluation of a parent adviser scheme at the London Hospital (Cunningham and Davis, 1985) has shown that many of the most vulnerable parents benefit from sensitive counselling and listening, even without explicit professional advice. In effect 'empowerment' and 'partnership', however defined, are unlikely to be effective without time, continuity and an awareness of the multi-faceted nature of family life, where special needs may be only one of a cluster of problems affecting parents at any one time.

The OPCS Report (Office of Population Censuses and Surveys, 1989) showed that only 38 per cent of parents interviewed had ever heard of voluntary organizations. As only 12 per cent of parents regularly saw a social worker, the number is perhaps not surprising. But referral to parent organizations right from the start will be a major step towards making sure that families know of all available services. Sixty-two per cent of the OPCS families had never heard of respite care. A mere 4 per cent used it. It is hard to believe that wider family needs would not have been better met if the families concerned had been introduced to local and national voluntary agencies from the first diagnosis.

An Individual Family Service Plan?

One way of ensuring that parents do know all about relevant sources of help — and are given appropriate advice about which of the often confusing melange of support systems offered to use — is the USA concept of the Individualized Family Service Plan (IFSP). The IFSP was introduced by Public Law 99-457 to replace the Individual Educational Programme (IEP) for children between birth and 3 years of age. As the Plan's name indicates, it addresses both the needs of the child and the needs of the family. The concept of a *Family* Plan is based on an acknowledgment (sadly often lacking in special needs services) that a balance needs to be struck between the 'best interests' of the child, parents, siblings and the ability and desirability of parents playing a role as 'educators', 'care-takers' or indeed their right to be 'ordinary parents'. In effect successful parental involvement in the ERA procedures will be negated by other unmet family problems.

The concept of a Family Plan also makes it easier to acknowledge cultural and other differences in child-rearing practices and to ensure that practical problems (like money, housing, equipment) can be resolved quickly and efficiently. Hopefully, Family Plans will also prevent families being offered excessive numbers of professional advisers (often with apparently conflicting advice). They should also avoid inappropriate pathological perceptions of families with a special needs child as 'handicapped families', and promote the recognition that *all* families are different in composition, needs, cultural heritage, past experiences and life stages. The philosophy behind such a Family Plan is encapsulated in Peter Mittler's citation of key factors for achieving the elusive and much pursued partnership with parents (Mittler, 1987), namely that:

> growth and learning in children can only be understood in relation to the various environments within which they are living;
>
> parents and professionals concerned about a child with special needs share a number of common goals;
>
> parents and the extended family are the most accessible adults when helping a child;
>
> parents and professionals each have essential information which needs to be shared amongst all who are concerned with the child's development.

Looking to the 1990s, we have many of the successful ingredients for such a partnership, but parity of esteem between parents, their professional advisers and the voluntary sector will only be achieved by continuous vigilance. In both the USA and UK we have education legislation which has begun to bridge the gap between pupil, educators, family and community. No one group is subordinate to the other. And all of us must accept the challenge of being *equal* partners with differing strengths, addressing a shared task, which is the education and growth of pupils and support for their families in the process. In effect, family life and the child's individual needs will best be strengthened if we remember that

> the most important thing that happens when a child with disabilities or special needs arrives in a family is that a child is born. The most important thing that happens when a couple become parents of a child with disabilities or special needs is that a couple has become *parents*. (Ferguson and Ash, quoted in Lipsky and Gartner, 1989)

Hence even the most specialist services need to become 'ordinary' and the ordinary special. They will also need to be appropriate to the major social and demographic changes.

References

BERRIDGE, D. and RUSSELL, P. (1987) *A Red Bus Next Time? A Review of Parents' Attitudes to Special Educational Provision*, London Borough of Haringey.

BRIMBLECOMBE, F. and RUSSELL, P. (1987) *Honeylands: Developing a Service for Families with Handicapped Children*, London, National Children's Bureau.

CAMERON, R. (1989) 'Teaching parents to teach children: The Portage approach to special needs', in JONES, N. (Ed.) *Special Educational Needs Review*, Volume 1, London, Falmer Press.

CUNNINGHAM, C. and DAVIS, H. (1985) *Working with Parents: Frameworks for Collaboration*, Milton Keynes, Open University Press.

DES (1978) *Special Educational Needs* (The Warnock Report), London, HMSO.

DES (1981) *The Education Act 1981*, London, HMSO.

DES (1985) *Better Schools*, Cmnd. 9469, London, HMSO.

DES (1986) *The Education (No. 2) Act 1986*, London, HMSO.

DES (1988) *The Education Reform Act 1988*, London, HMSO.

DES (1989a) *Our Changing Schools*, London, DES.

DES (1989b) *Circular 22/89: Assessments and Statements of Special Educational Needs: Procedures Within the Education, Health and Social Services*, London, DES.

GOACHER, B., EVANS, J., WELTON, J. and WEDELL, K. (1988) *Policy and Provision for Special Educational Needs: Implementing the 1981 Education Act*, London, Cassell.

HATCH, S. and HINTON, T. (1987) *Self-Help in Practice: A Study of 'Contact a Family' in Wandsworth*, Community Care/Social Work Monographs.

HEGARTY, S. (1988) *Meeting Special Needs in Ordinary Schools*, Windsor, NFER-Nelson.

HOUSE OF COMMONS (1987) *Special Educational Needs: Implementation of the Education Act 1981*, Third Report from the Education Science and Arts Committee, Session 1986–87, London, HMSO.

ILEA (1985) *Educational Opportunities for All?* (The Fish Report), London, Inner London Education Authority.

KRAMER, J. (1985) 'The 1981 Education Act in Derbyshire', *British Journal of Special Education*, 12, 3, pp. 98–101.

LALLY, M. *et al.* (1989) *Early Childhood Education: The Early Years Curriculum and the National Curriculum*, London, National Children's Bureau.

LIPSKY, D.K. and GARTNER, A. (1989) *Beyond Separate Education: Quality for All*, New York, Paul Brookes.

MITTLER, P. (1987) 'Family supports in England', in LIPSKY, D. (Ed.) *Family Supports with a Disabled Member*, New York, World Rehabilitation Fund.

NCC (1989a) *Circular No. 6: The National Curriculum and Whole Curriculum Planning: Preliminary Guidance*, York, National Curriculum Council.

NCC (1989b) *Curriculum Guidance Two: Curriculum for All*, York, National Curriculum Council.

NCC (1990) *Curriculum Guidance Three: The Whole Curriculum*, York, National Curriculum Council.

NELSON, E. (1989) *The Maze*, Camden Elfrida Rathbone, St. Margaret's, Leighton Road, London.

OFFICE OF POPULATION CENSUSES AND SURVEYS (1989) *Report 6, Disabled Children: Services, Transport and Education*, London, HMSO.

TOMLINSON, N. (1988) 'The debate: Curriculum and market — are they compatible?', in HAVILAND, J. (Ed.) *Take Care, Mr. Baker!* London, Fourth Estate Press.

WOLFENDALE, S. (1989) *All About Me*, London, Polytechnic of North East London and National Children's Bureau.

12 Annual Reviews: An Active Partnership

Nick Hughes and Barry Carpenter

Parental Contributions to the Annual Review Procedure

On a Monday morning in July 1988 Mr and Mrs Frost (names changed to preserve anonymity) attended the Annual Review meeting of their 4-year-old son, Michael. In holding this meeting Michael's school — a school for pupils with severe learning difficulties (SLD) — was fulfilling its legal obligations under the Education Act (1981) to formally review, at least annually, the provision being made for each pupil whose special educational needs were identified in the form of a written and legal Statement.

The arrangements for the Annual Review meeting were the same for Mr and Mrs Frost as they had been for the parents of seventy pupils already 'reviewed' that academic year. Mr and Mrs Frost had received an early invitation to the meeting and also, prior to the meeting, a copy of the teacher's report on Michael's progress. At the meeting itself they were welcomed and pleasantries were exchanged with the participants — the headteacher, Michael's teacher, the educational social worker (ESW), the medical officer and the educational psychologist. Mr and Mrs Frost then sat patiently and listened attentively while the teacher summarized her report and the medical officer commented on Michael's recent medical examination and read a brief speech therapy report. The educational psychologist then made comments on a period of observing Michael in class and the ESW commented on the success of respite care arrangements for Michael. Last, but not intentionally least, Mr and Mrs Frost were asked for their comments.

It was at this point that Mrs Frost did what no other parent in four years of Annual Review meetings had done. She produced from her pocket a dog-eared piece of paper, which looked suspiciously like a shopping list, and said, 'Our Michael's done that much at home this year we couldn't remember it all, so before we came out, we spent a bit of time jotting a few things down'. They then proceeded to relate Michael's achievements and their concerns for his future, using their notes as an aide mémoire.

This single piece of good sense on the part of Mr and Mrs Frost raised issues regarding the school's approach to parental involvement especially in relation to Annual Review meetings. Why, for example, were the parents the last members of the meeting to make a contribution? Were they not, in many senses, the meeting's focal point? Listeners and responders, yes, but equally, they were contributors of as many important views and as much important information as any one else. Given the need for parents to collect and organize their thoughts and prepare their contribution prior to the meeting, why had reports been prepared by an array of professionals but not by the parents? Was it precisely because the professionals had prepared reports and comments that their contributions tended to dominate the meetings?

Whatever the explanations, Mr and Mrs Frost's scribbled notes highlighted two interlinked problems: the school had not encouraged and enabled parents to make a written contribution to the Annual Review meeting and, perhaps because of this, had not really focused the centre of attention on parental perceptions during the meeting. This was not in keeping with the school's attempt to mirror current trends by developing an educational ethos of parental involvement and participation in all aspects of their children's education. Nor was it in step with the spirit of the 1981 Act which acknowledged the value of parental evidence by giving parents the right to make a written contribution to the formal assessment and reassessment of their child's special educational needs.

The parental right to make a written contribution to assessment raised a related issue, that of frequency and continuity. The schedules for assessment as required in the 1981 Act meant that parents would usually have the opportunity to report no more than twice in what, for a pupil with severe or profound learning difficulties, could be a school career spanning seventeen years. Should the parents not have the facility to make a written contribution more often than twice in seventeen years, and would not the Annual Review meeting be an ideal forum for that contribution to be heard? Such a facility would represent another step towards a more equivalent and collaborative partnership between parents and professionals which could serve only to benefit the educational development of the pupils concerned.

The Warnock Report (DES, 1978) stressed the need to increase parental involvement in education, and to foster an equal parent-professional partnership. The 1981 Act formalized this procedure. However, research (Goacher *et al.*, 1988) into the implementation of the Act found that some LEAs had made appropriate use of Statement procedures, but the procedures themselves were often time-consuming. Many Statements lacked specificity, and in practice the partnership between parents and professionals had been hard to achieve.

A recent report from HMI indicated that even when Annual Review procedures were good, there were instances in which parental views were incorporated or 'tagged-on', rather than presented in their own right. The report goes on to say: 'Parents' contributions varied widely, with some evidently very knowledgeable about their rights and responsibilities' (HMI, 1990, p. 13). Inservice training had been provided by some schools. This had considerably raised parents' understanding of curriculum matters and made them more aware of procedures (Carpenter, 1989; Carpenter and Cobb, 1990).

In the USA the effectiveness of the implementation of Public Law 94: 142 (the equivalent of the UK's 1981 Education Act) has, to a considerable extent, been attributed to the contribution of parent and voluntary organizations (Russell, 1990). Parents are actively encouraged to participate in the development of the individualized educational programme (IEP). Each objective set out for their child for the year is discussed with them, and parents must agree to these objectives before they can be accepted as part of the child's individualized programme.

Another significant difference between the 1981 Education Act Annual Review and the IEP in the USA is the inclusion of a section titled 'Parent Involvement/Training'. Written out on the IEP form is a space for an objective or activity required of the parent. Crean (1990) reports that this section of the IEP was most helpful as a lever to get unwilling parents actively involved with the special needs of their child.

The parents' need for personal contact and advice was recognized by the Warnock Report (DES, 1978) which introduced the notion of a 'named person' to act as an enabling counsellor and advisor for parents (Russell, 1985). The named person concept was weakly incorporated into the 1981 Education Act and consequently, according to Adams

(1986) there remains a case for extending the Warnock Report's idea to the creation of key workers who might be independent of LEAs and able to act as intermediaries for parents. In relation to the assessment procedures, the growing involvement of other counselling, guidance and befriending networks for parents, such as voluntary associations (see Wolfendale, 1989) and parent to parent self help schemes (Hornby, 1988) illustrates the parents' need for face-to-face support through a variety of modes (Carpenter, 1990a; Hornby, 1989).

The construction of parent-professional participation in the assessment procedures of the 1981 Act is best described by Wolfendale (1987a) as a 'process model' of equivalent expertise. The model takes account of the mutual and reciprocal involvement at each stage, and includes mutual tasks such as explaining, exchanging views, defining and agreeing a problem, formulating plans of action and so on. Clearly there are training implications for practitioners, a point recognized by the Fish Report (ILEA, 1985) and Wolfendale (1986). The process involves the development among parents and professionals of interpersonal and counselling skills; an aspect recognized by Cunningham and Davis (1985) and further addressed through the provision of workshop materials for cooperative working (Wolfendale, 1987b); and a training resource pack for working with parents (De'Ath and Pugh, 1986).

Parents and professionals each have essential information which needs to be shared amongst all who are concerned with the child's development (Mittler, 1987). This has not always been reflected in the practice arising from the 1981 Act. Fairfield School for pupils with SLD judged that they also were not entering into the spirit of the Act. The procedure they had adopted for the Act's formal Annual Review of pupils' special educational provision was not conducive to an equal parent-professional partnership. Parents perceived the Annual Review meetings as dominated by professionals and, therefore, found them somewhat daunting. In particular the school noted that parents were relegated to a role of listening and responding while each professional submitted and summarized a report on their child. Consequently the parents' contribution to the meeting was not equivalent to that of the professionals. The agenda of the meeting was largely dictated by the professionals and the partnership was far from equal. The intention, therefore, was to edge closer to perceived 'good practice' in parental involvement by exploring ways in which parents could be encouraged to become 'equivalent' partners with professionals, in the process of reviewing their children's educational progress and special needs provision.

In order to search for a solution to this problem a small, school-based pilot project was undertaken. Its aim was to devise ways of enabling parents to submit their own written views to the Annual Review meeting and to explore how parents might contribute differently to the meeting itself, so the part they played was equivalent to the other participants. In the context of the 1981 Education Act and the statementing procedure, Cranwell and Miller provided useful guidance. They found in particular that professional jargon — 'the use of technical terminology in situations where simpler alternatives exist' (Cranwell and Miller, 1987, p. 28) — was frequently misunderstood by parents. For example, jargon such as 'self image', 'cognitive development', 'audority', was misunderstood more than 80 per cent of the time. Cranwell and Miller found that parents used various strategies to overcome their confusion including ignoring, guessing and attempting to puzzle it out on their own. Parents seemed to prefer to try to fathom out the professionals' reports rather than risk ridicule and embarrassment by asking for explanations. Not surprisingly, these strategies resulted in worrying misconceptions amongst parents, especially as they tended to conclude that something else was wrong with their child or a disability was worse than anticipated.

In the light of their study, Cranwell and Miller made recommendations for writing reports: use no more words than are necessary; keep sentences short; and explain technical terms in simple words. They also advised that assessment and remediation techniques should be explained, figures and tables should be avoided, a glossary of terms should be provided, words with a high risk of misunderstanding should be omitted and, where technical terminology is unavoidable, it should be explained and related to the child's performance.

The school established three working groups comprising parents, teachers and staff from support services, all of whom were involved in the Annual Review process, who devised a Parents' Comments Form (PCF). The form was specifically designed to assist parents organize their thoughts on their child's educational progress and special needs, and to help them prepare their contribution for the Annual Review meeting by writing their thoughts down. The PCF was made up of a series of questions, which enquired about aspects of pupils' functioning. High priority was given to aspects of day-to-day management of children in the home because the working groups had identified this as the area most relevant to parents. Each question was illustrated with examples and care was taken to make the PCF as comprehensible as possible by avoiding professional jargon and providing translations for families with ethnic minority backgrounds. The questions on the PCF are listed below. The PCFs used with parents, which were delivered with an introductory and explanatory letter, have appropriate spacing between each question for parents to write their comments.

Parents' Comments for the Annual Review Meeting

Introduction
Please use this form to tell us how you think your child has altered both at home and at school. We would also like to know how you think we might, together, be able to help your child in the future.

Have there been any changes in your child's general health?
For example: general fitness; eating and sleeping habits; serious illnesses or accidents; periods in hospital; fits; diet or medicine, etc.

Have there been any changes in managing and looking after your child?
For example: lifting; feeding; dressing; toileting; washing; need for aids for sitting or walking; getting ready for bed or for school; keeping entertained; going out, etc.

Have there been any changes in what your child can do?
For example; looking; listening; sitting or standing; moving about; using hands to play with toys; drawing pictures; playing games; riding bike; using household objects; using money and shops; hobbies; leisure interests, etc.

Have there been any changes in what your child likes to do?
For example: favourite toys; music; watching TV; games; clubs, etc.

Have there been any changes in the way your child behaves?
For example: smiling; crying; happy or sad, good and bad moods; affectionate; temper tantrums; doing as told; helpful; selfish; shares; stubborn; cooperative, etc.

Have there been any changes in the way your child communicates and gets on with family and friends?

For example: smiling; crying; using sounds; looking at people; pointing; using gestures; using signs; using words; following what others say; starting conversations; chatting about events and people; getting on with parents, brothers, sisters, friends and strangers, etc.

Have there been any changes in the way your child can cope by him/herself?
For example: chewing; swallowing; feeding; drinking; using the toilet; dressing; undressing; washing; coping with being away from family; looking after belongings; keeping tidy; doing jobs; running errands; coping with growing up; coping with routines; getting out and about, etc.

Are there any improvements you would like to see in the future?
For example: in what your child does; in the way your child communicates, behaves and looks after him/herself, etc.

Have you noticed any changes in how your child gets on at school?
For example: likes or dislikes going to school; gets on with staff; gets on with other children; likes or dislikes school activities, etc.

Have there been any changes in the support you receive from people?
For example: school; doctor; social services; benefits; therapists; hostels; mental handicap team; baby sitters, etc.
Is there any support or advice that you would like in the next year?

Have there been any changes in your child's home circumstances or any special events which you would like us to know about?
For example; new baby; moved house; new special chair; new pet; holiday, etc.

General Comments
Please use the space below and over the page, to report any other views or concerns you may have. For example: any needs that you think your child and your family have; what you think of school and how it could help you; any general worries or concerns that your child or yourselves would like us to know about.

*Child's name*_____

*Parents' signature*_____

*Date*_____

Prior to their child's Annual Review, thirteen sets of parents were given the opportunity to submit their views using the PCF. An educational social worker (ESW) contacted each set of parents to answer any questions, allay any anxieties and offer help with the completion of the PCF. Six of the parents accepted this offer and another three declined only because they had been members of a working group and were, therefore, familiar with the PCF. Ten parents submitted their views to their child's Annual Review meeting using the PCF and nine of these parents attended the meeting itself. In the meeting the parents, not the professionals, presented their views first, using the information contained in their PCFs. This led to general discussion before the professionals summarized their reports and more discussion took place.

The pilot project was evaluated by means of a questionnaire and general discussion with parents and semi-structured interviews with professionals. The parents reported that the PCF, although a little repetitive and confusing in places, had helped them to prepare for the meeting and had improved the contribution they were able to make. None of the parents felt threatened by the PCF and all those who received assistance from the ESW valued it highly. All the parents reported an increased involvement in the meeting, some referring to the advantage of speaking first. All the parents felt that their contribution had been listened to and acknowledged and that the meetings were very worthwhile.

The strength of positive feelings expressed in the evaluation interviews suggest that the face-to-face contact was the *essential* ingredient not only in enabling the use of the PCF but also in the wider issue of seeking to develop a parent-professional partnership of equal expertise. The fact that the parents found the contact so helpful and rewarding says much for the quality of listening, communicating and counselling skills employed and bears out the views expressed in the literature by writers such as Aitkin (1988) and Cunningham and Davis (1985) regarding listening, the consumer model of parent-professional partnership and the new professionalism demanded by this approach. It illustrates that effective professional partnership with parents is not about filling in forms and making reports *per se*, but about the quality of the relationship that is built during this and numerous other activities. As McConkey expressed it, regarding the professional's role when working with parents, 'It's not what you do it's the way that you do it — that's what gets results (McConkey, 1985, p. 34).

The views expressed by the professionals also endorsed the use of the PCF. They felt that they had acquired more information from parents and a better understanding of the parents' point of view. They observed parents to be better prepared and more comfortable in the meeting through having a contribution of their own to make. The ESW reported that home visiting was a necessary service for parents as many needed assistance to interpret the PCF's questions and the visit itself concentrated parents' minds on the meeting and raised their awareness of its purpose and importance.

Another feature of home visiting requiring further thought is the problem of communicating with Asian parents. Significantly all three parents who did not complete the PCF were Asian. The ESW reported difficulty in making contact and in making herself sufficiently understood. This is a worrying feature for the school when the number of Asian children attending the school stands at 40 per cent and is increasing. Clearly, as well as the translations of the PCF into Asian languages an interpreter is needed for the person-to-person contact. Several parents, some of whom were Asian, volunteered to act as 'counsellors' with other parents. The idea of parent-to-parent contact has its attractions, as was demonstrated by the ease with which they counselled one another during the working group meetings. Since the availability of interpreters through the LEA is unreliable and somewhat impersonal, parent-to-parent contact may be a particularly appropriate solution to the problem of communicating with Asian parents.

One crucial aspect which will need further attention is the use made of the information parents give in the PCFs and during the Annual Review meeting. In her study Wolfendale (1988) found that some parents thought that submitting their views was an academic exercise because the professionals' views would always prevail. In this study teachers also expressed the same concern. It would seem likely that parents will only continue to submit their views if they see some beneficial outcomes from their reporting and participation in Annual Review meetings. This will require detailed recording of the decisions made at the meeting and assiduous follow-up work by the school, other professionals and LEA administrators to make sure that parents genuinely feel involved in a decision-making process which can bear fruit. It will also require the continuation of a regular system for evaluating the Annual Review process in which the parents make a major contribution.

Overall, the evaluation indicated that the pilot project had, in the majority of cases, achieved its purpose of helping parents submit written views and contribute on an equivalent basis to Annual Review meetings. General opinion was that the facility offered by the project, after revision of some aspects such as repetitive questioning, provision of an interpreter for ethnic minority families and more time for the meetings, should be made available to all the parents as a part of the school's routine Annual Review procedure.

The Interface with the National Curriculum

Circular 1/83 (DES, 1983) spoke in strong terms of a 'partnership between teachers, other professionals and parents'. However, practice over the next six years revealed that even in LEAs which encouraged parental participation, parents were not always able to take advantage of this opportunity. The parental contribution to the statementing procedures was often minimal or through silent assent.

To redress the balance, *Circular 22/89* (DES, 1989a) places new responsibilities on local authorities to ensure that parents are more closely involved in the assessment and statementing procedures. Parental contributions to the Annual Review procedures are again stressed in the circular: 'the views of the child's parents . . . should be included in formulating the outcome of the review and their attendance at review [is to be] encouraged.'

Whilst it is laudable that the validity of the parental contribution to the Annual Review process has been emphasized by *Circular 22/89*, unless parents are given enabling strategies to participate fully in this procedure they will again be peripheral participants in a professional-dominated forum. In addition to this, parents now face the prospect of being baffled by 'National Curriculumese'. As teachers and psychologists present their reports to Annual Review meetings they will inevitably be referring to the experiences the child has undertaken in the context of the National Curriculum, as well as the *Whole Curriculum* (NCC, 1990).

Indeed, parents may wish to ensure that their child is an active participant in the National Curriculum. The National Curriculum offers an equality of educational opportunity to all pupils. The pupils' entitlement is embedded in the first section of the Education Reform Act 1988 (ERA). For the first time in the history of education in this country the principle that all pupils attending maintained schools, including special schools, are entitled to a broadly based, balanced curriculum is enshrined in law.

In future, each Statement will be able to specify how the National Curriculum is to apply to the individual pupil. Although it may modify or disapply any of the requirements of the National Curriculum, *National Curriculum: From Policy to Practice* (DES, 1989b) stresses that 'the intention is not to make the statement negative in its impact'. Once entitlement to the National Curriculum is established, the issue becomes one of access for children with special educational needs, through carefully planned learning routes (Archer, 1989).

Lewis (1989) points out that to turn the 'ideal of the National Curriculum being for all into reality requires skilled modification of the curriculum'. As teachers grapple with this challenge, how will parents monitor that their goals for their child are not lost in an ever-changing curriculum landscape? Only through an open, honest partnership, based on mutual trust and respect, can parents seek re-assurance from teachers that their aspirations for their child are embodied in the child's curriculum programme. The Annual Review process offers an opportunity for negotiation and collaboration, and the PCF ensures that the parents' viewpoint is articulated alongside those of the professional contributions.

Curriculum Guidance Two: A Curriculum for All (NCC, 1989) sees access to the National Curriculum for children with special needs, as a challenge to the 'cooperation, understanding and planning skills of teachers, support agencies, parents, governors and many others' (p. 2). The Annual Review meeting can be the vehicle for this planning. It enables everyone to review their input to the child's educational programme, reappraise current goals, and plan for the future.

Parents remain to be convinced in practice that the National Curriculum can prepare their child with special needs for a fruitful citizenship in their community. The onus rests with the teacher to demonstrate this in practice, and to share ideas in the Annual Review meeting with parents. The curricular goals determined by the teacher should be blended with those identified by the parents. This blending through negotiation should evolve a holistic curriculum for the pupil applicable across the range of environments experienced by the pupil (for further discussions of these principles see Chapters 2 and 3 in this volume).

The ownership of the curriculum must be shared. Indeed *Circular 22/89* emphasizes the place of the pupil in contributing to the Annual Review procedure. Increasingly, through wider opportunities and raised expectations, young people with SLD are proving themselves capable of effective decision making in relation to their own life goals (Carpenter, 1990b). The Annual Review meeting could be an excellent training ground for children to voice their opinions and participate in decision making.

The opportunity of the PCF in the context of the Annual Review procedure, reinforces not only the necessity of parental contribution but also the validity. The PCF offers a way forward for parents to continue making their essential contribution in a climate of educational change, and where the Annual Review meeting may be an opportunity to understand a little more of how the National Curriculum relates to their child. Imaginitive curriculum planning, using a variety of teaching strategies and approaches, combined with the support and commitment of parents, teachers and professionals, will ensure that, through the Annual Review, the National Curriculum becomes a personalized curriculum, a 'curriculum for all'.

References

ADAMS, F. (Ed.) (1986) *Special Education*, Harlow, Councils and Education Press.

ARCHER, M. (1989) 'Targeting change', *Special Children*, October, pp. 14–15.

AITKIN, J. (1988) *Listening to Parents: An Approach to the Improvement of Home-school Relations*, Beckenham, Croom Helm.

CARPENTER, B. (1989) 'The curriculum for children with profound and multiple learning difficulties: Current issues', *Early Child Development and Care*, 46, pp. 87–96.

CARPENTER, B. (1990a) 'Joining Forces: Parental Participation in the Development of a Community Integrated Nursery', paper presented to the South Pacific Conference on Special Education, Auckland, New Zealand, January. (To be published in the *Australasian Journal of Special Education*).

CARPENTER, B. (1990b) 'A Post-16 Education Project for Students with Profound and Multiple Learning Difficulties', paper presented to the International Special Education Congress, Cardiff, Wales, August.

CARPENTER, B. and COBB, M. (1990) 'Learning together: Practice in an integrated nursery setting', in JONES, N. (Ed.) *Special Educational Needs Review*, Volume 3, London, Falmer Press.

CRANWELL, D. and MILLER, A. (1987) 'Do parents understand professionals? Terminology in Statements of Special Educational Need', *Educational Psychology in Practice*, 3, 2, pp. 27–32.

CREAN, S. (1990) 'Teaching special needs children — A comparison of two systems', in BAKER, D. and BOVAIR, K. (Eds) *Making the Special Schools Ordinary?* Volume 2, London, Falmer Press.

CUNNINGHAM, C.C. and DAVIS, H. (1985) *Working with Parents: Frameworks for Collaboration*, Milton Keynes, Open University Press.

DE'ATH, E. and PUGH, G. (Eds) (1986) *Working with Parents: a Training Resource Pack*, London, National Children's Bureau.

DES (1978) *Special Educational Needs* (The Warnock Report), London, HMSO.

DES (1981) *The Education Act 1981*, London, HMSO.

DES (1983) *Circular 1/83: Assessments and Statements of Special Educational Needs*, (Joint Circular with DHSS Health Circular HC [83]3 and Local Authority Circular LAC [83]2), London, DES.

DES (1988) *The Education Reform Act 1988*, London, HMSO.

DES (1989a) *Circular 22/89: Assessments and Statements of Special Educational Needs: Procedures Within the Education, Health and Social Services*, London, DES.

DES (1989b) *National Curriculum: From Policy to Practice*, London, DES.

GOACHER, B., EVANS, J., WELTON, J. and WEDELL, K. (1988) *Policy and Provision for Special Educational Needs: Implementing the 1981 Education Act*, London, Cassell.

HMI (1990) *Education Observed: Special Needs Issues*, London, DES.

HORNBY, G. (1988) 'Launching parent to parent schemes', *British Journal of Special Education*, 15, 2, pp. 76–8.

HORNBY, G. (1989) 'A model for parental participation', *British Journal of Special Education*, 16, 4, pp. 161–2.

ILEA (1985) *Educational Opportunities for All?* (The Fish Report), London, Inner London Education Authority.

LEWIS, A. (1989) 'A special need', *Junior Education*, March, pp. 10–11.

McCONKEY, R. (1985) *Working with Parents: A Practical Guide for Teachers and Therapists*, London, Croom Helm.

MITTLER, P. (1987) 'Family supports in England', in LIPSKY, D. (Ed.) *Family Supports with a Disabled Member*, New York, World Rehabilitation Fund.

NCC (1989) *Curriculum Guidance Two: A Curriculum for All*, York, National Curriculum Council.

NCC (1990) *Curriculum Guidance Three: The Whole Curriculum*, York, National Curriculum Council.

RUSSELL, P. (1985) 'The Education Act 1981: The role of the named person', *Early Child Development and Care*, 19, 3, pp. 251–74.

RUSSELL, P. (1990) 'Policy and practice for young children with special educational needs: Changes and challenges,' *Support for Learning*, 5, 2, pp. 98–105.

WOLFENDALE, S. (1986) 'Routes to partnership with parents: Rhetoric or reality?', *Education and Child Psychology*, 3, 3, pp. 9–17.

WOLFENDALE, S. (1987a) *Primary Schools and Special Needs — Policy, Planning and Provision*, London, Cassell.

WOLFENDALE, S. (1987b) 'Parents and professionals in cooperation: Workshop on developing skills for successful co-working', *Educational and Child Psychology*, 4, 3–4, pp. 100–109.

WOLFENDALE, S. (1988) *The Parental Contribution to Assessment*, Stratford-upon-Avon, National Council for Special Education.

WOLFENDALE, S. (Ed.) (1989) *Parental Involvement: Developing Networks Between School, Home and Community*, London, Cassell.

13   Entitled to Learn Together?

Ann Lewis

Introduction

Commentators on the Great Education Reform Bill (GERBIL), published in November 1987, argued that the integration of pupils with special educational needs (SEN) would be threatened by the proposed legislation (Haviland, 1988) and, at best, GERBIL was seen as doing nothing to strengthen the pro-integration stance of the 1981 Education Act (Wedell, 1988). Time has moved on; GERBIL has given way to the Education Reform Act 1988 (ERA) and it can be seen that special educators' representations have led to some changes to GERBIL, although these are not as radical as special education lobbyists would probably have liked.

Now debate about principles is giving way to addressing the practicalities of working within the ERA. We can be fatalistic and say, as many ordinary school teachers have said to me recently, 'Integration is a dead issue. Nobody cares about it, we're all just trying to keep our heads above water to meet the educational needs of "normal" children.' Alternatively we can hold on to a belief that integration is a valid educational goal and strive to find ways of promoting this, perhaps in spite of parts of the ERA. Other educational sectors provide good models of similar activity. For example, in the early years context powerful arguments as well as practical solutions have been put forward to try to ensure that a 'child-centred' approach is retained and fostered through the National Curriculum (for example, EYCG, 1989), despite the exclusively subject-based Programmes of Study and Attainment Targets.

The Integration of Children with SLD into Ordinary Schools

There has been considerable debate about the pros and cons of educational integration in Britain for over a decade (for a recent review see Lindsay, 1989), but Bennett (1987) has claimed that we still know little about the precise nature of interactions between 'normal' pupils and classmates with special needs. It is important that we know about the nature of this interaction if we are to claim that integration is consistent with the aims of the ERA and the working of the National Curriculum.

In this chapter I shall first review three recent and interconnected British studies that investigated young 'normal' children's interactions with classmates with Severe Learning Difficulties (SLD). The findings from these three studies will then be considered in the light of the ERA and the second part of this chapter will try to answer the question: can such integration continue within the requirements of the ERA and the National Curriculum?

The Context for the Three Studies

Two schools were involved in this work: one a first school (4–8 year-olds) and the other an all-age school (2–19 year-olds) for pupils with SLD. The heads of the schools decided that a group of ten children from a class of first school 6- and 7-year-olds would work, for one afternoon each fortnight, with ten children from a similar age group (4–8 year-olds) from the SLD school. The project took place over two years and involved two successive groups of ten children from the ordinary school (in the first year a relatively mature group of children was chosen for the project, but in the second year the ten children reflected a cross-section of ability) and two groups of ten children from the SLD school (the total lower school group, largely the same children in each year). In the first year non-verbal interaction was monitored and in the second year verbal interaction and attitudes were assessed.

The work was seen as part of wider personal and social education programmes in the two schools. The ordinary school staff hoped that the integration work would help their pupils to develop sensitivity towards others and a positive attitude towards particular 'special needs' children. The SLD school staff hoped that the same work would cultivate their pupils' independence and abilities to communicate with others. (Both schools agreed on the wider aims of the work — it was hoped that pupils' positive experiences with one another would foster the integration of people with SLD into local communities (Carpenter *et al.*, 1986; Moore *et al.*, 1987).)

The staff involved from both schools made joint decisions, after discussion, concerning the format, focus and structure of the integration sessions. Each session began with an introductory class activity for all the children. This activity was led alternately by a teacher from the special school and the class teacher from the ordinary school. The central (majority) part of each integration session focused on art and craft activities. Children were paired within the art and craft activity so that each child partnered a child from the other school. Children had a free choice of partner within this constraint.

There were discussions before the work began about the kinds of interaction which staff hoped would take place between ordinary and SLD school pupils. Various types of child–child learning were discussed as possible models for interaction. Different types of shared learning including buddy systems, peer tutoring, cooperative learning and collaborative learning were reviewed. The discussion led staff to the decision to focus on developing collaborative work in which each child made a different but complementary contribution to a shared task. An example of an appropriate collaborative activity was string painting in which the child with SLD dipped the string in paint and placed it on the shared piece of paper. This child's partner from the ordinary school then folded the paper in half and pulled out the piece of string, thus each child contributed to the end product.

Did the Ordinary School Children Like the Children with SLD?

Interviews were carried out with the ordinary school children near the beginning and at the end of a year of integration sessions. The interviews probed the ordinary school children's understanding of SLD as well as their feelings towards the children with SLD. In summary, the children with SLD were well-liked but not understood (Lewis and Lewis, 1987; 1988).

When asked to describe the children with SLD, very few of the ordinary school children made any reference to lack of ability. Overwhelmingly, and consistent with other developmental research on how young children describe others, the children with SLD were described in terms of physical characteristics: 'Some have got brown hair', 'Lucy's got a red dress'.

A particularly interesting aspect of the 6- and 7-year-old first school children's attitudes concerned the explanations which they held to account for the sometimes strange behaviours of children with SLD. At the beginning of the year the ordinary school children were told that the children with SLD had some form of brain damage but, regardless of this information, the ordinary school children often attributed behaviour of the children with SLD to sickness ('They're poorly'). One child believed that if his friend with SLD was given a Disprin he would be well again and would then resemble children from the ordinary school. Other ordinary school children initially believed that the children from the SLD school were normal but of a young age and would grow out of their difficulties. These comments were interesting as they showed that the ordinary school children sometimes ignored the 'obvious' (for example, that many of the 4- to 8-year-old children with SLD were of approximately normal size for chronological age) in favour of some more powerful cue to their level of development (for example, that, cognitively and linguistically, the behaviour of the children with SLD resembled that of normal 2- or 3-year-olds). Consistent with this view were comments made by many of the ordinary school children that when the children with SLD grew up they would have jobs such as teachers, taxi drivers, firemen or shop workers.

However, after a year of integration sessions these explanations were beginning to be questioned by the ordinary school children: the children with SLD were neither getting better, nor growing up as young brothers and sisters were doing. Many of these 6- and 7-year-olds remained confused about the nature of SLD. Several children began to express views that the real causes of the difficulties of the children with SLD were sensory ('They can't hear', 'Lot of them can't see properly'). Only one child came close to an understanding of SLD; she repeatedly described the children with SLD as having 'bad brains'.

This research, combined with other detailed studies of attitude change (see, for example, Katz, 1982, and Aboud, 1988, in relation to the development of ethnic attitudes) point to several ways in which teachers can foster ordinary school children's acceptance of others. The strategies differ across the infant and the junior school periods because of children's substantial developmental changes during this time. In the early school years (R to Y2) children need to be helped to express a range of emotions and not to perceive others dichotomously as either happy/good/positive or unhappy/bad/negative. Some children in this research avoided dichotomous judgments, by the end of the year of integration sessions, and described children with SLD as happy generally but also sad about some things.

Another important strategy in the early school years is to develop understanding and acceptance of different ways of responding to the world. Some children in this study understood and accepted double standards of teachers in relation to work (but not behaviour) of children with SLD and ordinary school children.

At junior school level (Y3 to Y6) three particular strategies may help children from an ordinary school to understand and accept positively children with SLD. First, ordinary school children need to be helped to focus on internal, rather than external, attributes of others (to shift from describing children with SLD as having particular physical features to describing them as, for example, being fun). Second, learning to attend to between-group similarities and within-group differences can help ordinary school children to be positive about minority groups, for example, to notice that a child with SLD shares an enthusiasm for certain sports with an ordinary school child while several children with SLD disagree about, for example, favourite foods. Third (and developing the acceptance of different world views referred to at an earlier level), older ordinary school children need to be helped to accept that at an abstract level, quite different world views are possible and acceptable, for example, that children and adults with SLD may have personal aims which differ from those of 'normal' peers.

Did the Children from the Ordinary School Have Much to Do with the Children with SLD?

Several striking findings emerged from analyses of whether and how ordinary school children interacted with children with SLD. Interaction was monitored in detail during the middle part of the session, that is, when the ordinary children and children with SLD were supposed to be working on joint tasks.

Interaction between ordinary and SLD school children occurred about one quarter of the time (24.3 per cent of observations). This is comparable with the frequency of child–child interaction found among preschool and primary school children in comparable situations (see, for example, Sylva *et al.*, 1980). Children had a strong preference for working with others of their own sex (as found repeatedly in educational and psychological research, for example, Oden, 1982). This same-sex preference applied whether it was an ordinary school child choosing a child with SLD or vice versa.

Levels of interaction between ordinary and SLD school children varied over the school year, with relatively little interaction at both the beginning (when ordinary school children often stared at the SLD children) or end of the year (when the ordinary school children had moved, intellectually, even further apart from the children with SLD). The change over the year, taken with findings from other research (for example, Sebba, 1983) suggests that there would have been greater interaction between the ordinary and special school children if similar cognitive or linguistic levels rather than similar chronological age had been the basis for grouping; for example, if the 5- to 8-year-old children with SLD had worked with ordinary preschool children of around 3 years of age. Interestingly, Byrne *et al.* (1988) report similarly that parents of children with Down's syndrome (most of these children attended SLD schools) found that their children were 'outgrown' by friends, and moved on to play with the younger brothers and sisters of children with whom they had been friends.

The importance of similarity of developmental levels in fostering positive interaction raises many difficult ethical and educational issues. If one pursues this line it leads to arguing for relatively homogeneous classroom groupings. This line has been advocated by administrators in some LEAs who have argued for the class grouping of children on the basis of levels attained in the National Curriculum. Yet the evidence from research into streaming (for example, Lunn, 1970) has shown that streaming intensifies children's positions. For example, children in lower streams drop even further behind their peers in other streams and develop increasingly negative self-concepts. The solution must surely be for a range of flexible groupings of children to be used so that, within or across classes, children with learning difficulties are sometimes in homogeneous groups but at other times in mixed ability groups, depending on the curricular aims of the activities.

The wide and widening cognitive and linguistic gaps between the ordinary and SLD school children might lead one to expect that interaction would be dominated by the ordinary school children. This did happen and was evident in both the actions and the talk of the ordinary school children. However, dominance can be seen as positive and enabling or negative and autocratic. Different ordinary school children reflected different kinds of dominance. Several ordinary school children ('enablers') gently encouraged children with SLD, taking them through activities in a careful step-by-step way, but other ordinary school children babied children with SLD by giving excessive amounts of help at every opportunity. A minority of the ordinary school children gave many demands to children with SLD, sometimes in a harsh and fierce manner. The characteristics of the enablers are considered more fully in the next section.

What Characterized 'Enabling' Children?

This research revealed some interesting characteristics of 'enabling' children and there are many parallels with work on effective peer tutoring (see, for example, Allen, 1976). The characteristics of enabling children are discussed more fully because they illustrate the types of positive interaction which the schools were hoping would develop, and provide models that other teachers may find useful.

{ In terms of non-verbal behaviours the enabling children were adept at managing the task with the partners with SLD without being overtly controlling.\ For example, they would subtly locate and have ready the various materials needed for the joint task. They would prompt the child with SLD non-verbally before trying to do the activity for the child. It is not clear from where the children drew this repertoire of behaviours or how it developed. There was no straightforward link with obviously likely precedents such as having a younger brother or sister. Similarly there were no simple correlations with ability or sex of the ordinary school child; boys and girls, more as well as less able ordinary school children became enablers.

Analyses of the ways in which enabling ordinary school children talked to children with SLD show that enablers' talk was characterized by careful step-by-step sequencing of instructions, orienting the child with SLD to the task (for example, 'Now we're going to make a duck'), responding to most of what the child with SLD said, even though this was often almost unintelligible, encouraging the child with SLD to show finished pictures or models to an adult and the frequent use of the first person plural ('Shall *we* play houses now?', 'That's *our* model'). These children were also proficient in re-phrasing comments to children with SLD in ways that were highly appropriate (for example, 'Let's do the red circle now' > 'Red now'). This type of re-phrasing of comments dropped the least meaningful parts and retained only the elements essential for communication.

Can, and Will, This Type of Project Be Continued Within the Bounds of the ERA?

One may ask, first, can the kind of work described in this project continue within the ERA (as outlined in statutory and advisory documents) and second, is this likely to happen? I believe that this work is compatible with the aims of the ERA but that those who support educational integration (a wide group encompassing parents and, crucially, governors as well as teachers) will have to work hard to persuade others of the validity and feasibility of that position. This point is developed further in the following sections.

A Common Curriculum

There is a strong, positive aspect to the National Curriculum in relation to integration. This is that it provides a series of common curriculum ladders for all children. *Curriculum Guidance Two: A Curriculum for All* (NCC, 1989) explicitly includes not only pupils with SLD but also pupils with PMLD within the common curricular framework. This common curriculum is an essential part of integration. I have argued elsewhere (for example, Lewis, 1988) that integration has been hampered by an absence of a common curriculum. How real is integration if the recognition of the individualized needs of pupils is so strong that classroom activities separate pupils with special needs from classmates? We have evidence from surveys (for example, ILEA, 1985a), HMI reports on individual schools (Lewis, 1986) and published case studies (for example, Booth and Statham, 1982) that pupils with SEN both in ordinary and special schools have often been isolated by individualized curricula and segregated by separatist systems of support. The principle that children with SEN should have access to the same broad and balanced curriculum as other children including, for example, Science and an emphasis on oral work in early literacy, is a positive aspect of the National Curriculum. This should be welcomed by special educators.

The National Curriculum provides a framework which is potentially highly supportive of integration, not just at a within-school level, but across special/ordinary schools. The National Curriculum provides a common language for detailed discussion of curricula. The fact that it is common to both sectors will help special school teachers to see links with what is happening in ordinary schools, and will help ordinary school teachers to recognize that what happens in special schools is not totally different from what happens in ordinary schools.

The gap in teachers' perceptions about what happens in ordinary and special schools was illustrated in the integration project described above. Initially the teacher from the ordinary school was apprehensive about what to do when it was her turn to lead the integration session. However, she borrowed art and craft curricular guidelines from the special school staff and was very surprised to find that 'It's just like the things I do now with my class!'.

It will be easier with the National Curriculum, than was previously the case, to develop continuity and progression across special and ordinary school curricula for individual pupils. The importance of this is illustrated in Bennett and Cass's (1989) cases studies of pupils transferring from special to ordinary schools, in which curriculum continuity was described as poor for three of the five pupils studied. Problems were particularly acute when the transition was made at mid-secondary, rather than the junior/secondary transfer stage. The use of National Curriculum Statements of Attainment to guide curricula decisions across special and ordinary schools is described by Archer (1989). He comments that a teacher from a special school will be able to match the curricular needs of a pupil from the special school with what the ordinary school has to offer (and vice versa), so that a pupil from the special school on, say, Level 3 of the Science curriculum can be placed in an ordinary school class in which Level 3 Science work will be carried out.

However, this approach needs to be used carefully otherwise it attributes a spurious precision to levels specified in the National Curriculum. There are anomalies in the National Curriculum documents with similar activities described as being at different levels in different subjects. For example, Science AT 13, Level 5, states 'Understands the idea of global energy resources and appreciates that these resources are limited' (DES and Welsh Office, 1989a) while the related statement 'distinguish between renewable and non-renewable resources' is presented at AT 7, Level 6, in the proposals for Geography (DES and Welsh Office, 1990).

It should also be recognized that pupils of differing levels can work together effectively on a common task, drawing on different but complementary skills as in the string painting task described earlier. This idea can be applied to tasks within the National Curriculum. For example, a game for a pair of pupils involving making 3D shapes from 2D card or plastic shapes could require one child to sort the shapes by colour (Science AT 15, Level 1) or shape (Mathematics AT 10, Level 1) and the other child to build the shapes into, for example, pyramids or cubes (Mathematics AT 10, Level 4) (DES and Welsh Office, 1989a; 1989b).

Another advantage of the common curriculum language provided by the National Curriculum is that special schools will be clearer about the resources available in the neighbouring ordinary schools and how these fit with the curriculum. Surveys of special schools' provision and curricular practices suggest that a major implication of the National Curriculum for special schools is that they will be pushed towards widening their curricula. One repercussion of this is that they may find that they lack resources needed for some work. A special school which wants pupils to do work on, for example, Level 4 of the Technology or Science curricula, will know that ordinary schools working at this level will need to have (and hence possibly available for special school pupils also) relevant equipment and materials. These might be too expensive for a relatively small special school to acquire. It would be reasonable for a system of sharing such resources between ordinary and special schools to develop. This might lead to a move-ment of pupils and/or resources and could work both ways. Some ordinary school pupils might benefit from a wide range of curriculum-linked resources on, say, early reading, while a special school might gain from access to specialized resources at secondary level.

The Nature of the Curriculum

The breadth of the educational aims stated in the ERA is another source of support for the integration of pupils with special needs. Section 1 of the Act states that the total curriculum should promote the spiritual, moral and cultural development of pupils as well as preparing them for adult life. All pupils in maintained schools are encompassed by these educational aims.

The aims of the schools involved in the integration work de-scribed earlier concerned preparation for adult life in the community as well as fostering children's individual sensitivities to the needs of people different from themselves. They are strongly consistent with the educational aims expressed in the ERA. The attitude interviews demonstrated that the children from the ordinary school were sensi-tive to the children with SLD and that, at least in the short term, the integration project met the aims of the ordinary school staff. Only time will tell whether or not the wider aims are met, although there is anecdotal evidence that positive attitudes towards the children with SLD were generalized to other contexts. Pupils at all stages of the special school were involved in some type of integration with local ordinary schools. Over time this meant that ordinary and SLD school pupils who had worked together in an infant school sometimes met up again in a middle-school integration project. The reports from staff indicated that both SLD and ordinary school pupils were excited and delighted by this re-meeting with earlier friends.

The effectiveness of this type of integration project in promoting positive attitudes is supported by a range of research into attitude change. That research indicates that positive attitudes to other groups are fostered more effectively through collaborative interaction than through (for example) simulations, role playing or multi-media presentations.

It is important that teachers and others recognize the breadth of the educational aims embodied in the ERA. They may turn out to be vulnerable, and certainly sit uneasily alongside the subject-centred Programmes of Study and series of Attainment Targets.

Group Work

A number of the National Curriculum Programmes of Study and Attainment Targets, particularly in English and Science (DES and Welsh Office, 1989c; 1989a), refer to pupils' abilities to work in pairs or groups, explaining things to another pupil. Part of the research into the integration project referred to earlier concerned analyses of talk between the ordinary and special school children (reported in Lewis, 1990; Lewis and Carpenter, 1990). These analyses show that the linguistic demands placed on both ordinary and SLD school children in the integration work probably exceeded any other communication demands they experienced in school.

The emphasis on children working collaboratively meant that the children persisted in attempts at communicating with one another. Virtually all comments spoken by children with SLD (usually only one or two words) were followed up by children from the ordinary school. Similarly when children with SLD appeared not to understand an instruction the children from the ordinary school generally re-peated and/or re-phrased utterances in attempts to communicate suc-cessfully. This is illustrated in the following example of a child from the ordinary school (Joe) trying to help a child from the SLD school (Micky) to make a tower with Lego bricks. This talk, all of which was by Joe, took place soon after the children had begun this activity.

Joe:

Put those two on	[instructing Micky to build the
Put those two on	tower]
Micky	
Micky	[getting his attention]
Put that [one brick] on	[dividing the task]
No	[giving feedback]
Bring it over	[small steps of the task]
Press it	[ditto]
Press on that	[ditto]
Oh Micky	
Micky	[trying to keep attention?]
Put it on	
No	[giving feedback]
Put it on down here	[re-phrasing, more explicit]
Come on	[encouraging]
Micky put this on	
Like that	[demonstrating]
Keep putting it on	

This extract shows how persistent Joe was in trying to communicate with Micky. Joe was not a particularly able child and had no younger brothers or sisters on whom he might have practised this kind of careful teaching. It is interesting that Joe did not immediately demonstrate to Micky what was required in placing one Lego brick on another but tried to get Micky to do it for himself first. The extent to which Joe's talk with a child with SLD pushed him linguistically is illustrated by comparing how Joe talked with Micky, with how Joe talked to Dan (a 6-year-old classmate) and Chris (a 4-year-old boy) during two sessions of similar activities.

Joe: *Dan:*

                 [making a print picture together]

Your turn

That'll do

                                   There's all those

Do another one

There you are

                                     OK

Finished now

                                 Let's go and show her

                 [picking up picture to show to the teacher]

This piece of conversation is much less demanding linguistically for Joe because the two children share so many assumptions and understandings about what is going on. Joe does not, for example, have to go into detail about what he means by 'your turn' or 'do another one', nor does Dan have to explain to Joe who he means by 'her' even though there has been no reference to anyone specifically. Joe, and probably you the reader, has guessed that 'her' means the teacher. Similar joint understandings are evident in the following short piece of conversation between Joe and Chris (a boy from the reception class) even though this was recorded within the first few minutes of the children meeting for the first time.

Joe:	*Chris:*
	[building a model from Lego]
	How did you make your car?
You get another one on top and fix them together	
	Do it again
Just copy off me Copy off that side	
	There done it

Recent work on oracy has drawn attention to the importance of the middle phase of childhood (that is, the primary school years) in children's language development. Although on starting school most children have acquired a substantial vocabulary and can use and understand it well, it is becoming increasingly clear that these children are still learners when it comes to sustaining a coherent conversation with another child. At this stage if one child says to another, 'That's my biro' and there is no response, the speaker does not know if this is because the listener has not heard, is deliberately ignoring the speaker or has heard but not understood. If the listener says 'My what?' or 'What's a biro?' then the speaker knows that the message has been heard and partly interpreted but not fully understood. The speaker also knows which bit of the message was unclear (that is, 'biro'). This gives the speaker a lot of useful information on which to base the next comment. It would be highly appropriate for the speaker to say next 'That's my pen'.

Several researchers (for example, Robinson and Whittaker, 1986) have shown that it is rare in infant school classes for children to be told explicitly when a comment has not been understood by the listener. Therefore the children with SLD in the project reported here may well have provided the children from the ordinary school with crucial, and otherwise infrequent, experiences for their development as conversationalists. The children with SLD often showed explicitly, usually non-verbally (such as moving away) or verbally (for instance, shouting) that they had not understood an instruction by a child from the ordinary school.

The National Curriculum documents make it clear that it is a curriculum for all children. Consequently the Attainment Targets concerning arguing one's case in a group are as important and as applicable to children with SLD, as to ordinary school children. The abilities of the children with SLD to defend their points of view were demonstrated in the talk between Rachel (a 6-year-old girl from the ordinary school) and Jane (a 5-year-old girl with SLD) when they were playing a dressing-up game. In this game the children argued about who should take on the roles of nurse and doctor. Jane, showing language skills which had not been evident at other times in school, made it clear that she wanted to be the doctor. (This event is described more fully in Carpenter and Lewis, 1989).

These examples concerning conversation between ordinary and SLD school children suggest that experiences occurring during the integrated sessions were important for developing the communication skills of both sets of children. Above all, the sessions gave a context to language development which was meaningful and in which communication served a real purpose.

Parental Choice

Many of the concerns about the National Curriculum and pupils with SEN reflect fears that parents will not choose to send their children to schools which appear to be poor in terms of published results of formal assessments. Consequently pupils with SEN will come to be seen as a drag on an otherwise healthy school, in terms only of published assessment results. This raises two issues, one about what parents look for in a school and another about what should happen to pupils with SEN in relation to Standard Assessment Tasks (SATs).

In relation to the first of these issues there is an assumption among those who fear that published results will automatically discourage schools from receiving pupils with SEN that parents share the DES's apparent concern with published assessment results as a (*the?*) measure of a school's health and desirability. This assumption is far from proven, and interestingly the many books and articles now appearing about how to sell your school to parents emphasize school climate as a key factor (for example, Dennison, 1989). Surveys of primary schools and parents (for example, ILEA, 1985b) repeatedly show that parents' priorities are for their children to be happy at school. Of course, many parents do care about academic standards but their priorities are about school climate at least as much as assessment results. This is a message which should be reiterated so that schools see pupils with SEN as a positive illustration of their caring attitude towards all pupils. One way in which schools may foster a caring school community is through the development of partial as well as full integration programmes.

Those involved in the integration project described here have often been asked about the reactions of children's parents to the work. This is interesting from the points of view of both the special and ordinary school children's parents. Parents of children from the special school were familiar with the principles behind the project and wholeheartedly supported it (Carpenter *et al.*, 1988). Parents of the ordinary school children similarly supported the work and were enthusiastic about their children's involvement. In the two years of the project described here only one parental complaint was received. This was made by the parent of an ordinary school child who was not involved in the project; the complaint concerned what she saw as her daughter's exclusion from the project. On the basis of this, admittedly limited, evidence there are no grounds for believing that parents will be negative about schools which practice integration of pupils with SLD.

The second issue raised here concerns publication of assessments. Two recent trends within the development of the National Curriculum reinforce concern about this issue in relation to pupils with SEN. There has been some back-tracking (SEAC, 1989) concerning teacher assessments and SATs as well as the role of the moderating process. The Task Group on Assessment and Testing (TGAT) model of combining teacher assessments with SATs, while problematic in terms of how two very different types of assessment could be combined, did allay fears about narrow SATs as the sole basis for reported scores. At the time of writing we can only make an informed guess about what SATs will look like but pupils with SEN are likely to fare particularly badly on formal, narrow tests. If pupils with SEN are on the same curricular ladders as other pupils but are excluded from formal assessment arrangements (that is, reported results but not ongoing teacher assessments) this would remove a possible obstacle to integrated work. There has already been a hint (from Angela Rumbold, when

Minister of State at the DES, in a parliamentary answer) that SEAC may recommend this course. (For further details see Chapter 17 in this volume).

Conclusion

The ERA does not rescind the pro-integration stance of the 1981 Education Act and the National Curriculum provides a common curricular framework for all pupils which, as I have argued above, can be used to support integration. The past decade has seen a wealth of comment, analysis and reflection about integration at both theoretical and practical levels. There is evidence that integration works and can be of benefit to special and ordinary school pupils, but it is also clear that effective integration does not come cheaply. In particular, there is a high cost in terms of commitment from practitioners and others if integration is to succeed. It is important that integration is kept on the educational agenda and that advocates of integration show how it can be fostered in this time of change.

References

ABOUD, F. (1988) *Children and Prejudice*, Oxford, Blackwell.

ALLEN, V.L. (1976) *Children as Teachers*, New York, Academic Press.

ARCHER, M. (1989) 'Targeting change', *Special Children*, 33, pp. 14–15.

BENNETT, N. (1987) 'The integration issue', *Junior Education*, January, pp. 8–10.

BENNETT, N. and CASS, A. (1989) *From Special to Ordinary Schools: Case Studies in Integration*, London, Cassell.

BOOTH, T. and STATHAM, J. (1982) *The Nature of Special Education*, London, Croom Helm.

BYRNE, E.A., CUNNINGHAM, C.C. and SLOPER, P. (1988) *Families and their Children with Down's Syndrome*, London, Routledge.

CARPENTER, B. and LEWIS, A. (1989) 'Searching for solutions: Approaches to planning the curriculum for the integration of children with severe and profound, multiple learning difficulties', in BAKER, D. and BOVAIR, K. (Eds) *Making the Special School Ordinary?* Volume 1, London, Falmer Press, pp. 103–24.

CARPENTER, B., LEWIS, A. and MOORE, J. (1986) 'An integration project involving a mainstream first school and a school for children with severe learning difficulties', *Mental Handicap*, 14, 4, pp. 152–7.

CARPENTER, B., FATHERS, J., LEWIS, A. and PRIVETT, R. (1988) 'Integration: The Coleshill Experience', *British Journal of Special Education*, 15, 3, pp. 119–21.

DENNISON, B. (1989) 'The competitive edge: attracting more pupils', *School Organization*, 9, 2, pp. 179–86.

DES (1988) *Education Reform Act 1988*, London, HMSO.

DES AND WELSH OFFICE (1989a) *Science in the National Curriculum*, London, HMSO.

DES AND WELSH OFFICE (1989b) *Mathematics in the National Curriculum*, London, HMSO.

DES AND WELSH OFFICE (1989c) *English in the National Curriculum*, London, HMSO.

DES AND WELSH OFFICE (1990) *Geography for Ages 5 to 16*, London, HMSO.

EARLY YEARS CURRICULUM GROUP (EYCG) (1989) *Early Childhood Education: The Early Years Curriculum and the National Curriculum*, Stoke on Trent, Trentham Books.

HAVILAND, J. (1988) *Take Care, Mr Baker!* London, Fourth Estate.

ILEA (1985a) *Educational Opportunities for All?* (The Fish Report), London, ILEA.

ILEA (1985b) *Improving Primary Schools*, London, ILEA.

KATZ, P.A. (1982) 'Development of children's racial awareness and intergroup attitudes', in KATZ, L.G. (Ed.) *Current Topics in Early Childhood Education*, Volume IV, Norwood NJ, Ablex, pp. 17–54.

LEWIS, A. (1986) 'Meeting special needs in infant classes: A discussion of evidence from HMI reports on individual schools', *School Organization*, 6, 2, pp. 245–55.

LEWIS, A. (1988) 'Children with special needs in primary schools', in CLARKSON, M. (Ed.) *Emerging Issues in Primary Education*, London, Falmer Press, pp. 123–40.

LEWIS, A. (1990) 'Six and seven year old normal children's talk to peers with severe learning difficulties', *European Journal of Special Needs Education*, 51, pp. 21–30.

LEWIS, A. and CARPENTER, B. (1990) 'Integration for children with severe learning difficulties: Discourse between six and seven year old non-handicapped children and peers with severe learning difficulties', in FRASER, W.I. *Issues in Mental Retardation Research*, London, Routledge, pp. 270–8.

LEWIS, A. and LEWIS, V. (1987) 'The attitudes of young children towards peers with severe learning difficulties', *British Journal of Developmental Psychology*, 5, 3, pp. 287–92.

LEWIS, A. and LEWIS, V. (1988) 'Young children's attitudes, after a period of integration, towards peers with severe learning difficulties', *European Journal of Special Needs Education*, 3, 3, pp. 161–72.

LINDSAY, G. (1989) 'Evaluating integration', *Educational Psychology in Practice*, April, pp. 7–16.

LUNN, J.B. (1970) *Streaming in the Primary School*, London, NFER.

MOORE, J., CARPENTER, B. and LEWIS, A. (1987) '"He can do it really" — integration in a first school', *Education 3–13*, 15, 2, pp. 37–43.

NCC (1989) *Curriculum Guidance Two: A Curriculum for All*, York, National Curriculum Council.

ODEN, S. (1982) 'Peer relationship development in childhood', in KATZ, L.G. (Ed.) *Current Topics in Early Childhood Education*, Volume IV, Norwood NJ, Ablex, pp. 87–117.

ROBINSON, E.J. and WHITTAKER, S.J. (1986) 'Learning about verbal referential communication in the early school years', in DURKIN, K. (Ed.) *Language Development in the School Years*, London, Croom Helm, pp. 155–71.

SEAC (1989) *Advice Note: National Curriculum Assessment and Testing*, London, SEAC.

SEBBA, J. (1983) 'Social interactions among preschool handicapped and non-handicapped children', *Journal of Mental Deficiency Research*, 27, pp. 115–24.

SYLVA, K., ROY, C. and PAINTER, M. (1980) *Childwatching at Playgroup and Nursery School*, London, Grant McIntyre.

WEDELL, K. (1988) 'The National Curriculum and special educational needs', in LAWTON, D. and CHITTY, C. (Eds) *The National Curriculum*, Bedford Way Paper 33, Institute of Education, University of London.

14 Equal Opportunities: Promoting Integrity and Respect

Sharon Jefferies

Disabled persons have the inherent right to respect for their human dignity. Disabled persons, whatever their origin, the nature or the seriousness of their handicaps and disabilities, have the same fundamental rights as their fellow citizens of the same age, which implies first and foremost the right to enjoy a decent life as normal and full as possible. (UN General Assembly Resolution: *Declaration on the Rights of Disabled Persons*)

Introduction

The uniqueness of the individual is the most important facet of any person and knowing the individual (having friends) is something desired by all. The ability to experience and handle emotions, to love and to be loved, to give and to receive, to choose and to reject, and to respect and be respected are some of the more important of human qualities. Are these those same qualities that educational establishments keenly deliver today?

Some two to three years ago, the National Curriculum and the Standardized Assessment Tasks seemed to cause many schools concern over their delivery of the 'whole curriculum'. At that time, for instance, there were worries that exact records would have to be kept of time spent on the core subjects, and that the curriculum would be assessment-led because of a desire to help pupils achieve when tested. It seemed that Local Management of Schools would mean that 'competitive tendering for pupils' might become either a reality or remain merely unpleasant fiction, given that fewer pupils equals less finance.

The question was this: 'Will schools forget or forgo developing the hidden curriculum?'.

The worst fears about the National Curriculum have not been realized. The document, *Curriculum Guidance Two: A Curriculum for All* (NCC, 1989), has done much to reassure teachers that the introduction of the National Curriculum and other educational initiatives need not displace the good practice and the imaginative innovations in curriculum development of which teachers in special schools can be rightly proud. In this chapter, examples of curriculum development and other initiatives at one school, the Newark Appletongate School in Newark, are used to illustrate the valuable contributions which have been made to the education of pupils with severe learning difficulties (SLD) throughout the country. In particular, there is an emphasis here upon the paramount importance of a commitment to provide equal opportunities for all pupils, as affirmed in the *Curriculum Guidance Three: The Whole Curriculum*:

> The curriculum must aim to meet the needs of all pupils regardless of physical, sensory, intellectual, emotional/ behavioural difficulties, gender, social and cultural background, religious or ethnic origins. All schools whatever their location and intake have a responsibility to promote good relationships and mutual respect.

> The ethos of a school should support the school's policy of equal opportunity by countering stereotypes and prejudice, reducing the effects of discrimination and helping pupils to accept and understand social diversity. (NCC, 1990, p. 13)

Of course, the theme of equality of opportunity has been further reinforced by the official recognition that all pupils share the right to a broad and balanced curriculum, including the National Curriculum.

For many years special schools have taken the opportunity to be involved in creative curriculum development (for examples see Baker and Bovair, 1990). Most schools have carefully constructed curriculum documents that serve to illustrate the individual pupil's state of skill acquisition; these are often criterion-referenced and broken down into such fine steps that all pupils can be seen to be achieving. The net result is that positive lists of development coupled with a 'pen picture' of the pupil can be used to provide a personal profile. This type of curriculum development was in evidence at the Newark Appletongate School, too. Nevertheless, a full curriculum evaluation was embarked upon about four years ago. The aim was to have a clear and precise set of objectives, individual files and regular curriculum development meetings. These provide automatic evidence to support the work of the teacher and, in fact, the school's raison d'être.

A full curriculum evaluation should seek to examine what is happening in the curriculum, retain that which is good, discard that which is not and move forwards developing new areas, maybe in a different style. The first of our findings indicated that for some pupils little or no progress had been made in a term or even in years. Therefore, this required urgent attention. We all believed that school should mean helping a young person to reach his or her full educational potential but, sadly, it was not possible to prove that this was happening for all and, after all, education was for all! Also, there was some agreement that the school population was changing — more students with profound and multiple learning difficulties (PMLD) were coming into the school and our more able pupils seemed to be going into ordinary schools. If this was so and if, as we heard, the National Curriculum was coming, we had strong reasons for allowing our curriculum to grow and broaden.

Developments in Early Years Education

First, we examined the area of early years education — particularly the Nursery. If every pupil deserved equal opportunities, why then did we segregate those with PMLD and place them in a 'special needs class'? Did the parents want this? Did the LEA? Did the fact that the special needs class had students aged from 3 to 19 years grouped together serve to illustrate good or bad practice? Indeed, did we value the individual, or was it merely cost-effective?

The decision was made that all new pupils should enter the Nursery without prejudice. It was easier to begin our desegregation with new pupils than those who had been afforded a protected environment for many years, since there would be no unlearning necessary. It was decided that staffing would be enhanced to facilitate this. Furthermore, a new class would be created — an Infant class that would take all pupils from the Nursery when they were 5 years old, again without prejudice. There was one problem — our existing curriculum did not have much to offer young children or those with PMLD. Working in a small team, staff established a new curriculum document for the Nursery/Infant group which embraced several important statements of principle:

1 The curriculum document should be relevant to every child.
2 Criterion-referenced assessment should be used. Assessment for assessment's sake has little significance; you must know where you are, where you are going and how you hope to get there.
3 A behavioural, yet humanistic, objectives style should be used.
4 Developmental charts should be utilized which would eventually include the objectives of the impending National Curriculum. At that time, having heard about testing at 7 years, we mistakenly believed that we might have to show why a child was not yet ready or when a child would be ready to move onto the National Curriculum.
5 The curriculum should contain subjects or experiences hitherto denied the youngest pupils and the pupils with PMLD, thereby promoting the beginning of equality of opportunity.

The curriculum document for the Nursery/Infant group produced by this small working party identifies specific areas: Early Experience, Cognitive Development, Self Help Skills, Personal Hygiene, Language Development, Gross Motor Skills, Leisure Skills, and Sensory Development. Some areas developed new experiences and, subsequently, new skills. We began horse riding weekly, hydrotherapy weekly, sensory work daily, wheelchair dancing weekly and 'aromatherapy' regularly.

Horse riding for all was a new concept for us. Respecting the degree of handicap in the past had meant that only the most able students went. Horse riding is a potentially dangerous activity and it usually follows that it means taking risks. However, using volunteers and reasonable staffing means anything is possible. Some of the Nursery Infant riders need three adults to each horse, some need only one but all now enjoy the experience of riding. We set up our own branch of the Riding for the Disabled Association and found their help and advice very useful.

Hydrotherapy or swimming for all does not happen easily when you do not have your own pool, and the previous experiences have been very much linked to physiotherapy in water or swimming lessons. However, thanks to friendly owners of a hydrotherapy pool and a minibus, we were able to offer equality of opportunity. Our hydrotherapy is based upon the Halliwick Method (see Stewart, 1990); it involves developing water confidence and experiences leading towards swimming independently but completed by all students with a one-to-one adult/student ratio. To the observer it resembles synchronized swimming in that a group of three children and three adults work together in the pool on a series of exercises and movements, with an extra adult to help each partnership when needed and to create differing water conditions. We bounce, we sway, we splash, we float . . . until we swim. The children have equality of opportunity and, as for the rest of the curriculum, assessment of progress in hydrotherapy is criterion-referenced and recorded. The record kept on each child is a series of positive 'I can' statements.

Sensory work (Longhorn, 1988) takes place both in the classroom and in our 'sensory room'. The sensory room was an old classroom, which has been decorated in pale pink with blackout curtaining and dimmed lighting. A section of the room has been made into a separate room for individual and small group work when it is desirable to heighten one of the senses without distraction. A full and varied range of equipment has been purchased, made or adapted to give every child equality of opportunity to develop their five senses. A pupil can feel vibrations, see flashing lights, taste new flavours, hear new sounds, touch new things . . . experience the world about us.

Wheelchair dancing activities developed at the school provide equality of opportunity in the area of dance. Different types of music are used ranging from waltzes to rap. We have ten dances which fit most tempos and are now able to facilitate experiences for our pupils of speed and movement of a variety previously untried. We have yet to master the Lambada! Like all of the experiences, wheelchair dancing requires one adult to each pupil and, once again, volunteers and our own 16+ students help us to provide this. The children show preferences for types of music and speeds of dance, enjoying every action-packed moment.

Aromatherapy (Price, 1983) is probably the newest curriculum activity that has spread through the school and is now practised in every class. This development owes much to INSET and continuing support provided by Maureen Hanse who has done much to develop the use of aromatherapy with pupils with SLD. During our curriculum evaluation we quickly realized that touch was restricted to clinical settings and, therefore, needed to be explored more fully. Massage is probably the oldest and simplest of all therapies. In traditional cultures, especially in the East, it is accepted as natural that people of all ages can benefit from regular massage, but in the West its use only quite recently spread to the field of education. Children and young people with SLD are subjected to much in the way of clinical touch by their teachers and nursery nurses in the management of their day-to-day bodily functions. Many young people with SLD are dependent upon adults in their world to give them the opportunity to feel cared for. Touch is generally felt to be good to give and good to receive, and most of us manage our 'touching time' within the confines set by society. But many young people with SLD do not follow the rules set by society and unknowingly touch persons that they casually meet, causing apprehension and misunderstanding. Opportunities to touch and be touched in appropriate settings had to addressed in school. All too often, we tend to be afraid to touch each other, yet, increasingly, research is showing the extraordinary effectiveness of touch, and touch is the core of massage.

Our own research into the sensory curriculum revealed that aromatherapy was ideally suited to this problem. It uses the art of massage, coupled with the use of essential oils, and provides a unique opportunity for the giver and receiver to communicate with each other. There is evidence that stroking animals reduces one's blood pressure, and stroking people can do the same. Massage can be stimulating or soothing and so it can make a person feel alert or relaxed, relieve tension, relax taut and aching muscles and induce a sense of well-being. For young people with SLD, who present challenging behaviour all too often, it can give a sense of worth. Of all the senses, touch is the first to develop. As babies, it is primarily through our tactile experiences that we explore and make sense of the world. Cuddles and strokes that we receive in infancy help us build to a healthy and positive self-image and nurture the feeling that, because we are touched, we are accepted and loved.

Aromatherapy has provided all our students with equality of opportunity to relax, to communicate and to feel valued. The pupils with PMLD receive aromatherapy from an adult. Of course, due to the profundity of their handicap and challenging behaviours, they are unable to give massage back to another. But the pupils in the Junior classes, the Senior classes and the 16+ Unit give and receive from each other, concentrating on heads, hands and feet. Freedom of choice is respected, although most of our students participate enthusiastically and with obvious enjoyment (Tompkins and Carpenter, 1990).

Any move towards creative curriculum development and the acquisition of new skills means identifying the skills required by adults working with the students, and finding appropriately qualified and experienced teachers to impart their skills. Inservice events have proved invaluable for gaining these necessary skills: non-teaching days enabling the whole staff to have hands-on experience and to share concerns; courses attended in and out of county; time for the staff with the INSET deliverer and the pupils present to work together;

and an opportunity to share developments with parents and governors.

Further Education

As the Nursery and Infant classes were desegregated we also opened up a 16+ Unit. Students had previously stayed on at school until 19 years and some curriculum development had been undertaken, but in a makeshift way. Acquiring a three-bedroom flat at the back of the school, and some funding to decorate and refurnish it, provided us with the opportunity to examine the curriculum for our most senior pupils. Should we promote a continuation of school or move on-wards? We took on board the good practice already happening and made a conscious decision to move towards a 'functional curriculum'. It was very clear from observing the students that they had learned much in school, but needed to be able to put that learning into practice in a real enviroment.

The 16+ students 'cut the umbilical cord' and moved into their flat with a teacher and a 'nursery nurse' (that is, teacher's assistant). They began to identify the necessary skills to enable the students to cope in the community. The principles adopted reflected the view that students have a right to be consulted about the curriculum and to make personal choices, and that the curriculum should reflect a chang-ing and growing society. Equality of opportunity was emphasized by affirming that every student should have access to the same curricu-lum, choosing personal components. Also, each student should negotiate with the teacher agreed aims and tasks; both teacher and student should understand why those skills and experiences were important and each student should work to their full potential.

Another separate curriculum document relating to the 16+ Unit was produced where the specific core curriculum has two com-ponents: a Primary Core Area, containing aspects of the curriculum applicable to all students, and a Secondary Core Area, containing aspects which are not necessarily applicable to all. The Primary Core Area includes Safety, Personal and Social Education, Recreational Skills and Community Experience. The Secondary Core Area includes Work Experience, Inter-personal Skills, the Duke of Edinburgh Award Scheme and Further Education Link Courses.

The students come into school only to complete community experience placements, follow up set tasks and for a weekly assembly. They prepare and cook their own lunch which, as in the real world, meets the needs of the day and time available (some days lunch is a snack, other days it is a two-course meal). The same menu is maintained for at least a half term with the view that practice makes perfect. The timetable is divided into whole-day or half-day blocks, with one day at the local FE college and one day of either community or work experience. At first, community experience comes in a protected and nurturing environment and when ready a student will move into work experience, that is, a real work placement. The timetable varies to meet the individual needs of the students, except that all attend the FE college on the same day. Even this is about to change to allow greater flexibility. The variations in the timetable mean that a good staff/student ratio can be achieved, thereby helping new or less confident students to have greater staff attention and time.

The new challenges facing our 16+ students, new freedoms and new routines, seemed exciting to us and yet we noticed a high level of unaccountable absenteeism. Closer examination of the curriculum suggested that this might be due to placing the students in a stress-loaded situation, in that there were high expectations of them and a very demanding timetable, where they had to make decisions, where they had to learn from both successes and failures (not as in the main school where one could enjoy almost error-free learning) and where they were expected to be grown up. Aromatherapy helped but it was not something students could easily practice on their own. Therefore, we were led to consider other methods of reducing stress. On the basis of our own experience of stress management for adults, we developed the use of a 'guided fantasy' which seemed to provide the answer. A special piece of music was made which is very soothing and quiet and lends itself to relaxation. The students now have a regular 'guided fantasy' which to date has been led by a teacher but, hopefully, in the near future this will be self-led and maybe a student will feel able to lead the group. Each student has a copy of the music and will be able to practise the guided fantasy at home when the need arises. The guided fantasy is a story about a journey to a quiet and calm place and then the return home, which is told by the teacher and enables the traveller to make the journey and return home feeling refreshed and relaxed. The travellers lie on the floor having completed a relaxing exercise and, closing their eyes, take a journey. The absenteeism has reduced and the students, and staff, seem better able to cope. Freedom of choice is respected as lying still is not easy for everyone. Initially, some students watched to see what it was like but now all join in.

The 16+ students had a whole morning spent on inter-personal skills and sex education so we could bring in 'relaxation time' to this part of the timetable. The aims were to reduce the level of stress felt using a technique that could be used at home or at school. Care, sensitivity, a little time, a quiet room and no interruptions are all that are needed to provide our students with a relaxing experience. We were unable to find an experienced stress counsellor, so we attended courses aimed at adults and then adapted techniques learned until we found one that suited.

With all our new curriculum areas we experienced and experience what the students experience, except that, if I am I and You are You, I cannot experience what You experience, and You cannot experience what I do. But both students and staff can share the road to that experience and empathy.

Policies on Equal Opportunities for the Whole School

Around the same time that this curriculum evaluation was taking place, other concerns were reaching us and making us think and consider our position in school, especially as regards Multicultural Education, Anti-racist Education, Gender-aware Education and Sex Education. If we truly believed in equality of education, then how would we ensure that everyone felt valued for themselves, that we respected cultural background and that we promoted equality, respect and integrity? Some statements commonly heard being uttered were starting to make us aware that we were forgetting so much in our struggle to offer equality of opportunity. In particular, people were effectively denying the cultural background and sexual rights of students with statements like 'I treat all my students the same — I couldn't even tell you how many black students I have' or 'Our students have enough difficulty knowing whether they are boys or girls' or 'Teach sex education? Why? You are only going to open up a whole new can of worms'.

Our small school in that small town had little to offer to promote any of these issues because a rich cultural diversity did not exist. Increase personal awareness and you must influence the ethos of the school — or do you open a 'can of worms'? Yet again, INSET was crucial. Training opportunities focused on the need to examine our own views as teachers, and as individuals, about living in a multi-cultural world, promoting gender-free education and providing students with information and understanding about their own sexuality.

Individuals attended staff development courses to increase their knowledge and perceptions in order to share these with the whole staff and, like many schools, we tried to improve our practice.

A Policy for Sex Education

The first of these areas that we decided to look at was Sex Education, not because we engaged in any prioritizing exercise but because the Education Act of 1986 meant that we had no choice. There is an expression that perhaps explains how most people feel when the subject of sexuality is brought up and that is 'Oh heck!' (followed by a hard swallow and a wiping of the brow). By law, governors, along with staff, had to agree on an accepted sex education curriculum for use in school or decide not to provide sex education. As a staff, we had identified a need for an area of the curriculum to be devoted to health education, but it became very clear that distinct lines appeared between health education and sex education. So we embarked on examining sex education in school, feeling quite strongly that whatever we did with pupils should begin when they were as young as possible and thereby continue our equality of opportunity policy.

Skills, attitudes, concepts and knowledge were discussed and prioritized. Existing work on self-help covered some of the skills but prime importance was placed upon sex education and, to that end, after collaborative discussion, a course for staff was planned. We looked for experienced teachers and enlisted the help of the FPA (Family Planning Association). It transpired during discussions that two of our sister schools were also interested in examining curriculum development in sex education, so we joined together to work on this area. Various individual members of staff had attended courses dealing with sex education and confirmed that, when planning a sex education programme, the attitudes to sexuality of the staff involved in teaching the content should be considered together with those of the parents and, most importantly, the pupils. To that end, three different questionnaires were devised and used with staff, parents and pupils. The pupils' questionnaire was used to determine what was already known without any 'formal' school input. A parents' questionnaire was used to gauge feelings, concerns and level of support for sex education. Finally, a staff questionnaire was used to ascertain feelings, concerns and previous experience.

The course planned with the FPA drew upon the three schools involved, with each school being represented by three teachers, three nursery nurses, and a parent governor. In addition to these, the county's two inspectors for special education were invited to join us. Team work is an essential part of any school's work but it is of paramount importance in special schools. Any curriculum initiative can fail or thrive through the level of active participation of all professions integral to the opportunities offered in the schools' curriculum. Governors have to review and consent to sex education being part of the curriculum and parents work in partnership with the school, so a fair representation of these different people needed to join together as course participants. A determined effort was made to have equal representation of males and females.

Much work has now developed from these early beginnings and a curriculum pack will be available for use soon. The three schools have gained much in the way of networking, sharing developments and producing a pack which prevents a feeling that the 'wheel is being reinvented'. Broader issues have been flagged and staff have had to work alongside, both in school and in another school, colleagues with whom they may not have come into close contact. The trialling of ideas, lessons and materials has been made possible because the project was formalized, with the LEA giving us some curriculum development time to use.

The areas written up include: Contact, Body Awareness, Feelings, About Me, Relationships, Sexual Feelings, Pregnancy, Birth, Parenting and Staying Safe, Body Language. As for all of the new curriculum, a pupil begins to receive sex education in the Nursery and continues through school. Of course, some issues are addressed only at a later age when it is age appropriate to do so; for example, contraception is covered in the Seniors. As with all the curriculum, equality of opportunity is primary in our thoughts which is why we did not produce a sex education document just for the Seniors. The type of work varies and incorporates much we had learned with regard to aromatherapy, stress management, and sensory/leisure work. Body labelling exercises may take place in the hydrotherapy pool, or while on a horse, or with an unclothed (anatomically correct) doll or using line drawings of a nude male and female. These activities certainly are not restricted to one lesson; they will be revisited time and time again at different stages in the pupils' school career. This is true of each curriculum area. (For further details on sex education see Chapter 15 in this volume).

Race and Gender

Gender bias and multicultural education provided us with even more food for thought. If equality of opportunity means that everyone is valued for themselves, that gender and culture are celebrated and that everyone regardless of degree of handicap has a right to a broad and balanced curriculum, then it seemed that we should work on gender and multicultural issues next. Once again, staff attended courses to heighten their own awareness. We had the good fortune to attend a six week staff development module as part of the LEA's staff development project (a one year involvement) which addressed multicultural, anti-racist education. Prejudice was examined and consciousness was raised. The first example of providing equal opportunities in a multicultural world was to examine the school library, to discard books that promoted either racism or gender bias and to purchase only books that promote gender equality and show all races and cultures positively. Any sexual or racial stereotyping is discouraged in school. The materials we use portray men and women of all races and cultures completing all tasks. We encourage our students to be equal and to treat each other with respect, empathy and sincerity. If racist name-calling occurs, it will be dealt with by all staff and not ignored. Ignoring racist remarks can be (unintentionally) signalling support for those remarks, and the students could believe it is acceptable to say or do something, when this is certainly not the case.

Challenging assumptions is hard work and promoting life in a multicultural world is not easy, especially if you live in a small town which does not enjoy a rich multicultural life. Assemblies can help to broaden perceptions but we are conscious of the tokenism apparent in the 'Three Ss Approach', that is, saris, samosas and steel bands. If the assembly is dealing with making bread, then it follows that it is natural to make breads of all types (chapatti, pitta, bread rolls) and to discuss what you would eat with them. Becoming aware of multicultural and anti-racist education has made us look towards work examining the first key words spoken and commonly used in a variety of differing languages and to understand more about cultures. If we are to offer equality of opportunity, we should be able to key everyday words with a child's mother tongue in the same way that we pair signs and symbols. Our view is that if a pupil has severe or profound learning difficulties, which often present communication difficulties, and they are exposed to one language at home and another at school, these problems are compounded.

This project is ongoing and will take some time to complete, but it is vital if we really believe in equality of opportunity. A greater understanding of the many differing cultures and ways of living needs to be fostered. This greater insight into what is socially acceptable for our students in their living situation can only serve to offer greater opportunities for them. Home culture is an extremely important facet of the person and being part of and celebrating your cultural heritage should be enjoyed by all. Greater understanding of each other fosters respect, and a more evenly developed, inquiring person. Parental partnership and community involvement should facilitate a better, more informed approach to providing a broad and balanced curriculum for our students.

Conclusion

A lot has happened in our small school in the Midlands in the past four years, and much is still to happen. Like our colleagues, we have had to address the National Curriculum, modify it to make it accessible to all, and dovetail into the existing curriculum work. We have had to cooperate more closely with our colleagues in ordinary schools by supporting desegregation, linking activities between schools, developing Records of Achievement, through TVEI-extension and by growing together. As with most schools, we take most things in our stride and somehow still manage to absorb creative curriculum development and thrive.

Equality of opportunity at our school means very simply that it matters that pupils can have a rich, varied and thoughtful curriculum where their personal self image grows and feels good and positive, where they can feel proud to be 'me' and happy to have us as friends, feeling enriched by knowing us, and where they can grow. Equality of opportunity is integrity, respect, humanity, and much more and should be fundamental to all that we do. In fact our school motto could be 'EQUAL OPS':

E   is for education, everyone's right;
Q   is for question — everyone should continue to find out more;
U   is for understanding — knowing about each other and respecting difference;
A   is for achievement — helping students to reach their optimum potential;
L   is for listening — using the advice and information available from different sources;

O   is for openings — take advantage of any learning situation for the good of the student;

P   is for proceeding forwards — if you know where you're going, you have some chance of getting there;

S   is for success — helping someone to succeed at something they want to do is fundamental to life.

References

BAKER, D. and BOVAIR, K. (1990) *Making the Special Schools Ordinary?*, Volume 2, London, Falmer Press.

LONGHORN, F. (1988) *A Sensory Curriculum for Very Special People: A Practical Approach to Curriculum Planning*, London, Souvenir Press, Human Horizons Series.

NCC (1989) *Curriculum Guidance Two: A Curriculum for All*, York, National Curriculum Council.

NCC (1990) *Curriculum Guidance Three: The Whole Curriculum*, York, National Curriculum Council.

PRICE, S. (1983) *Practical Aromatherapy: How to Use Essential Oils to Restore Vitality*, Wellingborough, Thorsons Publishers Ltd.

STEWART, D. (1990) *A Right to Movement: Motor Development in Every School*, London, Falmer Press.

TOMPKINS, A. and CARPENTER, B. (1990) 'A post-16 education project for students with profound and multiple learning difficulties', *Mental Handicap*, 18, September, pp. 105–8.

15 Health and Sex Education: A Cross-Curricular Theme

Jean Gawlinski

Content

Sex Education in mainstream schools has always been a controversial and sensitive issue, so it is not perhaps surprising that in many special schools the subject has been translated to a mere facet of health education, social skills, or relegated to the final year of school when the school nurse 'talked' to the leavers and produced a sepia film on the birth of a baby. The needs and abilities of pupils with severe learning difficulties (SLD) are so varied. A sex education programme devised for streetwise adolescents with SLD or emotional and behavioural problems would be as inappropriate for youngsters with profound and multiple learning difficulties (PMLD) as attempting to teach them Key Stage 3 Mathematics.

Certainly, however, it makes sense to construct the programme around a central theme such as 'Growing Up', in order to establish this concept in a child's mind as a key principle governing his or her awareness of him or herself and his or her behaviour towards others. As Ann Craft so aptly suggests:

> Parents, teachers and care staff are frequently able to say with a high degree of accuracy just how well a particular mentally handicapped adolescent can handle money or dress himself (*sic*), but it is all too likely that they will not be nearly so accurate in estimating the same adolescent's knowledge of sexual matters. Often these are taboo subjects and therefore not openly discussed. (Craft, 1982)

It is particularly important that parents should be fully involved, not only in the plans for their own son or daughter's sex education, but in the school's policy on this subject.

A review of normal sexual development may provide a starting point for group discussion. Consideration of the emotional, social and physical aspects of normal sexual development may form a relevant framework for the more specific discussion of pupils' needs. Use of forms, slides or radio cassettes can prove helpful. It would be useful if meetings for parents and staff were open to include parents of adults with SLD living at home, so that a number of the problems worrying parents such as masturbation, contraception, sterilization or uncritical promiscuity, can be discussed with the adult perspective. Parents' written questions might be invited if they prefer not to ask them openly.

What areas should be included in the structured programme for students with SLD? Hamre-Nietupski and Williams (1977) reported on one programme employed by twenty students with special educational needs (SEN) aged between 12 and 17. Five main components were devised: bodily distinctions; self-care skills; family members and relationships; social interaction; and social manners. Later a second phase built on the skills acquired in the initial programme. Parents and teachers decided that more sophisticated information was required concerning: growth distinctions and reproduction; self-care skills; and social skills and social manners.

The authors reported that, with very few exceptions, the students mastered the objectives in the component areas and were also able to generalize their newly acquired understanding. This successful programme has been revised and extended. If and when goals are achieved, it is important to reinforce the knowledge and behaviour and reconsider the position. Perhaps a student's capabilities have been underestimated; clear, realistic goals are essential.

Topics included under sex education vary but a typical selection might be those covered by the *Life Horizons* slide series (Kempton, 1988) which are:

1 Parts of the body
2 Sexual life cycle
3 Reproduction
4 Birth control
5 AIDS and other sexually transmitted diseases

6 Building self-esteem and establishing relationships
7 Moral aspects of sexual behaviour
8 Marriage
9 Parentage
10 Preventing or coping with sex abuse.

Other examples of programmes are those produced by the Mill Lane Adult Training Centre (Mill Lane ATC, 1980), and Bender, Bender and Valletutti (1985) which state clear objectives and suggested activities, while Fischer, Krajicek and Borthick (1973) provide detailed teaching suggestions, although the areas covered are more limited. Monat (1982) gives extensive details on topics to be covered in a programme for people with SEN as does Kempton (1975). McNaughton (1983) has adapted health education material for pupils with SEN. The staff at Rectory Paddock School (1983) give suggestions, and Hilary Dixon and Gill Mullinar (1986) provide a framework, suggested preparation and activities within their resource book. They believe that central to their strategy is the concept of self-esteem and that a major part of human dignity is feeling good about oneself. Students are then more likely to develop non-exploitative caring relationships and are themselves less likely to be exploited by others. A fuller view of the resources available is provided by Craft (1987), who also lists distributors, and Dixon (1988).

Teaching

Adolescents with SLD find it difficult to grasp concepts that are neither concrete nor visible, hence teaching methods must be selected which provide clear, unambiguous and frank communication. This need can be met by the use of slides, drawing books, photographs, films, or videotapes, the most useful of which are those which can be used selectively to enable teaching programmes to be individualized. Important issues arising in relation to teaching methods concern how many pupils should be taught together, should the sexes be mixed, should all teaching be on an individual basis, and who should undertake the teaching. There is no single obvious choice but many options, and the set up, class groupings and staffing available may dictate the answers to some of these questions.

Who Teaches?

The most important consideration is that the teacher concerned feels confident to talk about personal subjects in a matter-of-fact, basic way and knows the pupils in the class or group. As Craft (1982) adds: 'A sense of humour and an honest, direct approach are very necessary.' A teacher in a special school who takes the senior pupils may be the most suitable person to explore growing up and its implications in a regular lesson period. Lower down the school a less formal approach may be more appropriate. The class teacher may do the teaching but if he or she feels uncomfortable with certain issues another member of staff may be enlisted. If all adults involved with the pupils are aware of, and in agreement with, the approach taken in a school, use can be made of the 'teachable moment', dealing with topics as they naturally arise; for example, the birth of a pupil's brother or sister.

Welfare assistants (that is, teachers' assistants) in special schools play an active part in the education of pupils, particularly with girls' menstruation, and so should be involved in the setting up of programmes. The author has found their contribution to be invaluable. A nurse, social worker or psychologist may also make a contribution to a sex education programme. This needs to be carefully planned as bringing in an outside 'expert' to do the teaching may cause problems as 'the outsider', unfamiliar to the pupils, may be unable to gauge the teaching at the appropriate level or to capitalize on conversations or situations which arise outside the formal teaching time. It is essential that the people involved in teaching sex education are sensitive to the pupils' individual needs. However, it is not so much who, but the how and what that are important.

The Grouping of Pupils

Large groups may be unrealistic because of the likely range of previous knowledge and experience of the participants. Also pupils are more likely to express their anxieties in a small informal group. On the whole, though, individual teaching is impracticable and time consuming but may be necessary where the problem of inappropriate behaviour arises.

It may be considered appropriate to mix the sexes in teaching situations to enable comparisons of roles to take place in the group. It is also sometimes suggested that female and male staff members teach students together. If more than one teacher is involved in each session, it also reduces the likelihood of problems arising where accusations of misconduct or misinformation have been made.

Setting up a Health and Sex Education Programme

Legally the governing body of the school must decide whether sex education is taught and if they decide in favour they are responsible for drawing up a sex education policy. In practice the headteacher, head of Personal and Social Education (PSE) or the staff collectively often draw up the policy. This is usually presented at a meeting of the governing body and amended if necessary.

The following are a few guidelines for setting up a health and sex education programme, although there are no hard and fast rules.

> *Liaison with parents and care staff*: a special school may send out a letter to parents to inform them of the planned programme. It is a good idea to hold a meeting or a series of workshops so that parents can talk through the very real anxieties they may feel. Parents' reactions may vary. Some parents may feel that they would prefer to give their child sex education and this is to be applauded, although it might be helpful to hear what attitude these parents have towards their children's sexuality. They may also welcome advice about suitable books and leaflets they can use with their children.
>
> In areas where there are children from ethnic minorities it will be especially necessary to find out the views of parents concerning sex education. The religion of such parents may specifically forbid the imparting of information to mixed groups of boys and girls. On the other hand the strong family ethos of some religious denominations may be very favourable to teachers' efforts. Other parents may feel embarrassed about speaking to their children about sex and may feel relieved that the staff of the school take on this role. They can, however, play an important part in backing up what is being taught. To do this they will need to know what topics are being covered and to be as closely involved as possible. Here workshops have, in the author's experience, proved to be the most effective means of communication. Parents often feel less inhibited

in talking of their children's sexuality once they hear other parents with similar concerns and anxieties.

When to begin sex education: sex education cannot be premature, a child can only learn what he or she can understand, but it may come too late to prevent unnecessary worry to the youngsters, their parents or care staff. With young childern abstract lessons will probably not be very effective but everyday situations can be used to make the child more aware of his or her own body and to teach him or her to develop appropriate social behaviour. An early stage in sex education would be concerned with motor, sensory and self-help skills, for example, in cleanliness, proper use of toilet, and reacting sensibly to bodily functions. It should also include the development of self-awareness, naming different parts of the body, having attention drawn to developments in older people of the same sex, and referring to differences in the physical development of the sexes.

The Family Planning Association has evolved a philosophy for sexual development for people with SEN. It includes the following ten points under the title Sex Education for Mentally Handicapped:

1   Provide relevant information on sex as people with SLD have less opportunity to pick up information from the same sources as other people.
2   Teach people with SLD about their own bodies and help them see themselves like other people.
3   Help them find an expression of their sexuality that best suits their abilities and needs.
4   Help to enable them to enjoy the company of both sexes by acquiring social skills.
5   Help them understand and learn the responsibilities of a sexual person.
6   Help them communicate about sex and develop a language with them to do so.
7   Assist them to develop realistic goals.
8   Teach them ways of avoiding situations in which they may be sexually exploited.
9   Help them not to become involved in inappropriate sexual behaviour that might make them socially unacceptable.
10   Give them information and help with birth control, remove anxiety, and prevent attitudes of over-protection.

Setting Objectives

Some special schools have set out specific objectives from which staff choose those most relevant and immediate. Such objectives have included getting pupils to:

> identify sexual differences between males and females;
> care for the body during menstruation;
> react to erections and ejaculations as normal bodily functions;
> identify and practise social customs related to acceptable sexual behaviour;
> practise socially acceptable behaviour with members of both sexes;
> learn strategies to avoid sexual abuse;
> discuss sexual development;
> discuss pregnancy and birth as normal bodily functions;
> discuss the nature and purpose of the family unit;
> practise birth control where appropriate.

In helping the pupils reach these objectives, staff should bear in mind not only that their mental and physical development, but also their sensitivities, need considering. Pupils need to be taught to behave in a socially acceptable way, particularly when they reach adolescence. For example, in advance of menstruation girls may be introduced to older girls who have already menstruated or should be prepared for this development in simple, practical, and realistic ways.

Consideration, as well as frankness, is required of staff. They must be aware of the important role they may play as counsellors to pupils who have emotional and other problems. Although every pupil will need sex education, staff who do not wish to should not be expected to carry through a sex education programme. However, all should be expected to participate in staff discussion and understand the goals. Staff must be sensitive to the views and feelings of parents, although they may differ from their own.

Levels of Understanding

Parents of pupils with SLD often need help in appreciating that it is normal for all humans to develop secondary sexual characteristics and to want to show and receive affection by touch, warmth and body contact. As Craft (1982) observes: 'The biological clocks of severely mentally handicapped individuals may be set at a slightly different rate from those of their normal peers but set they are and cannot be stopped'.

As with pupils with moderate learning difficulties, it is helpful to discover what individuals do know about gender, reproduction, and sexual behaviour. It may be helpful to work with a manual such as Fischer, Krajicek and Borthick (1973) which allows parent and teacher not only to gauge levels of understanding but also to become familiar with the language used by the individual to describe behaviour and body function.

Craft (1982) stresses the importance of setting goals because it requires us to make decisions about the degree of complexity of our input. An example of a frequently asked question is, how much and what specifically do we want the girl with SLD to understand or do about her menstruation? Craft gives the following considerations:

> It is a normal occurrence and happens to all women. This can only be conveyed by the attitude of the person helping the girl.
> The girl knows that each time her period starts she must tell (by word or sign) a carer so that she receives the help she needs in managing menstruation.
> Can she be taught to care for herself during the period? Pattullo and Barnard (1968) suggest a behaviour modification programme may help to achieve this.
> The girl maintains modest behaviour, changing her sanitary pad in private or with a helper. She does not show or tell everyone else what is happening.

The most basic component is emotional security (that is, having periods is normal) together with self-care, and appropriate social behaviour. Craft describes this so aptly:

> Explanations can be widened rather like ripples from a most simple core, according to the individual's level of understanding. In this particular example of menstruation the next ripple would be the simple biological explanation of periods. The further ripple would consider the relationship of the menses to reproduction. Some youngsters with moderate learning difficulties may well be able to go even further and grasp the social implications of fertility. (Craft, 1982)

Slang Terms

For those able to use or respond to words, sex organs should be given their correct names or appropriate modification alongside familiar or slang terms used by pupils. It is important to recognize the use of these slang terms as an important part of the sex education process, since youngsters with SLD may have problems equating a name used by a doctor to that used by their peers.

Suggested Topics

The health and sex education programme may be best placed in the context of PSE but in so doing it is vital that it does not get 'brushed under the carpet'. Biological and physical facts can be used as a starting point for much of the social learning that will help those with SLD to understand themselves and other people better.

The biological aspects need to be taught in their social context. Areas that should be covered include:

How the body works — the skeleton, muscles, skin, heart, five senses, etc.

Good health — personal hygiene, safety, handicaps.

Puberty — physical changes in adolescents, emotional changes, increase in sexual drive and interest, start of menstruation, nocturnal emissions.

How does growing up change us?

Understanding ourselves and others — recognizing our own moods.

Daydreams about sex.

Menstrual hygiene.

Wet dreams.

Masturbation.

Expressing ourselves.

Relationships and different kinds of love.

Behaviour on a 'date'.

Public and private behaviour.

Good and bad manners.

The biological aspect and social context can extend as far as is appropriate ultimately to include birth control techniques and the responsibilities of parenthood.

Child Sexual Abuse

This very real social problem has been highlighted in the media recently as the number of reported cases has been steadily increasing throughout the world. It is a problem which affects a wide range of children and is of particular concern to parents and teachers of pupils with learning difficulties, due to problems in communication and in learning socially acceptable behaviour. The children's vulnerability may be compounded if they already feel devalued and rejected. However, as the author has experienced, 'with care and sensitivity most children with moderate and severe learning difficulties can be taught to protect themselves from people who may harm them — bullies, strangers, and adults known to them' (Gawlinski, 1989).

Preventing Sexual Abuse

The *Good Sense Defence* programme by Kidscape (Elliot, 1986) teaches children how to recognize and deal with potentially dangerous situations, including the possibility of sexual assault, without making them fearful or mistrustful of normal everyday affection. The programme, which comprises approximately four lessons, starts with a lesson on general rules in looking after oneself, what to do if lost, how to make an emergency phone call, and the importance of telling parents where one is going. The programme progresses into lessons of a more specific nature, for example:

To say 'No' — if anyone, even someone they know, tries to touch them in a way which frightens or confuses them.

To cope with bullies — to ignore them if possible, to get help and always tell an adult.

To tell — that adults need to know about problems to be able to help.

To yell — that it is OK to yell, if they think they are in danger from someone who might harm them. Also they are taught how to yell really loudly, in case of emergency.

Not to talk to strangers — what is a stranger? How to recognize and deal with approaches from strangers, including tricks and bribes.

The relationship and sensitivity of staff with pupils is of paramount importance if staff are to handle the Kidscape *Good Sense Defence* programme adequately and are able to give pupils the feeling of trust to confide in staff about any 'bad' touching they may have experienced. Pupils with SLD are often confused about what constitutes 'good' and 'bad' touching which cannot be ignored. This can be introduced to younger children, as Michelle Elliot (1988) suggests, with the kind of touches pets like and dislike progressing to the kind of touching children like and dislike, for instance, too much tickling. This discussion can, at the appropriate time, include discussion on parts which are not touched by others, that is, those parts 'covered by your swimsuit'. Obviously this whole aspect of 'good sense defence' needs to be taught with extreme sensitivity, particularly as there may be sexually abused pupils in the class. This type of discussion can give these pupils the confidence to disclose information to their teacher or parent or to say 'NO' to further abuse.

Pupils with Profound and Multiple Learning Difficulties

The students with PMLD are at a particular disadvantage because they are at the receiving end of often intimate but impersonal touch; dressing, toiletting, menstrual care, bathing and feeding. One way of giving touch a place is through games and exercises and massage where touch and body contact can be encouraged, helping to firm up muscles, relax tenseness, foster confidence and trust, and allowing the opportunity for increased awareness of 'self' and 'other'. Physiotherapists may help in this.

The Knills' package on *Body Awareness, Contact and Communication* (Knill and Knill, 1986) is extremely useful for this area of the curriculum and has proved invaluable for all pupils with SLD, but particularly for pupils with PMLD. Warren's book, *Drama Games for Mentally Handicapped People* (Warren, 1981) also gives plenty of ideas. Teaching should be by means of short uncomplicated sentences supplemented by simple visual material such as pictures, body puzzles, and felt cloth figures.

The Need for Privacy

Given that it is normal for all humans to have sexual feelings and gain pleasure from warmth and touch, where and with whom in a specific environment can a particular individual express what he feels sexually? If the answer is nowhere with no one, that should lead to a reassessment.

Could more privacy be given? Could a more flexible approach be made to students holding hands, hugging, sitting with an arm round each other — providing the person being touched does not object?

Although it might be argued that schools are not the place for such behaviour, three points are relevant: such behaviour does occur in any normal school, mostly out of sight of the eyes of authority. Pupils with SLD are perhaps over-efficiently supervised; most pupils with SLD are remaining in education until age 19, spending the greater part of their day in the only place where they are able to see their friends; and left to themselves, pupils with SLD usually do not want to do more than cuddle, kiss, hug or hold hands with a special friend.

Appropriate Behaviour

Social situations and good manners are best acted out in role play to demonstrate appropriate and inappropriate behaviour, work which can be supplemented by the use of slides or photographs.

Behaviour modification programmes are necessarily systematic and can be very successful both in teaching specific self-care skills and in substituting acceptable public behaviour for acts which are unacceptable, such as open masturbation, or potentially dangerous, such as indiscriminate kissing and hugging.

Clear and specific corrections of behaviour are needed. 'Don't do that! That's not very nice, is it?' may have very little meaning to a pupil with SLD. 'Johnny, don't play with your penis here' should be followed by telling him where he can go. It is concern about masturbation which often causes most distress to parents.

A number of points are made by Craft (1982):

> Masturbation is a natural and normal human activity for both males and females. It is not realistic nor desirable to attempt to stop an individual from every erotic act.
>
> The peak of sexual interest and activity is usually the late teens so in the long term time will decrease the inclination.
>
> Open masturbation may be engaged in for a wide variety of reasons, besides the physical release and satisfaction that orgasm brings. It is, for example, an extremely effective means of catching parental or staff attention, also of comforting oneself if something has not gone right.

Before beginning any systematic reshaping of behaviour, teachers and parents should keep a record, as with any inappropriate behaviour, of what is happening immediately before an individual began to masturbate, how long the activity continued and what happened afterwards. A pattern may emerge; for example, it may become obvious that the individual is being excluded from some game or enjoyable pastime or that a particular person is exciting for him or her.

Constructing the Programme

This may well take several months as teachers bring their own knowledge up to date and review the material available. Using audio-visual aids can be most helpful, but care should be taken in introducing anything produced for mainstream adolescents as the commentary can be confusing and the slide pictures may raise more questions than they answer. Individual pupils have, for example, wondered why their bodies do not have written labels indicating the position of the vagina, breasts and so on.

Games which provide an opportunity to build trust and acceptance all help; for example, suggestions offered in *Sexuality and Mental Handicap* (Dixon, 1988) are suitable for more able pupils. Some special schools watch television programmes like *Let's Go* and *Merry Go Round*, which can be a helpful lead into a talk or discussion. Flexibility is essential as one cannot always gauge how much material to use in one lesson. Sometimes just one slide or picture can prompt enough talk and discussion to fill a session. Pupils need time to ask questions and clear up misunderstandings. For example, a youngster quoted by Craft (1982) reported after 'a very interesting lesson' that he had learnt about 'peanuts and overcoats'. He had misheard two words new to him, 'penis and intercourse'! What are needed basically are simple explanations related to pupils' own experiences of changes in the body and emotional feelings.

Evaluating the Effectiveness of Teaching Programmes

Evaluation of the effectiveness of sex education programmes cannot be undertaken without prior consideration of the goals of sex education. The goals may be expressed positively in terms of pupils showing appropriate sexual behaviour or negatively in terms of a reduction in inappropriate sexual behaviour. More specific objectives may be planned and evaluated when using visual aids such as slides and outline drawings.

Watson and Rogers (1980) noted that those pupils who indicated that teachers had been responsible for their sex education scored higher on the knowledge scale than those who indicated family or friends. This suggests some support for the value of formal programmes. Attempts have been made to test sexual knowledge before and after a sex education programme. Penny and Chataway (1982) found that sexual knowledge increased on post tests and continued to increase after completion of the programme, which the authors concluded may not be solely attributed to the programme. They suggest that the small teaching situation may have facilitated information exchange.

One welcomes attempts to measure changes in pupils' knowledge and behaviour. However, where this is impossible, some indication of the effectiveness of sex education may be sought from teachers' reports, which is a simpler, although probably less valid, approach. Kempton (1978) found that teachers reported positive effects of the sex education programme on the students' behaviour, with greater appropriate expression of sexual feelings and desires both verbally and in action, and many teachers noted that more communication about sex took place.

Use of Teaching Cards

The author has found that the most appropriate and useful evaluation and teaching materials for adolescents with SEN are the SPOD (Association to Aid the Sexual and Personal Relationships of People with a Disability) Teaching Cards which also test the pupil's knowledge of the male and female body, menstruation, sexual intercourse and other aspects. For example, one card illustrates a pregnant woman. The teacher's card accompanying this gives the objective: know that a baby grows inside its mother and that sexual intercourse can initiate this.

Questions:
 Which woman is having a baby?
 How can you tell?
 How long is the baby inside the mother before it is born?
 Do you know how the baby is started?
 Can a couple have intercourse without starting a baby?

Why do some people have babies?
Why do some people decide not to have babies?

Suggestions:
Describe simply how intercourse can lead to pregnancy, pointing out that the baby grows in a part of the mother's body
called the womb. [It refers here to another diagram.] Describe
how the baby is born with as much detail as is appropriate to
the pupils' comprehension. Task analysis record sheets may be
used in teaching and evaluation.

Staff and Parent Training in Sexuality and Special Educational Needs

Various agencies provide training to staff and parents on sexuality and
SEN. These courses vary in content and approach but generally
include a balance of four areas: Attitudes, Knowledge, Teaching
Content, Teaching Method. Detailed suggestions of content and
methods for staff training programmes can be found in Kempton
(1983) and Kempton and Foreman (1976). The Family Planning Association Education Unit organizes one, two and three-day courses
for teachers and other professionals working with people with SEN,
including 'made-to-measure' courses at the request of a school or
group of schools.

The evaluation of the effectiveness of staff training programmes
raises similar problems to those raised by the evaluation of teaching
sex education to students. If staff training is effective in terms of
enabling staff to change the pupils' behaviour, the results may be
unobservable. Brantlinger (1983) found that sexuality training was
effective in producing attitude change; staff and parents becoming
more liberal on post tests. However, as the author indicated, it is not
clear whether these changes in attitude actually made a difference
subsequently to the staff and parents' interactions with young people
with SLD.

Participants on one-day workshops do not appear to change their
attitude or behaviour. Sebba (1981) and Shaddock (1979) suggested
that workshops need to be longer to be effective. Staff attitudes at a
one-week workshop run by Judy Sebba for the Cambridge Institute
of Education in 1982 seemed to become more diverse after the course
than at the start of the course. This may have been due to discussion
of the issues raising complexities that participants had not previously

considered. More participants felt confident about talking to parents after they had completed the course.

Future Trends

Social attitudes to sexuality in those with SLD may be considered to have reached the tolerance phase of Kempton's 'elimination/tolerance/ cultivation scale', cited in Sebba, 1981. Hence, there is still much progress to be made to assist youngsters with SEN generally to exercise their rights to fulfil their sexual and emotional needs as others do. The first steps would seem to be to provide more practical training for parents and staff in order to encourage positive attitudes and inspire confidence. It is neither realistic nor desirable to expect to reach a consensus on sexual attitudes, and staff who do not wish to become sex educators should not be put under pressure to do so. However, sex education could be integrated into initial and inservice courses for many professional groups, rather than being an elective option or covered in a few hours as in current teaching training programmes (May, 1980). Furthermore, attempts could be made to evaluate inservice courses in terms of their effectiveness in changing both staff and pupils' behaviour, and consideration be given to which course activities are most effective in producing such change.

References

BENDER, M., BENDER, R. and VALLETUTTI, P.J. (1985) *Teaching the Moderately and Severely Handicapped*, Volume 2, 2nd edition, Austin, Texas, Pro-Ed.

BRANTLINGER, E. (1983) 'Measuring variation and change in attitudes in residential care staff toward the sexuality of mentally retarded persons', *Mental Retardation*, 21, 1, pp. 17–22.

CRAFT, A. (1982) *Sex for the Mentally Handicapped: A Guide for Parents and Carers*, revised edition, London, Routledge and Kegan Paul.

CRAFT, A. (1987) *Health, Social and Sex Education for Children, Adolescents and Adults with a Mental Handicap: A Review of Audio-Visual Resources*, London, Health Education Authority.

DIXON, H. (1988) *Sexuality and Mental Handicap: An Educator's Resource Book*, Wisbech, Learning Development Aids.

DIXON, H. and MULLINAR, G. (1986) *Taught Not Caught: Strategies for Sex Education*, Wisbech, Learning Development Aids.

ELLIOT, M. (1986) *Good Sense Defence for the Young: Kidscape — Programme for Prevention of Sexual Assault on Children*, London, Kidscape Ltd.

ELLIOT, M. (1988) *Keeping Safe — A Practical Guide to Talking to Children*, revised edition, London, Bedford Square Press.

FISCHER, J.L., KRAJICEK, M.J. and BORTHICK, W.A. (1973) *Sex Education for the Developmentally Disabled: A Guide for Parents, Teachers and Professionals*, Baltimore, MD, University Park Press.

GAWLINSKI, J. (1989) 'Good Sense Defence', *Special Children*, 32, 9–10.

HAMRE-NIETUPSKI, S. and WILLIAMS, W. (1977) 'Implementation of selected sex education and social skills to severely handicapped students', *Education and Training of the Mentally Retarded*, 12, pp. 364–72.

KEMPTON, W. (1975) *Sex Education for Persons with Disabilities that Hinder Learning*, Duxbury Press.

KEMPTON, W. (1978) 'Sex education for the mentally handicapped', *Sexuality and Disability*, 1, 2, pp. 137–44.

KEMPTON, W. (1983) 'Sexuality training for professionals who work with mentally handicapped persons', in CRAFT, A. and CRAFT, M. (Eds), *Sex Education and Counselling for Mentally Handicapped People*, London, Costello Education.

KEMPTON, W. (1988) *Life Horizons:I* and *Life Horizons:II* (teaching slides and handbooks), Felixstowe, Concord Film Council.

KEMPTON, W. and FOREMAN, R. (1976) *Guidelines for Training in Sexuality and the Mentally Handicapped*, Philadelphia, Planned Parenthood of Southeastern Pennsylvania.

KNILL, M. and KNILL, C. (1986) *Body Awareness, Contact and Communication*, Wisbech, Learning Development Aids.

McNAUGHTON, J. (1983) *Fit for Life*, Basingstoke, Macmillan.

MAY, D.C. (1980) 'Survey of sex education coursework in special education programs', *Journal of Special Education*, 14, 1, pp. 107–12.

MILL LANE ATC (1980) 'Health and sex education programme for mentally handicapped adolescents and adults', *Teaching and Training*, 18, 2, pp. 56–9.

MONAT, R.K. (1982) *Sexuality and the Mentally Retarded*, San Diego, College-Hill Press.

PATTULLO, A.W. and BARNARD, K.E. (1968) 'Teaching menstrual hygiene to the mentally retarded', *American Journal of Nursing*, 68, 12, pp. 2572–5.

PENNY, R.E.C. and CHATAWAY, J.E. (1982) 'Sex education for mentally retarded persons', *Australia and New Zealand Journal of Developmental Disabilities*, 10, 1, pp. 21–6.

RECTORY PADDOCK SCHOOL (1983) *In Search of a Curriculum*, 2nd edition, Sidcup, Robin Wren Publications.

SEBBA, J. (1981) 'Sexuality and mental handicap', *Apex*, 18, 4, pp. 116–18.

SHADDOCK, A.J. (1979) 'Sexuality and the mentally retarded: Attitudes and knowledge of participants in a one-day seminar', *Australian Journal of Mental Retardation*, 5, 8, p. 316.

SPOD (1982) *Sex Education for Mentally Handicapped People* (teaching cards and handbook), London, SPOD.

WARREN, B. (1981) *Drama Games for Mentally Handicapped People*, London, RSMHCA.

WATSON, G. and ROGERS, R. (1980) 'Sexual instruction for the mildly retarded and normal adolescent: A comparison of educational approaches, parental expectations and pupil knowledge and attitude', *Health Education Journal*, 39, 3, pp. 88–95.

16 TVEI and its Relationship to the National Curriculum

Bill Cassell, Sylvia Lindoe and Carolyn Skilling

TVEI in Leicestershire

All pupils share the right to a broad and balanced curriculum, including the National Curriculum.... The range of needs to which this principle of entitlement applies will vary from the profound and multiple disabilities which are experienced by a minority of pupils and call for life-long support to the sometimes less apparent educational problems. (NCC, 1989, p. 1)

The right to share in the curriculum defined in Section 1 of the Act does not automatically ensure access to it, nor progress within it. (*ibid*)

The first quotation is rapidly becoming a central article of faith in discussions about pupils with special needs, although perhaps the second quotation remains the most pertinent.

Thus, although the arrival of the National Curriculum has brought with it the acceptance, willing or otherwise, that young people with special educational needs are entitled to a breadth of curriculum experience comparable to that of their peers, the strategies for achieving the breadth of provision, and the resources for supporting it, remain an issue. Indeed, 'sharing in the curriculum' is not necessarily an adequate concept on its own, and 'access' could be seen to imply a concept of a curriculum which exists independently of pupils — not necessarily the most helpful starting point for planning in a special needs context.

The National Curriculum can, of course, provide a helpful framework for looking at the common range of experiences and areas of skill and knowledge which schools should be aiming to provide; but an additional dimension in planning can be given by looking at intended *outcomes* for the learner. This consideration of outcomes is given a specific focus through the Technical and Vocational Education Initiative (TVEI) — a focus which reinforces the concept of an equal entitlement, and which also directs attention to the organization of teaching and learning.

A recent restatement of aims by the TVEI Unit of the Training Agency describes the intention thus:

> TVEI's role is to help produce a more highly skilled, competent, effective and enterprising workforce for the 1990s. It is a bold long-term strategy, unique amongst nations, for investing in the skills of ALL our young people 14–19 in full-time education and equipping them for the demands of working life in a rapidly changing highly technological society. It does this by:
>
> > relating what is learnt in schools to the world of work;
> > improving the skills and qualifications of all, in particular in science, technology, information technology and modern languages;
> > providing young people with direct experience of the world of work through real work experience;
> > enabling young people to be effective, enterprising and capable at work through active and practical learning methods;
> > providing counselling, guidance, individual action plans, records of achievement and opportunities to progress to higher levels of achievement.

There may be certain tensions resulting from the application of these principles to students with severe learning difficulties (SLD), but the emphasis on *all* young people is categoric, and also very helpful. In Leicestershire it has been welcomed largely because it has provided financial and philosophical support for the further development of a broader curriculum, and for planned progression within and beyond that curriculum. TVEI funding has enabled special schools to address the fundamental issues of designing and resourcing a curriculum which ensures access to the experiences and opportunities which would lead to the outcomes identified by the TVEI Unit.

Leicestershire's provision includes seven schools for pupils with SLD, and it would be appropriate to look at some of the particular ways in which they have responded to the challenges and opportunities outlined above. During the TVEI extension programme, they each received an annual sum approximately equal to their school capitation, as well as increased non-teaching time for school TVEI coordinators, and the support of advisory teachers and LEA TVEI staff, part of whose role was to support the planning process and to facilitate links with mainstream schools and colleges. Much of the planning was done as part of a County Special Schools' Consortium, which provided mutual support, as well as an effective dissemination structure.

As a result, specific curriculum development has been undertaken in the following areas:

the use of microtechnology and Information Technology (IT) as aids to learning and to communication, and the development of pupil competence in their everyday use;

recording achievement using a variety of strategies and formats, and developing the use of Records of Achievement within and beyond school;

the development of Science and Technology teaching, particularly in the contexts of limited resources and facilities, lack of specialist staff, and restricted pupil mobility;

progression and continuity of pupils' educational experience from 14 to 19, and particular concern for the transition from school to 'adult life', at whatever age this takes place;

provision of experience of the 'world of work' whether directly or indirectly, and establishing its relationship to the curriculum;

the development of more effective Personal and Social Education, including the part played by guidance and counselling;

establishment of purposeful links with mainstream schools and colleges;

further development of appropriate curricular structures, including the use of modules, and the broadening of teaching and learning approaches.

Obviously many of these areas overlap, such as the use of IT in developing Records of Achievement, or the use of links with Colleges of Further Education as part of a structured transition from school to a wider society, while also forming part of a developing modular curriculum. Nevertheless, it would be convenient for the present purpose to deal with them separately.

Applications of IT

Increased availability and extended use of microtechnology is in many ways the most obvious application of TVEI funding, and the range of uses is extensive. As an example, one school concentrated on applications for students with profound and multiple learning difficulties (PMLD). Items which they purchased included computer joysticks, a head-operated tilt-switch and grip touch-and-go switch for use with a range of devices as well as with computer programs.

All these devices have environmental control applications as well as their role in operating information technology. They also seem to have a part to play in developing physical coordination. In addition, they acquired a Mains Controller and Reward Box, with a variety of switching mechanisms, which essentially is used to develop cause and effect associations, with variable timings and age-appropriate rewards (see Chapter 10 in this volume).

At this stage it is worth highlighting a point which this school and many others — mainstream as well as special — have made about certain TVEI-derived developments. Having acquired new equipment, and modified their curriculum, they are concerned that progress will be hindered by some very basic problems: maintenance and replacement of equipment following the ending of TVEI funding; the extra time needed to set up equipment; and staff training needs. These issues are under discussion.

Other developments and applications of IT include the purchase of programmable robots; the provision of extra printers for use by students with poor control over writing, or no writing at all, in many cases with the Records of Achievement as the focus; and the purchase of appropriate software and keyboard adaptations. These things are not new, but TVEI funding, and the support and implementation structures associated with it, have provided schools with more than simply financial means; they have provided time — time for staff to analyze and to plan, to work together and to reflect jointly on progress. They have provided a stimulus for change, and a set of yardsticks by which to evaluate it. These observations can be amplified as we consider other areas of development.

Records of Achievement

Records of Achievement have constantly been an explicit TVEI priority. Initially, many people had serious reservations about the value of

Records of Achievement for young people with SLD, which included: the conceptual difficulties with defining 'achievement'; the inability of many pupils to have a hand in the production; the danger of their being a record of decline; the concepts of 'negotiation' and 'owner-ship'; youngsters' understanding of the process; the issue of who might be 'users'; and the question of pupils' recognition of their own achievements.

Acceptance of TVEI funding, however, has meant acceptance of the obligation to develop Records of Achievement, and experiences have been instructive, in respect both of the perceived value of the process, and of the strategies employed.

Methods of compiling Records of Achievement have naturally included video, dictation, word processing, audio tapes, photographs and staff comment. Fundamental to the success of the more ambitious approaches, such as compilation of video profiles, are factors such as staff time and technician support. And again, question marks hang over their sustainability. Thus one school observes that,

> a large proportion of our TVEI resources have been used to develop video profiles, purchasing equipment and tapes, pro-viding technician time and non-teaching support. Without TVEI resources this would not have been possible. We have worked on standardizing material on the tapes and providing continuity over the age range. Improvement in the quality of recording has been another area of work. Staff are also being trained in editing and dubbing. The management of this in-volves liaising with thirty students, nine staff and a technician, and much of the work can only be done during school hours at the expense of teaching time.

Certainly there is a significant 'curriculum challenge' in moving from this developmental stage to a situation where outcomes and values are clear, logistics are resolved, and organization is more harmonious. But if the school acknowledges the value of the process and has found an approach which in some sense 'works', then it will attempt to maintain the structure, and one would suggest that LEAs and central government should be able to support its efforts.

Regardless of the strategies or the technology employed to pro-duce a Record of Achievement, the whole process is very limited and of relatively little value unless the school first of all defines for itself exactly what would constitute an achievement for each of its pupils; secondly, ensures that there are opportunities for such achievements (and, indeed, that much curriculum planning is geared to ensuring that they happen); and thirdly has a means of explicit acknowledgment and celebration of achievement. Whatever the formal means of such acknowledgment — certificates, assemblies, displays — there are certain patterns of curriculum organization which can help define and facilitate recognizable achievements.

Modular Approaches

One such organization pattern is the adoption of a partial or complete modular structure. Modules have the potential to offer short-term, clearly-defined targets, specifically geared to student needs, and with the possibility of defined and recognizable achievements.

Many of the modular approaches which have been funded by TVEI are planned and delivered jointly with local Colleges of Further Education (FE). At their best, such links serve a wide range of purposes, providing a curriculum that is broader and more relevant to students' age groups and specific needs. They develop social skills and qualities of independence, and are part of a planned involvement with the community. Together with National Curriculum requirements, Sections 5 and 6 of the Disabled Persons Act, and an evolving role of other agencies such as the Careers Service and Social Services, this kind of link is part of a multi-professional approach to continuity and progression in education from 14 to 19 and to the process of transition from child to adult services.

Links with an FE college provide the opportunity for learning to take place in a more adult environment. There is access to a wide range of opportunities of a vocational nature, such as the use of workshops for skills training, as well as shared use of canteen and student union facilities, college and community familiarization, work preparation and independent living skills. There is an obvious advantage in sharing the links with students from mainstream or other special schools. Links of a modular nature prove most popular, thus broadening the range of options available. The college is able to plan more objectively and students benefit from the preparation for transition to full or part-time FE courses.

Close liaison between college and school staff can facilitate movement towards a joint 16+ curriculum, one that is related and complementary to both establishments. In addition to offering full and part-time courses to school leavers, colleges also provide similar modular link arrangements with Social Services day centres for people with learning difficulties. There are significant moves towards the post-school placement of students with SLD becoming more fluid and client-centred. Social Services departments are more actively seeking the opinions, needs and wishes of the client group in designing service principles towards a new mode of day care for people with learning difficulties. Rapidly diminishing is the large institutionalized day centre. The new model advocates a 'mixed economy' of care, enabling the client to spend appropriate lengths of time in education (FE/community), employment (supported, sheltered or open), or using local amenities.

College-based modules have covered a wide range of activities including Hairdressing, Music, Keep Fit, Leatherwork, Pottery, Woodwork, Home Maintenance, Cookery and Horticulture. An example serves to illustrate how the design of modules can draw together independence training, social skills, assessment issues, teaching strategies, and collaborative planning. The module was in Microwave Cookery.

Example 1: Module in Microwave Cookery
The module comprised seven two-hour sessions of cookery and one session of evaluation. Nine students attended the course, six males and three females. Students continued to work in established pairs.

Two innovations proved very successful. The course tutor provided pictorial recipes that she had drawn herself. Most of the students were able to follow these and this greatly increased their ability to work independently. Repeating recipes on consecutive weeks proved very useful, and students made noticeable progress from the first to the second attempt at a dish.

There were some problems, however. A sudden replacement of microwaves in the last week of the course confused both students and staff. This led to a consideration of the variety of microwaves that the students used and which they preferred. This was a complex issue involving students' differing abilities. For one student, for example, the most important feature was a clear read-out while for another the degree of manual dexterity required was the critical factor. Generally the basic, often older, machines were the ones that proved most successful for the students to use. Through all five Microwave Cookery modules lack of time has been a critical factor. It seemed particularly noticeable this time, as students were doing so much more for themselves and consequently taking longer. A couple of the recipes, though simple, were too time-consuming for the allotted two hours. Others (for example, the corned beef hash) were excellent.

All the students in the group improved noticeably during the course, some making excellent and even astonishing progress. Two students were more or less able to complete the recipes independently, although measuring and quantities tended to be problematic, despite a variety of methods being explored to resolve this difficulty. Hygiene continues to be another area that needs continual reinforcement. The element of self-assessment that we have tried to introduce has also been problematic. Although students are much better at answering straightforward questions, the communication skills required for judging their own performances require much further development. Lack of time at the end of sessions did not help this situation.

Example 2: SPECIAL school/college link course
While some modules are 'one-offs', other schools have developed year-round modular programmes.

Modular Programme 1988/89

Autumn Term
1a Using the College — 12 weeks × half day.
Familiarization with key areas of the college. Independent mobility within and between the buildings and use of a range of college facilities. Assessment of the level of functioning of individual students.

1b Road Safety — 12 weeks × half day.
Use of pelican and zebra crossings, working towards independent mobility in the town centre and identification of specific locations. Increasing levels of independence, from supervised large groups to small groups/pairs 'shadowed' by members of staff. Awareness of social and cultural context of the town.

Spring Term
2a Brooksby Agricultural College Project — 6 weeks × half day.
Pre-vocational introduction to horticulture, agriculture and construction as areas of employment. Taster activities practising a range of basic skills and use of tools and equipment. Travel by public transport.

2b Information Technology — 6 weeks × half day.
Recording achievements on Brooksby project using word

processing — inputting text, correction, saving and printing. Students produced a newspaper for friends and staff at school.

3a Use of Leisure (Winter) — 4 weeks × half day.
Introduction to a range of community facilities, particularly appropriate to cold seasons. College leisure centre, town library and museum. Practising basic skills and assessing facilities.

3b World of Work — 4 weeks × half day.
Appreciation of the purpose of work, different jobs, health and safety and attributes of various jobs.

Summer Term
4a Community Service — 6 weeks × half day.
Making links with the day centre for people with physical handicaps, offering a shopping service to housebound in-dividuals. Awareness that students can make a contribution to society and progression of community independence.

4b Getting About — 11 weeks × half day.
Extension of autumn term Road Safety module but looking at orientation in a wider context. The module introduces simple map reading and timetables. Students will prepare for the residential visit to Yorkshire by finding out about the area from maps and tourist literature. We will also look at how to get there by public transport. Emphasis on using buses and trains, and students will organize their own short visits to local leisure areas.

5a Use of Leisure (Summer) — 5 weeks × half day.
Introduction to a range of outdoor activities, including canoeing on the river and use of public recreational facilities, such as tennis courts, putting and bowling. Practising and assessing basic skills such as booking and paying for facilities.

Residential Experiences

It is clear that one aim of such a course is to provide a structured set of experiences which will develop social skills and independence.

Residential visits are a parallel part of the course and are also supported by TVEI funding. Three schools in Leicestershire have developed a collaborative residential course, with a significant outdoor pursuits element, using TVEI funding and supported by an advisory teacher for Special Educational Needs (Outdoor and Physical Education). The course takes place at the county's Outdoor Education Centre at Aberglaslyn in North Wales, and has been a learning experience for staff at the Centre, as well as the students. The advisory teacher worked with students before the course, familiarizing them with equipment, and developing confidence in activities such as climbing and canoeing.

Staff also went through a similar process, so that they understood the nature of students' experiences. (A spin-off from this was that some staff went on to complete approved instructors' courses in these activities, so that they can run their own student courses). The course leader comments:

> One thing that is obvious from the courses I have been involved with, is how the staff expectations of what the students can achieve have improved. For September 1990 it is hoped, conditions permitting, to involve the students in a five-mile estuary canoe trip in kayaks and open (Canadian) canoes, and to build on the rock climbing experience so that some students are involved in climbing hundreds rather than tens of feet. It was proved in the 1989 course that students can walk eight miles and climb a 2865 foot peak in the process. The students do enjoy camping out overnight. The expansion of the activities has come about through the now experienced Aberglaslyn and school staff (teachers and support staff); the activities are arranged to challenge all students at whatever level they are working at, so as to achieve, and, most importantly, to enjoy their experience.
>
> It must be stated that the course is not wholly concerned with physical activities: there are trips to castles and the shops; there are chances to see the countryside and be involved with the locals; there are visits to the beach for barbecues and bonfires, and sing-song sessions at night in a clearing in the woods; walks along a disused railway line, through a tunnel which you need a torch for (and don't get!), so a friend or/and a member of staff is available to grab hold of. In essence the course is balanced, challenging yet giving time to relax and eat ice cream.

In this outdoor education programme, as in other areas of curriculum development, a variety of aims and purposes overlap. There are, for instance, elements of Personal and Social Education, of progression towards independence, and of links beyond school.

Mini-Enterprise Initiatives

In another ambitious development, we see work-related activities coming together with elements of Science, with preparation for life outside school and with the National Curriculum. This particular initiative is described by the school as a 'mini-enterprise', although this to some extent sells it short and perhaps gives a feeling of the entrepreneurial taking precedence over the educational. The schools' description of the project is worth reproducing at length, not because it is out of the ordinary, but because it illustrates a comprehensive approach to curriculum planning which merges school aims, TVEI aims and National Curriculum aims.

How the mini-enterprise developed
The school entered the LEA's TVEI extension in September 1987 and joined other special schools in developing the theme 'Preparation for Adult Life'. The chosen curriculum vehicle for this approach was horticulture. The school is extremely fortunate in possessing a bungalow adjacent to the main site and with the support of the Special Needs Science advisory teacher it was decided to use the garden as an educational resource.

In the first year a heated greenhouse was purchased and the mini-enterprise was conceived as a means of selling surplus garden produce. The bulk of the fruit and vegetables was to be used in the bungalow in cookery lessons and the preparation of meals. The mini-enterprise was given the title of 'Bungalow Bargains'. The title described the main venue of the enterprise and also indicated that it was essentially a 'cottage industry'.

The enterprise expanded from its initial horticultural base to include preserves, pastries and craft items. Recently the range of activities has been further increased by the purchase of a badgemaking machine and photocopier for the bungalow. Thus the enterprise activities cover a wide range of learning experiences and enable the pupils' skills to be expressed in a practical and rewarding manner.

To date the main outlet for sales has been through school fêtes, Mencap Society Fêtes, lunchtime stalls for school staff and 'mail order' to parents and friends of the school. In the summer of 1989 the enterprise ran a stall in the main shopping street of Hinckley and sold direct to the public. Students helped 'man' the stalls and the experience helped to develop confidence and self-esteem.

The proceeds from the sales are deposited in a building society account. Students are involved in the 'bookkeeping' and help to decide how the profits should be spent. To date the enterprise has purchased a freezer to facilitate the storage of foodstuffs as well as purchasing small household and garden equipment. The enterprise has also purchased records and tapes of the students' choice.

At present most of the support funding for 'Bungalow Bargains' comes from TVEI. In future years the enterprise must become increasingly self-financing. The present policy is to purchase the larger items needed while funding is available.

TVEI at the school has been important in developing Science and Technology in the curriculum and the mini-enterprise is seen as a relevant and practical method of delivering Science, Technology and of course has many other curricular implications.

What the enterprise seeks to achieve

The mini-enterprise exists in order to provide learning experiences that enhance independence and self help. The mini-enterprise activity is seen as complementing the curriculum for senior students. It aims to provide students with work-related experiences and the opportunity to learn a range of skills, for example, handling money, in an adult setting. The aims of the enterprise project are:

- to provide students with SLD with a range of work-related experiences;
- to provide senior students with SLD with an opportunity to learn a range of skills such as basic finance, within the framework of a relevant and rewarding educational experience;
- to provide students with work-related and commercial experience within the school environment and, where possible, in the wider community;
- to provide students with opportunities to experience a variety of commercial disciplines, such as production schedules, advertising, selling and budgeting, and to participate in the decision-making process;
- to provide, through the enterprise, a motivation for participating in a range of curricular activities and, through the commerical

need for quality, encourage the highest standards of endeavour in the work undertaken.

At the time of writing (August, 1989), students in the two senior class groups work on the mini-enterprise with the bulk of the work taking place in the bungalow. Since 1986 the bungalow has been the class base for the 16–19 age group. The class curriculum places a high priority upon the development of skills relevant to the home and community. Students are able to practice a wide range of domestic skills, for example, purchasing and preparing food, cleaning and re-decoration, garden maintenance and responsibilities of living in a 'family'-type community. The mini-enterprise was developed as a means of delivering cross-curricular experiences: art, cookery, horticulture, science, maths, design and technology, and communication skills to a group of students with SLD in their last years of schooling. The concept envisages student participation in a range of relevant de-cisions. These would include: what to make, how to make it, where and how to sell it and what to do with the proceeds.

Learning skills arising from the mini-enterprise activities are listed under the following headings: finance, production and selling.

Finance:
The experience of using an account: students need to visit a local building society to make deposits and withdrawals and need to make out and sign the appropriate forms.

Using money in real situations: students will need to handle money when selling or counting up after a sales promotion. In both cases accuracy is essential.

Cost and value: students will be involved in the decisions about pricing and will therefore have experience in a practical way of differ-ent costs of items and their relative value. This will develop a greater understanding of the cost of the things they wish to buy.

Budgeting: students will be involved in deciding how much of the income they will spend on equipment and materials and how much can be spent upon 'reward' items such as records. Realistically these will be guided decisions but at least the students have the opportunity to experience the process and have some effect upon it.

Production:
To date, the mini-enterprise has produced and sold a wide range of items. These include craft items such as Christmas decorations, foodstuffs such as cakes and chutney, manufactured items such as badges and recipe books, and horticultural items such as plant cuttings, excess fruit and vegetables, tomato plants and bedding plants. The wide range of goods ensures that students on the enterprise are involved in very different production techniques and skills. Summarized, these include:

> Home economics: Cookery and kitchen management. Hygiene in food preparation. Using kitchen tools and domestic technology such as kettles and microwaves. Selecting, weighing and measuring ingredients.
>
> Horticulture: Garden management, safe and proper use of tools, planting and harvesting.
>
> Art and craft: designing and making items by hand, using print and stencil kits, using sewing techniques.
>
> Manufacturing: Using computers and word processing, using photocopiers, using light production machines and sewing machines. Using equipment safely.

Selling:
> Technology: Using word processors, printers and duplicating equipment to produce advertising notices and leaflets.
>
> Design: Making posters and information leaflets.

It can be seen from this summarized list that a wide range of learning experiences, essential to a successful lifeskills programme for students with severe learning difficulties, can be delivered through mini-enterprise.

The school went on systematically to match many of the tasks undertaken by students against various Attainment Targets which had been suggested at that time in the draft proposals of the Design and Technology National Curriculum Working Group (DES and Welsh Office, 1989a). These covered 'Economic and Industrial Understanding' (NCC, 1990) as well as materials, tools, aesthetics and organizing and planning. In the statutory order for Technology, many of these attainments are still present in the Design and Technology Capability profile component. They include:

Pupils should be taught to:

> develop a product and how to market, promote and sell it;
>
> develop effective pricing, promotion and distribution;
>
> calculate costs and make decisions on price; etc. (DES and Welsh Office, 1990)

They also drew in Mathematics and Science Attainment Targets as part of their planning. Relevant Maths Attainment Targets would include:

Pupils should:

> select the materials and the mathematics to use for a task; plan work methodically;
>
> record findings and present them in oral, written or visual form as appropriate. (DES and Welsh Office, 1989b)

And among the relevant Science Attainment Targets would be:

Pupils should:

> identify, and describe simple variables that change over time, for example, growth of a plant;
>
> know that plants and animals need certain conditions to sustain life;
>
> know that living things respond to seasonal and daily changes. (DES and Welsh Office, 1989c)

Resources Implications

It is apparent that TVEI developments have been part of an integrated process and that clear and explicit links have been made with National Curriculum planning. This project drew on the support of the advisory teacher for Special Needs with a specific brief for the development of Science in special schools. Another part of his role has been to develop a system by which large and/or expensive items of Science apparatus not normally owned by special schools have been purchased centrally and made available for loan. He comments as follows:

> This has involved the schools in curriculum and resource planning exercises that have in themselves been useful.

Microscopes, incubators, skeletons or circuit boards need to be booked in advance and teachers therefore have to decide not only what they want to borrow, but why they want it, how they will use it, and when.

TVEI funds were made available to augment the apparatus loan service by providing smaller items of apparatus which together have formed module kits for topics such as 'Making Things Move', 'Hot and Cold', and 'Materials'.

Recently one special school, which by the efforts of staff and parents, has raised enough money to provide a new Science and Technology resource base, has had TVEI money made available to enhance their stock of apparatus on semi-permanent loan. It has been agreed that the resources of the school should then be made available to other special schools. In another case TVEI funds are being used by special schools on a particular Technology project. When the project is completed the apparatus has been offered to the loan service for use by other special schools not involved in the project. These examples of collaboration and cooperation between schools are to be commended and where ever possible emulated.

The introduction of the National Curriculum has ensured that Science is offered to all our pupils as part of their entitlement to a broad and balanced curriculum. There is much in the Programmes of Study in Science that is already being taught in schools. TVEI has helped schools to identify what is relevant in their curriculum and to address their curriculum with greater thought than previously. It has enabled long-term planning to occur and has helped to provide the resources and to fund the additional support that pupils need. In this way it has helped to ensure that pupils make meaningful progression from one topic to another.

It is hoped that having benefited from the improved curriculum that TVEI funds have helped to provide, schools are able to retain the benefits as the funding is reduced and finally ceases altogether.

Collaboration

The element of collaboration has been further built in to current planning in that a group of schools within the Special Schools consortium, having made Science and Technology a priority for further development, are jointly planning four Science and Technology Activity Days. These will include workshop activities in the schools, and visits to centres of interest, such as museums, local industry and field centres. A significant area of curriculum development will thus be undertaken on a shared, collaborative basis, with materials produced jointly, National Curriculum elements considered jointly, external support being provided more cost effectively, inservice activities being enriched, and links with mainstream schools being established. This is clearly a way of working which is worth fostering and sustaining.

Similar collaboration is planned in the development of approaches to Personal and Social Education (PSE), where staff are being released from teaching in order to develop materials and strategies. In the context which we are describing, where TVEI is encouraging the development of a curriculum which takes more note of the world outside school; where the National Curriculum asserts an equal entitlement for all students; and where the expectations of pupils with SLD are rapidly broadening, the role of PSE, and of guidance and counselling, becomes fundamental. It is, however, an area full of difficulty. In respect of TVEI influence, it is not the easiest or most obvious sphere of development, because mere availability of funding does not lead to change. And there are other obstacles, real or imagined, such as the scope of genuine life choices for students, especially those with PMLD, or the common tradition that guidance and counselling are aimed at parents rather than pupils. Nevertheless, if the curriculum for students with SLD is being expanded, and if more emphasis is being placed on independence and on the process of transition, then we need to take a very close look at the quality of the guidance process.

Links with the National Curriculum

If we attempt to sum up the way in which TVEI has acted as a mediating factor in considering the application of the National Curriculum to students with SLD, there seem to be several strands to the process. We start with a situation where the National Curriculum establishes the notion of 'entitlement' for all students, but does not necessarily define just what it is that they are entitled to, nor the best way of ensuring they can get it. The process of implementing one LEA's TVEI policy has in many respects established some ways not only of identifying these entitlements in terms of experience, but has also provided a planning and support mechanism which explicitly addresses questions of access. It has also led relatively painlessly into the age of the development plan.

Thus we could for convenience identify three discernible strands running through the implementation process. First, there is the identification of specific curriculum issues, such as Science and Technology, which deserve attention. Second, there is the development of various ways of assessing and recording students' experiences and abilities across their curriculum, primarily through a Record of Achievement. And thirdly there is an underlying concern to place their curriculum experiences in a context of planned and structured progression, both within and beyond school. This is seen through the use of FE Links, the emphasis on guidance, the development of action plans, and the development of work experience, among other things. Overlaying these elements is a continuing integrated support and planning structure. Schools are required to analyze their situation and establish targets drawn from a combination of their own aims and wider LEA intentions; they have access to external support, advice and expertise; financial 'pump priming' is available, as is extra time for key staff to manage the developments; and progress is monitored and evaluated by the school in conjunction with the LEA.

The result in respect of curriculum provision could presumably be an interesting balance of the various aims and interests of the school, the LEA and the government. If, however, the process has operated as it should, with teachers in control, then it will have started with the needs of each individual child, and ended with the school being better able to identify those needs, to plan appropriate targets and programmes, and to go as far as possible towards meeting them, thus ensuring that the concepts of 'access' and 'entitlement' apply not so much to *all* pupils as to *each* pupil.

Note

All quotes in this chapter, unless otherwise identified, come from Leicestershire teachers' unpublished reports or personal interviews with them.

References

DES AND WELSH OFFICE (1989a) *Design and Technology for Ages 5 to 16*, London, HMSO.

DES AND WELSH OFFICE (1989b) *Mathematics in the National Curriculum*, London, HMSO.

DES AND WELSH OFFICE (1989c) *Science in the National Curriculum*, London, HMSO.

DES AND WELSH OFFICE (1990) *Technology in the National Curriculum*, London, HMSO.

NCC (1989) *Curriculum Guidance Two: A Curriculum for All*, York, National Curriculum Council.

NCC (1990) *Curriculum Guidance Three: The Whole Curriculum*, York, National Curriculum Council.

17 Assessment, the National Curriculum and Special Educational Needs: Confusion or Consensus?

Martyn Rouse

Introduction

In this chapter I intend to consider why recent proposals relating to the assessment of pupils with learning difficulties within the National Curriculum are causing confusion and concern for many of the professionals involved. I should then like to suggest how it might be possible to preserve, develop and share with the wider educational community, those promising assessment practices which are already occurring in many special education settings.

Overview

It is possible to discern an emerging pattern of development in terms of assessment practice in special education. Until relatively recently the field was dominated by psychometrics (psychological measurement). Increasingly many of the assumptions which underpinned this approach have been questioned and a new perspective of educational measurement has begun to influence practice. Briefly this change can be seen as the movement:

> *from* assessment of the learner's ability, aptitude and deficits which involved ranking and comparison;
>
> *to* assessment of the learner on the curriculum against predetermined criteria;
>
> assessment of the curriculum and its delivery;
>
> involving learners in their own assessment;

teachers becoming reflective practitioners assessing not only the learner but also themselves, the curriculum and the classroom context.

Any overview which attempts at this particular time to pinpoint our current position in the assessment debate, to describe the journey which brought us to this point and also to suggest possible future directions, would be very much easier to achieve if it were possible to stand still, look up and take a few bearings. However, the sky is cloudy, the sea is rough, and familiar landmarks are disappearing from view as the vessel in which we are travelling is propelled by external currents of considerable force. In addition, these currents are not even running in a constant direction. We find ourselves in an eddy consisting of conflicting advice, confusing messages, and, for the special education community in particular, the feeling that the decision makers are not always aware of our existence.

I shall return to some of the reasons for this confusion later in the chapter, but first I should like to consider the meaning and purposes of assessment, for it is a lack of clarity in the minds of some policy makers and professionals that has caused much of the current confusion.

What is Assessment?

For the purpose of this discussion I intend to take a broad definition of assessment. Assessment is more than merely testing, and whilst testing may be part of the wider activity of assessment, we are reminded by Salvia and Ysseldyke that 'testing and assessment are not synonymous. Assessment in educational settings is a multifaceted process that involves far more than the administration of a test' (1985, p. 5).

Assessment involves the collection of evidence about which judgments are made. In turn there are fundamental questions relating to what constitutes evidence as well as about the 'who' and 'how' of making judgments. Munby provides a useful starting point when he suggests that assessment must: 'involve a judgment; be based on certain criteria; be concerned with attainment or performance of an individual or a group; be based on criteria which are relevant to the particular performance or attainment being considered' (1989, pp. 11–12).

I will argue later in this chapter that assessment should do even more than this. It should be fundamentally concerned with improving the quality of teaching and learning. Unfortunately, too much assessment practice in the past did not attempt to address this issue at all. However, teachers have always made judgments about their pupils. Sometimes the evidence upon which these judgments were made was collected by the systematic use of techniques which have shown themselves to be extremely useful. In other cases judgments were based upon little more than intuitive, subjective reactions to events and individuals. There are other techniques for collecting evidence, including the use of commercially produced standardized tests which, although widely used, have become increasingly discredited in the eyes of teachers and many other professionals.

It could be argued that there was too much testing and too little assessment in the past. As part of the evidence collected by the Task Group on Assessment and Testing (TGAT) (DES and Welsh Office, 1988), it was estimated that up to 90 per cent of primary schools used some form of standardized tests and that 75 per cent of LEAs either insisted or encouraged schools in this practice. In many cases, testing occurred as part of the educational calendar. Secondary schools would test their first year intake on arrival, primary schools would regularly test 'reading attainment', often using tests which did not reflect the school's reading curriculum. When questioned about the benefits of such practice some heads and teachers would claim that 'we have always done it', 'the parents want it' or 'we like to compare standards from one year to the next'. In too many cases little action followed what was an expensive exercise both financially and in teacher time. Results would often be locked in filing cabinets or sent to the LEA never to be heard of again. Testing in some schools and LEAs had become a ritual, part of the liturgy of the school year, which served no purpose other than being a 'security blanket' to provide comfort. It is hardly surprising that such practice became increasingly discredited. It was separate from the curriculum and provided no useful information in helping to guide curriculum decision making. Goldstein (1989) provides a powerful case against what he calls 'separate assessment', arguing instead for 'connected assessment'. This distinction between separate and connected assessment is useful in reminding us that curriculum-based assessment (connected assessment) has become increasingly common in special education settings. Tucker describes curriculum-based assessment as 'the ultimate in teaching the test, because the materials used to assess progress are always drawn directly from the course of study' (1985, p. 200).

The End for Psychometrics?

The science of mental measurement or psychometrics dominated the development of many assessment procedures. Education, particularly special education, has always been vulnerable to psychometric influence, although Wood (1986) suggests that this is less so than before. The dominant position which was held by educational psychologists and test producing agencies over assessment practice has only recently been challenged. Until this challenge, education was, in the words of Wood,

> lacking a distinctive and self-confident view about the purpose of testing in schools and about what kinds of tests were suitable and unsuitable, it has, rather like a client state, looked on helplessly as psychometric doctrines and practices have been installed and put to work. (1986, p. 185)

It could be argued that special education owes its existence to certain psychometric assumptions, particularly the belief that ability is distributed evenly throughout the population in the so-called 'normal curve' in which the special education population is located in the bottom left-hand corner. Rarely was it pointed out that the normal curve is a statistically derived distribution and not a matter of fact.

The most fundamental weaknesses in using psychometric techniques which are designed to compare pupils with each other, is that there must always be losers. Getting on for 50 per cent of the school population will be below average! Improvement, progress or development is rarely celebrated, because some pupils will always be at the bottom when compared with other pupils. However, we find it difficult to leave behind many of the assumptions derived from psychometrics, because, in the words of Goldstein, 'the psychometric model provides the most potent influence on our thinking ... it has become very difficult to separate that model from our whole understanding of what assessment is or can be' (1989, p. 140).

Many traditional forms of assessment which were based upon psychometric theory assumed that the mental attributes being tested actually existed independently of the context in which they were tested. These attributes were seen as existing within the pupils. The consequence of this assumption led many pupils to being given what were in effect life sentences because judgments were being made based upon this inappropriate evidence. The data collected had little to say about the pupils themselves, only about where they stood relative to others on some fictional scale; nevertheless, position on this scale, however uninformative about what you could do, and could not do, was tremendously decisive in the matter of life chances (Wood, 1986). Gould emphasizes the consequence of such decisions when stating, 'few tragedies can be more extensive than the stunting of life, few injustices deeper than the denial of an opportunity to strive or even hope, by a limit imposed from without, but falsely identified as lying within' (1981, p. 29). We needed techniques of assessment which would not merely tell us where pupils stood relative to other pupils but procedures which would indicate what it was that pupils could do or could not do, did or did not know. We required systems of assessment which would celebrate achievement.

The publication of Glaser's (1963) paper introduced the notion of criterion referenced testing and contrasted it sharply with norm referenced testing. Wood (1986) suggests that this was the point at which educational measurement began to detach itself from classical psychometrics. The break is not yet complete, and there are those who would argue that the influence of psychometrics is still profound (see, for example, Goldstein, 1989). This leads to considerable confusion, as techniques derived from traditional approaches are often being used for purposes for which they were not designed. And yet, the evidence has been present in every classroom; the difficulty has been in deciding which evidence is significant and how it should be collected, recorded and reported. Harlen (Harlen *et al.*, 1977) summarized this dilemma when she stated, 'children are showing their attitudes and abilities all the time in their normal work. They are always telling us all we need to know about their characteristics if only we can receive and interpret the messages'. Perhaps it is a lack of understanding about the purposes of assessment that is the cause of much of the current confusion.

Trends in Assessment

As a result of growing dissatisfaction with traditional forms of assessment, the late 1970s saw an increasing interest in holistic approaches to assessment which were multifaceted, continuous and naturalistic. These trends could be shown thus:

Traditonal	*More recent*
Experts	Teachers
Outside the curriculum	Curriculum related
Comparative	Personally referenced

Measures ability/aptitude	Measures attainment
Occasional	Continuous
Pupils passive	Pupils active
Allows only a few to succeed	Allows a wide range of success
Supports the selection process	Supports personal development
Norm referenced	Criterion referenced
Assessment private	Assessment negotiated

The trend towards these more recent approaches to assessment has been well explained by Bridges (1989), Goldstein (1989) and by Wood who points out that compared to psychological measurement, educational measurement,

> deals with the individual's achievement relative to himself (*sic*) rather than to others;
>
> seeks to test for competence rather than intelligence;
>
> takes place in relatively uncontrolled conditions and so does not produce 'well behaved' data;
>
> looks for 'best' rather than typical performance;
>
> is most effective when rules and regulations characteristic of standardised testing are relaxed;
>
> embodies a constructive outlook on assessment where the aim is to help rather than sentence the individual. (Wood, 1986)

Purposes for Assessment

The central purpose of educational assessment is to help with the process of decision making. The type of procedures to be used should depend upon the decisions which need to be taken. When the procedures employed do not match the purposes, confusion and mistakes will occur. There are many writers, for example, Nuttall (1989), Popham (1981) and Reason (1989), who stress the importance of matching assessment techniques with the decisions which need to be taken. Because there is a wide range of assessment purposes it is naive to assume that one set of assessment techniques would be sufficient to meet all demands.

An extensive list of purposes could be produced. It might include:

screening and identification of pupils who may require additional support;

referral for special placement based upon legal requirements;

ranking or grading pupils;

allocating scarce resources, eg., places in higher education, or speech therapy;

helping teachers to plan the curriculum;

evaluating pupils' learning;

helping pupils to review their own learning;

evaluating the effectiveness of teaching;

providing information for colleagues;

monitoring standards;

comparing schools;

providing information for others outside school (e.g., parents or employers). (Ainscow, 1988)

These purposes could be grouped into those which were mainly concerned with the process of: selection; evaluation and accountability; and improving the quality of teaching and learning. There is likely to be some overlap between these groupings and perhaps it may best be represented by Figure 17.1.

I would argue that there is no single assessment technique which would by itself hit the bull's eye of the Assessment Target (see shaded area in Figure 17.1). A range of procedures are needed if the demands of all the purposes listed above are to be achieved.

Assessment and the National Curriculum

The National Curriculum marks a watershed for the development of assessment practice in England and Wales. For the first time ever, nationwide programmes of assessment will monitor pupil progress and the achievement of Attainment Targets within the National Curriculum. Whilst many of the proposals incorporated within the Education Reform Act 1988 (ERA) have caused considerable debate, it is the proposals for national assessment and the publication of the results, together with local management of schools (LMS), open enrolment, and the school's ability to opt out of local authority control, which are causing most concern. Taken together, these proposals

Figure 17.1: The Assessment Target

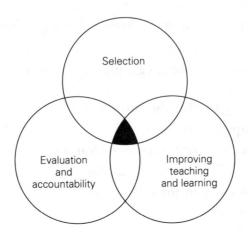

attempt to bring the pressure of 'market forces' and competition between schools. It has been suggested by some that this will encourage all schools to 'get better'. However, critics argue that market forces and competition between schools gives the controlling power to the consumer and is likely to create a relationship between parents and schools, not built upon cooperative partnership, but on buying and selling (NUT, 1990). The losers in this competition will be the pupils in the less well regarded schools as the human and material resources are reallocated to the 'successful' schools. The possibility of this leading to the creation of 'low achieving schools' which may be found in particularly disadvantaged socio-economic areas is a grim prospect.

It is also intriguing to speculate about how special schools will be 'compared'. Clearly the use of crude league tables is even more inappropriate. Perhaps the futility of this prospect will encourage those people, who feel that ordinary schools can be compared on the basis of test results only, to reconsider. They must surely realize that, whilst it is necessary for the community to know more about schools, the sorts of information required must cover a wide ranging set of effectiveness factors, or 'performance indicators'. League tables based on assessment results are insufficient.

There is little doubt that pupils with special educational needs (SEN) are unlikely to be valued customers in ordinary schools in such a climate. Not only are they expensive to provide for, but they are likely to distort the published results for the school, unless by some complex procedure of exceptions their results are excluded. Such arrangements will undermine the entitlement for *all* pupils to receive a broad, balanced and relevant curriculum. It is not possible to consider all the issues relating to 'disapplication' and 'exclusion' within this chapter but readers who are interested in this topic are advised to refer to Norwich (1989). Perhaps the most controversial aspect of the assessment proposals is the inclusion of pupils as young as 7 years old, an age at which, as Desforges (1989) points out, in many countries, children have only just started school. This aspect of the controversy was fuelled by the comments of Oliver Letwin, a member of the Hillgate Group, a right-wing pressure group, whose ideas underpin many of the proposals of the ERA. On a BBC *Panorama* programme about the National Curriculum, he suggested that testing 7-year-olds was a good idea because, for those who were struggling, the sooner they knew they were 'failures' the better!

A National Framework for Assessment

In order to provide a framework for the development of a national system of assessment and testing, the Government set up the Task Group on Assessment and Testing (TGAT), under the chairmanship of Professor Paul Black, to provide guidance for the subject working groups about assessment arrangements.

The TGAT was requested by the Secretary of State for Education, in a letter dated 30 October 1987, to develop a system of assessment which would be capable of serving a number of purposes. 'These include diagnostic or formative purposes ... summative purposes and purposes concerned with publicising and evaluating the work of the education service' (DES and Welsh Office, 1988, Appendix B, p. 2).

A sense of relief greeted the publication of the TGAT report. Not only was it a good read, it was free, politically astute and managed to please most people. In the face of considerable pressure from those who wanted to stress only the summative and evaluative functions of assessment, it proposed a system which was integrated with the curriculum, stressed the importance of teacher assessment, and suggested that practical tasks could replace traditional pencil and paper tests. The TGAT report was accepted by the Government and its proposals formed the basis of the national framework for assessment announced by the government in June 1988. These proposals have been incorporated within the terms of reference for each of the subject working groups. However, each of the subject groups is requested to offer advice in broad terms about assessment and testing in relation to the Attainment Targets which they recommend.

The national framework for assessment and testing calls for:

> Attainment Targets to be expressed in up to ten levels of achievement;
>
> a combination of teacher assessment (TA) and national externally set standard assessment tasks (SATs);
>
> the results of the SATs and TAs to be used formatively to help better teaching, and summatively to inform parents about their child's progress at the ages of 7, 11, 14 and 16;
>
> standards to be safeguarded by comparing teachers' assessments with the results of the standard assessment tasks and with the judgments of other teachers both internally and externally through a system of moderation.

The TGAT report stressed the importance of linking assessment to the curriculum, and if one examines the reports of the subject working groups which have been published at the time of writing, the influence of the TGAT proposals is profound. Indeed, a cynic might argue that it is not so much a National Curriculum, more a national system of assessment and testing.

It is interesting to note that the government decided to separate the national oversight of the curriculum from assessment, giving responsibility for the curriculum to the National Curriculum Council (NCC) and responsibility for the assessment arrangements to the Schools Examination and Assessment Council (SEAC). If the aim was to produce a national system of curriculum based assessment, why was it necessary to separate these two functions other than for reasons of power and control? The balance of power between these two bodies shifts in subtle and, to the outsider, inexplicable ways. Could it have anything to do with 'divide and rule', with the Department of Education and Science (DES) pulling the strings?

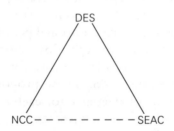

The TGAT Report managed to produce a creative compromise between the seemingly incompatible demands of formative, summative and evaluative purposes of assessment by concluding that assessment data can only be used for all these purposes if they are initially collected and used for formative purposes. However, Elliot (1989) suggests that it may in fact have done us a disservice by claiming that they are not incompatible after all. A number of other writers referred to earlier, particularly Nuttall (1989) and Goldstein (1989), would argue, as I have already mentioned, that different assessment purposes need different assessment techniques.

The TGAT report argued strongly against the use of norm referenced tests and age related comparisons on the grounds that they cannot show the progress of individuals. Instead they come down strongly in favour of criterion referenced assessment linked to statements of attainment within the National Curriculum. Elliot (1989) argues, however, that specifying statements of attainment is to standardize learning outcomes so that performances of individuals and groups can be publicly compared. Withers and Lee go even further in this argument and suggest that there is little difference between norm and criterion referenced assessment, except that the latter is more benign and acceptable. They argue that the criteria are in themselves norm referenced in that the criteria represent standards of achievement likely to be reached by children of different ages.

> That the criteria themselves are norm-referenced is apparent when one considers that our interest in this child not yet being able to read relates to the fact that she is seven years old and not seven months, for at seven months the criteria are not applicable. (1988, pp. 181–2)

This apparently hard line view does have a ring of truth about it when one looks at some of the recent publications from NCC and SEAC. For example, in *The National Curriculum: A Guide for Parents of Secondary Pupils* (NCC, 1990) the ten levels of achievement are shown as the floors of a building with progress depicted as a lift going up the outside in a glass cage. The levels (floors) are then related to what pupils will learn at various ages. This is another clear indication of achievement being linked to age related targets which are derived from 'norms'.

Further confusion has been caused by the decision to subordinate teacher assessment (TA) to standard assessment tasks (SATs). The TGAT report recommended that the eventual grading of each pupil would result from an equal contribution from TA and SATs. SEAC has now suggested that when the TA and the SAT differ, it will be the result of the SAT which takes precedence. This advice, which has been accepted by the Secretary of State for Education, has made the system even less acceptable in the eyes of many teachers because it stresses the importance of the summative and evaluative purposes at the expense of the more important formative functions of assessment. It also devalues the teachers' role in the process suggesting that the cumulative knowledge of several years is less reliable than information produced by a 'one-off' assessment task. Also adding to the confusion currently are the whispered stories about chaos from the schools in which the SATs are being piloted. It is difficult to know what the SATs will finally look like, since their development is shrouded in secrecy (NUT, 1990).

It would appear, then, that the summative and evaluative purposes of assessment, not only underpin the exercise of specifying Attainment Targets, but also the detailed arrangements for producing 'grades' for pupils. If this does indeed prove to be the case once the system is in operation, then the political pressure to impose a system of evaluation on the education system will have won the battle. Teachers might then, as they have been known to do in the past, subvert those aspects of the system which are not in the interests of pupils. Teachers are only likely to accept a national system of assessment which can be shown to improve the quality of teaching and learning. The battle is still to be fought.

Assessment and Special Educational Needs

There are two major elements involved in the assessment of pupils who are experiencing difficulties in learning. The first concerns decisions relating to placement. In other words, (who gets special education? In England and Wales these arrangements have been formalized within the statementing procedures of the 1981 Education Act. The second, and more relevant to this debate, concerns the monitoring of pupils' learning within the classroom setting together with an evaluation of classroom process.)

(The traditional view of assessment asked the question, 'What is wrong with the child? ... What are his/her strengths and weaknesses?' It stressed the need to know the child's intelligence and about any 'psycho-neurological dysfunction'. Where problems existed, they were assumed to exist 'within' the child.) A critique of these approaches can be found in Salvia and Ysseldyke (1985) or Ainscow (1988). More recent approaches ask the question 'What does this child need in order to optimize learning, growth and development?'. It adopts what is known as an 'ecological perspective' in that it is as interested in the learning context (that is, the curriculum, the teaching, the organization of the school and classroom) as it is in the learner. It takes a broader, multifaceted, naturalistic view of assessment in which the teacher plays the central role. The rationale for adopting such approaches is well described by Ainscow (1988). But how can these new approaches to assessment be reconciled with the recommendations of SEAC and the National Curriculum subject working groups? The glib answer might be, 'with difficulty'. However, I hope to be able to demonstrate that there are grounds for (unwarranted?) optimism. Sadly, the good news is not to be found in most of the documentation emanating from SEAC or the NCC, except at the level of simplistic platitudes or pious exhortations.

The TGAT report had little to say about the issues relating to the assessment of pupils with special educational needs other than recommending flexibility and the establishment of a separate special unit within SEAC to produce testing materials and assessment procedures sensitive enough to respond to the needs of these children (DES and Welsh Office, 1988, paras. 168–9). In a later publication, *A Guide to Teacher Assessment* (SEAC, undated) issues relating to special educational needs are again discussed in a short section. As Wedell points out, 'There is no indication of an awareness that the issues raised in this context form a continuity with problems in the evaluation of achievement in general' (1990, p. 3). There is not the space to go into detailed criticism of the publication within this chapter, but in conversations with teachers, I have heard regular complaints about the complex cross-referencing system and the outmoded references to diagnostic assessment leading to remedial help. There are useful sections, particularly within Chapter 2, but sadly special needs issues are dismissed in one paragraph next to a section on communication difficulties.

The SEAC booklets do not consider the difficulties and uncertainties relating to whether curriculum progression can be demonstrated by ten equal levels of achievement or indeed whether it is possible to structure learning in such a linear manner; what will happen when a pupil achieves Level 5 but can not do Level 2 of a particular Attainment Target?

There is, of course, no reference made to those pupils whose learning difficulties are so severe that they will spend years working on Level 1. McNab (1990), in an amusing and perceptive article, considers whether there is anything below Level 1; Level 0, for example? The SEAC booklets are unhelpful on this, and like NCC's *A Curriculum for All* (NCC, 1989), give no help in how progress between the achievement levels will be assessed and reported. The assessment section in *A Curriculum for All* (*ibid*) is particularly disappointing. It amounts to two sentences and a quote from *SEAC Recorder*, No. 2 (SEAC, 1989).

If the official documentation is not providing the necessary guidance, where should we turn? I believe we already have many of the answers. The issues relating to the assessment of pupils with learning difficulties have been high on the agenda of the special education community for quite a time. This is a view which is even endorsed by a government minister. In a recent speech, Alan Howarth, Under Secretary of State for Education and Science, pointed out,

> I have been struck by how advanced teachers in the SEN field are in the field of assessment. Perhaps I should not find that surprising, as assessment has always been an integral part of SEN work. I do not think that I go too far to say that teachers of children with SEN are in the forefront in the cycle of setting objectives, monitoring achievement, reconsidering approaches and so on. In that sense, teachers of pupils without special educational needs have much to learn from you. (1990, p. 50)

There is greater confidence about assessment within the special education field for a number of reasons. This confidence arises from development in a range of procedures and initiatives both in special and ordinary schools, including annual reviews, involving other adults (for example, non-teaching assistants) in the assessment process, support teaching, involving pupils in their own assessment through initiatives such as Records of Achievement, Certificate of Pre-vocational Education and profiling, daily monitoring, the graphical representation of progress, precision teaching and computer assisted data storage to improve record keeping. I could go on, but the point is made. Within the special education community we have the professional base upon which to build a system of assessment which will improve the quality of teaching and learning for *all* pupils.

Possible Future Developments

Some of the encouraging developments in assessment practice in both special and mainstream settings have been mentioned, but many of them share a common weakness. They are, with certain exceptions, concerned with the assessment *of* students, rather than assessment *with* students. The fundamental purpose of most approaches is concerned with assessing learners, either by looking for their difficulties, or by looking for progress on the curriculum. Whilst there is an important place for curriculum based assessment, particularly within the National Curriculum, there is a growing need, particularly in times of rapid change, to develop systems and approaches to assessment which use naturalistic enquiry and involve the students as active participants, whilst at the same time considering the classroom context and other ecological variables.

Such approaches could radically influence teaching and learning by providing teachers with evidence, not only about pupils and their progress, but also valuable information about a range of factors which influence the effectiveness of teaching. These factors include the curriculum, classroom management, the organization of resources and student/teacher interaction. I would argue that by empowering teachers in this way more radical reforms are more likely to occur than if assessment procedures are imposed from the outside.

However, I appreciate this will not be easy. If progress is to be made we need systems of assessment and recording that, according to Ainscow,

> recognize the complexity of classroom life;
>
> pay attention to intended *and* unintended outcomes;
>
> allow opportunities to reflect upon the process of learning *for teachers and students* [my words added in italics];
>
> take account of contextual factors; and
>
> respect the views of all participants. (Ainscow, 1988)

To this list I would add: 'are an integral part of the teaching and learning process'.

From this list it will be clear that the central role in this process can only be played by the teacher. For many years, teachers have tended to devalue the knowledge they were acquiring all the time about pupils' learning and development, because assessment 'experts' told them that their views were subjective and unreliable. In certain cases, this may have been true, but in the best classrooms, many of which were in special settings, the quality of the information was richer, more valid and certainly more useful than data generated by most formal techniques.

The task then is to provide a forum for professional debate within the profession about the purpose, nature and practicalities of assessment. Crucially, there then need to be opportunities to share and collaborate with colleagues on naturalistic forms of assessment. By working together in the same classroom, through shared observation, by comparing perspectives, the expertise can be developed. But it is almost impossible, in my opinion, to learn about this alone. Given the shortage of time currently available, these suggestions may seem rather impractical and idealistic. I believe the time can be found by looking at many of the arrangements which already exist in schools, such as co-teaching, support teaching and peer coaching in which teachers work together. It is, after all, a staff development issue and if it is to be done properly then time has to be found to enable it to happen. Through such a process, in which teachers reflect upon their own practice and see themselves as learners, real and not merely rhetorical change can occur.

The aim is to develop assessment procedures which do not happen to students, they involve students. It lets students into the secrets of assessment by encouraging them to review their own learning. It is a process which helps students to understand themselves as learners. Such approaches are applicable in all settings. I have seen it successfully used with young adults with SLD, with teachers on inservice courses and in preschool settings with children as young as 3 years old. It can make students less dependent on the teacher for feedback and has been shown to have a powerful motivating effect. Also, by enabling the pupils to share the responsibility for assessing and recording their own learning, the burden on the teacher may be reduced. The promising work which has resulted from the introduction on Records of Achievement (ROA) has much to offer in this direction (Broadfoot, 1986; Broadfoot *et al.*, 1989), although at the time of writing future funding for the project is uncertain. An interesting element in many of these recent initiatives in assessment, particularly with older students, has been the right of the assessed to negotiate aspects of the assessment with the assessor. James (1989) provides an interesting critique which links the part played by negotiation in student assessment, with teacher appraisal and naturalistic enquiry. It is a development not without its difficulties. There are unresolved, perhaps unresolvable, tensions arising from the imbalance of power between the assessor and the assessed. Can students' self assessments ever have parity with teacher assessments, or is one likely to be regarded as more important than the other? Perhaps there is an interesting parallel here between the relative status of teacher assessments and SATs in the National Curriculum. This imbalance of power in negotiated assessment may be even more obvious in special education settings for a number of reasons. Withers and Lee (1988) argue that this should not prevent negotiation from taking place, because it can open up the assessment process for scrutiny. The process may also enhance learning, because students find it easier to understand what is expected of them. They no longer have to guess the teacher's intention and it helps them to understand themselves as learners. These are powerful reasons for using such approaches.

The arguments in favour of moving towards such approaches are in my opinion overwhelming. They will enhance the professionalism of teachers in the assessment process, and go some way towards counteracting what could be bad news if those who seek to stress the evaluative functions of assessment get their way.

Conclusion

It is obvious that this is a time of great uncertainty and confusion in the assessment debate. The ERA, the National Curriculum and the associated assessment proposals have provided a focus for this debate. Whatever proposals eventually emerge from government about the relative balance of formative, summative and evaluative functions of assessment, we must not be allowed to be overwhelmed by systems designed to compare schools and which are only capable of saying that some of our students are still working at Level 1. It is essential to preserve and nurture those forms of assessment which will enhance our professionalism, improve the quality of teaching and learning, and celebrate the achievements of our students across the whole of their development.

The special education community has much to offer colleagues elsewhere. Join the debate, get involved, especially in staff development activities and moderation arrangements, you may have more to offer than you have to learn. In this way future developments can be influenced and when the current storm of uncertainty has settled, we may be able to look back and say, some good came out of it after all.

References

AINSCOW, M. (1988) 'Beyond the eyes of the monster: An analysis of recent trends in assessment and recording', *Support for Learning*, 3, 3.

BRIDGES, D. (1989) 'Pupil assessment from the perspective of naturalistic research', in SIMONS, H. and ELLIOT, J. (Eds) *Rethinking Appraisal and Assessment*, Milton Keynes, Open University Press.

BROADFOOT, P. (Ed.) (1986) *Profiles and Records of Achievement*, London, Holt, Rinehart and Winston.

BROADFOOT, P. *et al.* (1989) *Interim Report of the National Evaluation of Extension Work in Records of Achievement Schemes*, Bristol and Milton Keynes, PRAISE and Open University Press.

DES AND WELSH OFFICE (1988) *National Curriculum: Task Group on Assessment and Testing: A Report*, London, HMSO.

DESFORGES, C. (1989) *Testing and Assessment*, London, Cassell.

ELLIOT, J. (1989) 'Conclusion: Rethinking appraisal', in SIMONS, H. and ELLIOT, J. (Eds) *Rethinking Appraisal and Assessment*, Milton Keynes, Open University Press.

GLASER, R. (1963) 'Instructional technology and the measurement of learning outcomes: Some questions', *American Psychologist*, 18, pp. 518–21.

GOLDSTEIN, H. (1989) 'Psychometric test theory and educational assessment', in SIMONS, H. and ELLIOT, J. (Eds) *Rethinking Appraisal and Assessment*, Milton Keynes, Open University Press.

GOULD, S.J. (1981) *The Mismeasure of Man*, New York, W.W. Norton.

HARLEN, W. *et al.* (1977) *Schools Council Progress in Learning Science Project: Match and Mismatch*, Edinburgh, Oliver and Boyd.

HOWARTH, A. (1990) 'Long day's journey into light?', *British Journal of Special Education*, 17, 2.

JAMES, M. (1989) 'Negotiation and dialogue in student assessment and teacher appraisal', in SIMONS, H. and ELLIOT, J. (Eds) *Rethinking Appraisal and Assessment*, Milton Keynes, Open University Press.

MCNAB, I. (1990) 'Tangles and crossed wires', *British Journal of Special Education*, 17, 1.

MUNBY, S. (1989) *Assessing Recording Achievement*, Oxford, Basil Blackwell.

NCC (1989) *Curriculum Guidance Two: A Curriculum for All*, York, National Curriculum Council.

NCC (1990) *The National Curriculum: A Guide for Parents of Secondary Pupils*, York, National Curriculum Council.

NATIONAL UNION OF TEACHERS (NUT) (1990) *A Strategy for the Curriculum*, London, NUT.

NORWICH, B. (1989) 'How should we define exceptions?', *British Journal of Special Education*, 16, 3.

NUTTALL, D. (1989) 'National assessment: Will reality match aspirations?', *Education Section, Review 13*, British Psychological Society.

POPHAM, W.J. (1981) *Modern Educational Measurement*, Englewood Cliffs, Prentice Hall.

REASON, R. (1989) 'Evidence of progress?', *British Journal of Special Education*, 16, 4.

SALVIA, J. and YSSELDYKE, J. (1985) *Assessment in Remedial and Special Education*, 3rd edition, Boston, Houghton Mifflin.

SCHOOLS EXAMINATION AND ASSESSMENT COUNCIL (SEAC) (1989) *SEAC Recorder*, 2, London, SEAC.

SCHOOLS EXAMINATION AND ASSESSMENT COUNCIL (SEAC) (undated) *A Guide to Teacher Assessment*, London, Heinemann for SEAC.

TUCKER, J.A. (Ed.) (1985) 'Curriculum based assessment' *Exceptional Children*, 52, 3 (special issue).

WEDELL, K. (1990) 'SEAC's guidance on teacher assessment', *British Journal of Special Education*, 17, 1.

WITHERS, R. and LEE, J. (1988) 'Power in disguise', in BARTON, L. (Ed.) *The Politics of Special Educational Needs*, London, Falmer Press.

WOOD, R. (1986) 'The agenda for educational measurement', in NUTTALL, D. (Ed.) *Assessing Educational Achievement*, London, Falmer Press.

The Future in the Light of the Challenge

18   Training for Change: School-based INSET

Anita Gadsby

Why School-based INSET?

During the eleven years that I have been Head of my present school, a major part of my role has been concerned with the professional development of staff — enabling the school to develop and grow in response to constant changes. Encouraging teachers to continue to learn new skills and to adapt to new circumstances, in a period of unprecedented change for special education, has been a challenging but rewarding experience. Why school focused inservice training (INSET)? If we continually seek to improve the quality of teaching and learning, school-based INSET is a way of achieving this upgrading (Casteel, 1984).

Planning for Change

Schools with good leadership are ready for the implementation of the National Curriculum because they see it as part of the challenge of new opportunities for their pupils and are open minded about the outcomes. They are able to adjust their own teaching style and goals to meet new demands and to plan positive ways forward. They are not daunted by having only part of the picture, some of the answers at any one time; they are prepared to search for alternatives and to collaborate to make things work.

A Healthy Organization — Organized for Change?

According to Balshaw (1989), change in education is most likely to be effective if:

it meets the perceived needs of those who will have to implement it;

there is support from senior personnel;

it is based on realistic goals which have been set by the participants;

there are effective procedures for evaluating the development of the project;

inservice training opportunities are provided which relate to the concerns of the participants;

opportunities are provided for participants to support one another.

INSET for special educators of pupils with severe learning difficulties (SLD) has to address complex issues. Developing realistic goals and effective procedures for a group with such complex and multiple learning difficulties is not easy. The development of present curriculum models for this field of special education has been in response to a variety of influences. Parental expectations, early diagnosis and intervention, research into learning difficulties, social trends towards normalization, emphasis on integrated learning and independence, the need for preparation for life skills, the presence of a growing population of multiply handicapped pupils in special schools, have all played a part in influencing current thinking and determining needs, often in a dynamic and innovative fashion but sometimes in an uneven, disjointed way. The introduction of a National Curriculum has focused attention on the need to deliver a curriculum model which addresses the entitlement of all pupils, whatever their degree of disability, in a systematically planned way and does away with a narrow, exclusive curriculum model.

The crucial factor in having 'innovation' adopted is not merely the attractive nature of that innovation but is first and foremost about people who accept and use it and are in a frame of mind to do so, whatever the difficulties (Hewett, 1989). Hewett refers to this 'culture of development'; reflecting teachers who are able to be openly self-reflective about their teaching. Because of the far reaching implications of the National Curriculum on the provision of education for pupils with SLD it is essential that each institution is in a healthy state to meet the new demands. A healthy state implies an organization with clear curricular policies, understood and supported by all staff, parents, governors, and support services, together with strategies that enable all pupils to take full advantage of the curriculum. It suggests the need for teams of multi-professional staff ready and able to work effectively together to deliver the curriculum in a wide variety of settings. It demands a whole school approach to development. It implies time and training to implement the many necessary changes. How are schools to effect this level of readiness for change, when time is the one element not negotiable?

INSET for the National Curriculum involves the reappraisal of systems within the school, special and ordinary. The task may be more complex for those mainstream schools providing a full-time curriculum for pupils with SLD. The processes, however, can be seen to be similar. It requires a state of readiness on the part of the school to be able to carry out the necessary evaluation of present systems.

Leadership

HMI clearly identified in *Ten Good Schools* (DES, 1977) that a common element in such schools is effective leadership and a climate conducive to growth, where emphasis is laid on consultation, team work and participation. Effective professional management requires organized staff collaboration (LEAP, 1989). The implementation of the National Curriculum demands a style of leadership concerned as much with the interactive learning of individuals and groups of staff, teaching and non-teaching, as with the pupils. It is no longer possible for curricular decisions to rest with one or two individuals, since the implications for delivering the National Curriculum affect the whole institution. Similarly, a democratic style of leadership requires members of the senior management team, other than the Head, to develop skills for motivating people. Management training when based in school enables whole teams to learn to take equal responsibility for the healthy growth of the institution.

A recent report from the School Management Task Force to the DES contains proposals to improve management training in schools. It suggests that all teachers need management training and should get it, and that training should move away from off-site to a school-based approach using on-the-job experience and the support of colleagues ... school management requires a team approach (Lodge, 1990).

Training for Delegation

There are a number of reasons why some Heads are reluctant to delegate. The skills required in participative management are far more demanding and require more resourcefulness than does a more conventional autocratic style. Although the risks may be greater the rewards are in a feeling of shared responsibility for successes and failures (Warwick, 1983).

In any school there may be the need from time to time for short term curriculum development work to be undertaken by different teams. Training is required in order that staff are able to work within a variety of cooperative groups. A number of LEAs are providing training for senior management in schools and colleges by 'buying in' training packages which focus on training for whole school development. The Coverdale Consultancy in Interactive Teamwork (Coverdale Management Training, 1989), LEAP Management in Education (LEAP, 1989) and the Special Needs Action Programme (SNAP) (Ainscow and Muncey, 1983) are some notable examples.

Effective Teamwork Training

Devolvement of good practice is dependent upon a networking system of support for senior staff wishing to encourage a more collaborative style of leadership. Whole school training days provide opportunities for exploring the range of personal skills available both within and between institutions. A healthy institution has within it a variety of teams of people who are able to collaborate effectively to plan and carry out tasks in a given period of time with results that are satisfactory to all team members and which move the organization forward. All members of a staff team will need to learn teamwork skills in order that there can be greater collaboration on the implementation of the National Curriculum, through shared responsibility.

Effective teams must taken account not only of the tasks to be done but also the strengths of individuals within the team. This requires sensitivity to and familiarity with the ways in which others in the school work. Training time spent on team building activities needs to focus on the processes of working together. At this time of major changes, the skills of effective listening, observation, honesty and flexibility, using each other's strengths and knowledge for tasks to be done, using time efficiently and delegation have never been more crucial to the successful growth of schools. In addition, attention to the task process, defining the job to be done, gathering information and looking at success critieria for the best outcomes are some of the skills necessary for managing changes in whole institutions. The successful management of personal and group time is vital so that tasks are completed, decisions are implemented and progress is reviewed. Short term 'action research' teams are one way of reviewing curriculum developments.

Good Communication

Training time spent on the building of communication skills and evaluation of systems for good communication within the school can be most effective in enabling staff to own new developments. It is important to identify the ways by which consultation and decision making happen within a school. The processes of information sharing are complex and need to be understood and owned by all. Exercises in improving listening skills are an important element of training for effective teamwork; active listening, not the passive, half-hearted sort of thing that people do when they are waiting for a gap in the verbal traffic so they can edge their way into it, is what helps communication most (Coverdale Management Training, 1989).

Entitlement

The National Curriculum requires schools to give access and entitlement to all pupils. The requirement to offer all National Curriculum subjects presents a direct challenge to special educators planning for the needs of the most profoundly handicapped. Many schools have already disbanded their 'special care units' and have amalgamated such groups of youngsters with the more able. Experience shows that these pupils benefit and perform at unexpected levels when exposed to more stimulating opportunities. The National Curriculum needs to be approached in this same spirit of expectation that there will be some benefits for all pupils rather than the assumption that it will not be relevant to some groups. Providing breadth and balance in the curriculum needs careful consideration. A number of schools are becoming involved in planning through regional working groups. The North West Regional Group has over thirty LEAs represented; the West Midlands group has a similar role. Cluster groups of schools are studying aspects of the curriculum for pupils with SLD in relation to the National Curriculum. Work at each school base supports and reports to the regional groups which are in turn supported by HMI. In this way a national evaluation of the implementation of the National Curriculum for pupils with SLD is developing. This is an excellent way for school teachers to have access and to contribute to developments in the wider national field of special education.

Awareness Raising Training

Special educators need to be aware of both the requirements of the law to teach the National Curriculum, and the timescale for implementation. There was initially much debate in schools about whether the National Curriculum would be relevant to the needs of pupils with SLD. Schools undertook two additional training days in 1989–90 for raising teachers' awareness of the National Curriculum. There is a fear of the vast new language of the National Curriculum; training needs to identify what the National Curriculum terminology means, to enable a common language to be developed within the school. The new terminology has to be clearly understood by all teachers, governors, and parents. In some schools parent governors have joined in staff training for the National Curriculum in order to develop knowledge and understanding of the tasks schools face.

The training pack developed for the National Curriculum INSET Activities by the National Curriculum Council (NCC, 1989), has helped schools to identify what was already known, and what was not clear. Activities that enable teachers to voice anxieties about the National Curriculum, when led by a tutor with knowledge of the problems with which all teachers are struggling, can help to focus on the skills and strengths within the institution. This initial awareness raising training provided opportunities for teachers to look at such issues as cross-curricular planning, recording and transfer between primary and secondary phases and to set some realistic timescales for school development and implementation.

Integrated Education

In the past, special schools traditionally expected each teacher to have the expertise to teach all subjects to a small group of pupils. The introduction of the National Curriculum has focused attention on new ways of delivering a broader range of subjects through developing contacts with other schools. INSET which crosses school barriers and involves teachers in training with mainstream as well as other special schools is valuable in removing barriers to change. Cooperation and collaboration in curriculum delivery need to be positively promoted. Hegarty (1987) and Hodgson, Clunies-Ross and Hegarty (1984) highlight how school-based courses between special and mainstream schools have grown out of staff discussions on needs for development. Mainstream schools face many challenges in providing for the curricular needs of pupils with SLD. Most special schools have broadened the curriculum in recent years to encompass the needs of youngsters developing autonomy and the need for an independent life style. A shared responsibility for pupils' learning may be difficult to implement, yet integrated education requires a change of perspective and thinking about collaborative approaches.

Curriculum Audit and Evaluation

Ownership of the curriculum rests with the whole school staff. INSET, therefore, must involve the whole school in an evaluation of the present curriculum, its delivery, the school's resources, current assessment procedures, record keeping and styles of teaching. This is an excellent piece of INSET work for the school since whole teams must collaborate to come to agreement on what is currently provided. Day, Johnston, and Whitaker (1985) remind us that the underlying assumptions for school evaluation are that:

> better understanding of the organization and policies ... could improve the opportunities and experiences provided in classrooms;
>
> systematic study and review allows the school to determine, and to produce evidence of, the extent to which they are providing the quality of education they espouse;
>
> a study of school policies can help teachers identify policy effects which require attention at school, department or classroom level;
>
> many policy issues cut across classrooms and require collective review and resolution;
>
> there are many learning experiences, (field work and extra-curricular activities, for instance), which do not take place in the classroom and which require the cooperation and appraisal of the whole school;
>
> participation in a school self-study gives teachers the opportunity to develop their professional decision-making skills, enlarge

their perspectives, and become better informed about the roles, responsibilities and problems of their colleagues.

School evaluation needs to take account of such issues as:

Curriculum details
Schools will need to look at the degree of breadth and balance in present curriculum for each age group through:

>assessment of the time spent on each subject;
>assessment of time spent on other activities such as therapy and travel to get access to subjects or activities and subjects not covered;
>cross referencing the National Curriculum with the present curriculum.

Subject headings
There is a danger in assuming that the National Curriculum introduces totally new ideas and working practices for SLD schools. Whilst schools are rightly concerned to preserve all the positive aspects of the present curriculum, the reality is that much of what is established good practice in such schools is enshrined in National Curriculum documents. The core curriculum subjects can be seen to encompass many of the learning activities already provided — perhaps under another name. Thus aspects of a 'sensory-motor' programme and 'cognitive development' become part of the Maths, English and Science curricula and can be identified through Programmes of Study. The National Curriculum provides the opportunity to sharpen and clarify what is now taught, and to avoid inappropriate activity for some children. Teachers need to be encouraged to look to assimilate present good practice within the guidelines of Programmes of Study. On examination many include exactly the kind of activities in which special schools are engaged. A whole school approach to terminology is vital for accurate recording and relaying of information to others.

Modular planning
Mainstream schools offer the opportunity to special schools to take part in the curriculum through modular courses, which give short-term opportunities for pupils to experience and learn. This is one way of ensuring broad and balanced content whilst allowing for the pace of individuals, who may repeat a modular course as necessary.

Existing schemes of work

How uniform are they throughout the school? How does whole year planning relate to them and are whole school approaches used for some schemes? Primary colleagues may have valuable experiences to share with special schools in the development of cross-curriculum themes.

Organization

Within the school, the grouping of pupils and the likely need for changes to enable the National Curriculum to be accessible to all and for the changing populations of special schools must be addressed.

Accommodation and resources

There may be a need to make changes both in the use of school-based physical resources and accommodation in other schools. The audit will show the quality, availability and effectiveness of existing resources for delivery of a broad based curriculum to all pupils.

Staffing

Traditionally staff in special education have been expected to have skills in all subject areas, across whole age ranges. Clearly schools will have areas of expertise and discrepancies in curriculum cover. There may be a lack of subject knowledge in special schools — training alongside mainstream colleagues can help in the introduction of the National Curriculum. Deployment of staff for such a changing organization will be an important issue for each special school to consider. An opportunity exists, however, because of the expertise gained in all-age schools, to show how the learning in children's early years supports later curriculum developments, since special school teachers are very familiar with working across phases within their own organizations.

Roles and responsibilities of staff

The role of the Curriculum Development Coordinator (CDC) is as crucial to the overall development of the school as is that of the Staff Development Coordinator (SDC). (These roles may be combined and/or given other titles elsewhere). Schools need to consider such responsibilities in the allocation of additional allowances. Where such duties are held by teachers other than the Head there is a greater feeling of ownership of the curriculum and the development of the school, by the whole staff. Training for these roles is being provided centrally by some LEAs, enabling further sharing of ideas with mainstream colleagues. Many schools are establishing a model whereby every teacher has a responsibility for overall supervision and development of a particular curriculum area, although s/he may not have the sole teaching input into that subject. In this way, smaller schools can share the load equally amongst staff and develop agreement on the optimum use of staff time. Teachers with a curriculum responsibility can play a crucial role in disseminating information to colleagues, support staff, governors and parents. As INSET is required for a particular subject area the teacher responsible may convene a working party, for example, to produce or amend the school's policy document. The draft can be endorsed and implemented by the whole staff with monitoring by the subject and curriculum coordinators. The CDC may be given responsibility for gathering together information for the curriculum audit.

Specialization
Special schools have established a strong tradition for training in independence and life skills — with support, some of these skills could be handed back to parents. The special school needs to accept the limits of its roles — it is no longer possible to provide a diet of everything every week. Good home-school liaison ensures that parents are well informed, supported, and guided towards other professionals for help which the school cannot give.

Quality of teaching and learning
Styles of teaching will need to be reviewed since different approaches will be necessary in different situations. Pupils learning in a variety of situations need to be aware of the social behaviours that are the norm. Collaboration between special and mainstream teachers can ensure a more uniform style of management of pupils. Many mainstream colleagues coming into contact with pupils with SLD for the first time are unsure of teaching approaches. Special schools need to involve others in training to develop new ways of negotiation.

Timetabling
There is evidence of some confusion between 'the timetable' and 'the curriculum' in special schools. The National Curriculum demands clear recording of what is taught in subjects, levels of Key Stages, ATs and periods of time spent on each subject. Timetabling methodology needs to be part of whole school training in order that these issues, together with the use of accommodation and resources

(including staff) can be shown. Timetabling must take account of the possible options for curriculum delivery and the best use of resources to obtain the required model. Planning which takes account of mainstream timetabling for curriculum access is particularly complex and may require the model more familiar to such schools — that of a whole year plan. All-age special schools may find this exercise particularly taxing since there needs to be continuity and progression shown throughout the school.

Time

Amounts of time spent on subjects across the school as well as class by class, with the tradition of offering open-ended time to some curricular activities, on the premise that pupils with SLD need more time to learn, have to be examined in the light of requirements for more breadth and balance in the National Curriculum. Teaching time needs a whole school rationale for the allocation of time. There may be differences between theory and practice in the amount of time pupils are taught — what is reasonable teaching time for special needs? Should there be the same variations as for mainstream pupils? How are schools to organize this within the constraints of travel arrangements? There need to be whole school discussions and agreement on the appropriateness of half day events taking place on a weekly basis — still a common feature in many special schools. The time involved in travel for such activities must be set against the actual teaching time, the wider outside experiences of some pupils, together with other options (such as encouraging groups of parents to enable their children's access on a regular basis to such activities out of school time, thus concentrating the school's energies on those most in need of such a weekly programme). The length of the school day may need to be considered in the light of parity with mainstream schools and the needs of different age groups.

Time management

Teachers can feel stressed by the pace of new initiatives and the lack of sufficient time to read, absorb and implement. Sharing the load through effective team work is one way of relieving the pressures. Meetings which are planned so that time management has a priority equal to the agenda, will usually allow for decisions to be made and action taken. Individual members of the team may be encouraged to address their own agenda items, presented in a coherent way with positive proposals for implementation. In this way, teams do their own work and consensus is more easily reached. Time management is particularly difficult for small schools, with few teachers. Joining in training activities with teams in other schools can help to speed up the processes of policy decision making. Schools may choose to use some Local Education Authority Training Grants (LEATGs) funding to enable teachers from a group of special schools to meet together. Activities, such as the preparation of draft statements and schemes of work on particular curriculum subjects which are then taken back to their respective schools for shaping and implementation, are becoming a feature of staff development in special education.

Assessment, recording and reporting arrangements
These have been areas of particular strength in special education and many schools are well placed to adapt existing systems to the requirements of the National Curriculum. There are strategies for ongoing assessment, task analysis and reporting to parents which can be shared with mainstream colleagues. Schools will need to address the issues of monitoring and assessment of cross-curricular approaches — where is the individual child in that? How is it possible to prioritize objectives for individual children within a topic? Ainsworth (1989) argues that the development of whole school approaches to assessment leads not only to a better understanding that each individual is worthy of equal opportunity within the school community, but also that through involving the individual pupil in the continuous appraisal of his/her performance more positive attitudes can be developed on the part of pupil and teacher alike.

Location of resources
Special schools cannot provide for the total resource needs of the National Curriculum without access to the wider community. Development of the strong tradition of using the community and other schools to access learning will enable delivery of the National Curriculum in a broad and balanced way. It will be essential for the school to have close contact with mainstream colleagues during this process of evaluation because of the implications for a devolved curriculum and integrated provision. The Technical and Vocational Education Initiative (TVEI) is one initiative which is enabling such planning to take place. The nature of the introduction of the National Curriculum will determine the pace of such an exercise since it seems inevitable that continual evaluation and assimilation will be necessary for several years as new subjects are introduced. 'Where' the curriculum is accessible will become an increasingly important consideration for SLD schools. Training needs to take account of what is required by the

National Curriculum and TVEI and what is available in the locality of the school. (Increasingly special schools are using Science lab time, drama studios and IT facilities in secondary schools, whilst sharing cross-curricular topics with primary schools, for example). Valuable lessons can be learnt from mainstream schools engaged in similar processes. Colleagues involved in TVEI can glean valuable help from cluster schools when planning such new initiatives. Headteachers need to promote a positive view of the benefits that pupils can gain from the National Curriculum and a supportive attitude towards colleagues who are anxious about the timescale of changes.

Conclusion

The loss of initial training for special education together with the introduction of new legislation has led to the need for a major change in delivery of professional development through school-based activity. Staff in special education must learn to give away their knowledge and skills, be prepared to engage in consultancy, demystifying expertise, exercising evaluation systematically and working in a more open collaborative way (Hegarty, 1987). In assessing the value of training, it is important to have some means of measuring outcomes — whether performance on the job actually improves (Everard, 1986). Increased awareness at all levels of the positive benefits to be gained in working cooperatively and planning efficiently must lead to improved opportunities for children to gain the best advantage from their learning. Finally, the best organizations know that people count, everyone's cooperation is necessary (excellent companies require and demand extraordinary performance from every employee) and seek to support that. Excellent *schools* are no different.

References

AINSCOW, M. and MUNCEY, J. (1983) 'Launching SNAP in Coventry', *Special Education: Forward Trends*, 10, 3, pp. 8–12.

AINSWORTH, B. (1989) 'How to help the ship along: An evaluation of effective support teaching', in AINSCOW, M. (Ed.), *Special Education in Change*, London, David Fulton Publisher with the Cambridge Institute of Education.

BALSHAW, M. (1989) 'Special schools and ordinary schools: It's not what you do, it's the way that you do it', in BAKER, D. and BOVAIR, K. (Eds) *Making the Special Schools Ordinary?*, Volume 1, London, Falmer Press.

CASTEEL, V. (1984) 'Special needs and school-focused in-service education', in BOWERS, T. (Ed.) *Management and the Special School*, Beckenham, Croom Helm.

COVERDALE MANAGEMENT TRAINING (1989) *Coverdale Review*, Coverdale Management Training, Regent St, London.

DAY, C., JOHNSTON, D. and WHITAKER, P. (1985) *Managing Primary Schools: A Professional Development Approach*, London, Harper and Row.

DES (1977) *Ten Good Schools: A Secondary School Enquiry*, HMI Matters for Discussion Series, No. 1, London, HMSO.

EVERARD, K.B. (1986) *Developing Managemet in Schools*, Oxford, Basil Blackwell.

HEGARTY, S. (1987) *Meeting Special Needs in Ordinary Schools: An Overview*, London, Cassell.

HEWETT, D. (1989) 'The most severe learning difficulties: Does your curriculum go back far enough?', in AINSCOW, M. (Ed.) *Special Education in Change*, London, David Fulton Publishers with the Cambridge Institute of Education.

HODGSON, A., CLUNIES-ROSS, L. and HEGARTY, S. (1984) *Learning Together: Teaching Pupils with Special Educational Needs in the Ordinary Schools*, Windsor, NFER-Nelson.

LEAP (1989) *Local Education Authorities Project Management in Education INSET Initiative*, Milton Keynes, BBC.

LODGE, B. (1990) 'Talent spot future heads, LEAs told', *Times Educational Supplement*, 16 March, p. 3.

NCC (1989) *An Introduction to the National Curriculum* (INSET Training Pack), York, National Curriculum Council.

WARWICK, D. (1983) *Decision Making*, Education for Industrial Society, London.

19   Teacher Education: The Changing Focus

Christina Tilstone

Introduction

The impact on schools and other educational establishments of the 1988 Education Reform Act (ERA) has been traumatic and far-reaching. The effects have, however, not been wholly negative and the introduction of one part of the Act, the National Curriculum, has resulted in a welcome evaluation of current practices by schools and teacher education establishments or, to use the current jargon, they have been made 'to undertake a curriculum audit'.

It is evident that such a wide ranging and penetrating analysis of the curriculum has shown that not all the activities in schools before 1988 were bad. Much that has been built on a sound understanding of a range of theories and on self-critical classroom experience needs to be retained. There is, however, a danger that the National Curriculum with its emphasis on regular testing and assessment may encourage teachers to place a greater emphasis on those parts of the curriculum that can be most easily tested and to neglect the effective domain.

Historical Perspectives

The Act had been preceded, in the 1980s, by criticism at all levels of current standards. Special Education suffered particularly from these comments and it is therefore useful to consider the development of specialized courses for teachers of pupils with severe learning difficulties (SLD).

The 1944 Education Act made Local Education Authorities responsible for the education of 'handicapped' children. An estimated 10 per cent of such children were, however, considered 'ineducable' and became the responsibility of the Local Health Authorities. The most 'able' of this 10 per cent were 'cared for' in Occupation Centres, later to be called Junior Training Centres; the remainder were placed in institutions for the subnormal or remained in their own homes and lacked any public provision or resources. The medical profession was solely responsible for educational decisions about such children, who were classified as 'mentally handicapped' or 'mentally defective'.

The first Occupation Centres were opened by philanthropists, and were voluntarily funded. By 1959 there were 435 run by Local Health Authorities, and only twenty were the responsibility of voluntary bodies (Pritchard, 1972, p. 82). The staff of these centres lacked any form of recognized training but were usually caring, committed and well motivated.

A voluntary organization, The National Association for Mental Health (now, MIND) acknowledged the need for staff training, and set up one year courses. Standards improved and although these courses now appear to have been very basic, compared with our present BEds, much of the development and the practice had an intellectual stringency leading to a child-centred approach to teaching, influenced by the seminal ideas of Rousseau (1712–1778), Seguin (1812–1880) and Montessori (1870–1952).

The 1959 Mental Health Act was progressive and the changes that followed are reflected in the substitution of the term Training Centres for the previously named Occupation Centres. Unfortunately, the assumption still prevailed that as the children concerned were believed to have low mental levels, it followed that they were also emotionally and socially retarded. Consequently, the staff of the centres tended to adopt a nursery/infant school curriculum regardless of the age of the pupils. The image of the 'subnormal' (the term used by the 1959 Mental Health Act) was of a perennial 'Peter Pan' with fixed and rigid limitations on the knowledge and skills that he or she could acquire.

Gunzburg, a psychologist working at Monyhull Hospital in Birmingham, did much to challenge this notion. His ideas were influential and, as subsequent research began to indicate the real potential of these children (Clarke and Clarke, 1958; O'Connor and Hermelin, 1958; Luria and Vinogradova, 1959; Luria, 1961), the need to provide better training for the staff of the Junior Training Centres was recognized. In 1964 a new body, the Training Council for Teachers of the Mentally Handicapped, coordinated training, and the duration of the training courses was increased from one to two years. From this point a new professional began to emerge with a comprehensive knowledge of normal child development, assessment and behavioural psychology. Mildred Stevens, an innovative practitioner in the 1960s and 1970s, and the organizer of the Manchester Training Course, emphasized that good teaching was based on rigorous observation, systematic assessment, thorough analysis and sound technique. In her books *The Educational Needs of Severely Subnormal Children* (1971) and *Observe Then Teach* (1978) she stressed the importance of a creative curriculum, a structured approach to individual programming, and the value of parental support. Her influence is still evident in many teacher education courses today.

Such pioneers made it obvious that 'mentally handicapped' children were capable of benefiting from a rich and varied education, and that with early help they could achieve much more than had previously been thought possible. The 1970 Education (Handicapped Children) Act brought 'handicapped children' into the education system; Junior Training Centres became Special Schools; and the 24,000 children involved became entitled to 'Special Education' (Heddell, 1980).

Thus the 1970s can be seen as a turning point in the development of education services, with the recognition that the handicapped had the same rights to education and to the services of professionally trained teachers as any other members of society.

A pragmatic response to this belief was the establishment of 'Mental Handicap' as the main subject on a number of initial teacher training courses. New BEd courses were then developed, the theoretical base of which included a philosophical and conceptual approach to the curriculum for all pupils.

Such courses were able to recruit students with wide experience and who were firmly committed and well motivated. The high quality of entrants was recognized by the Warnock Committee and the courses were seen as 'a means of attracting candidates of good intellectual and professional ability to work with severely handicapped children' (DES, 1978, p. 232). The Committee did, however, express some concern at the narrowness of this specialized initial training and recommended careful monitoring by HMI. In addition, it emphasized the need for specialist inservice courses of one year full time, or the equivalent.

In 1984 the Advisory Committee for the Supply and Education of Teachers (ACSET) recommended that initial teacher training courses designed to develop the skills necessary for teaching pupils with SLD should close. Such courses, it was proposed, should only be offered as inservice training for those teachers who had experience with pupils with SLD. Unfortunately, no additional funding was allocated and the consequences of these decisions, apparently taken without consultation, have been more serious than the envisaged shortage of newly trained teachers of pupils with SLD. Colleges have found that the inevitable result of the rundown of their specialized initial training courses has been the break up of teams of experienced teacher educators. The knock-on effect has been the closure of those specialist inservice courses which policy makers had assumed would ensure the continuation of a regular supply of teachers of pupils with SLD. To date, no clear solutions to the problem have been suggested.

The particular difficulties of teachers struggling to keep up the standards with diminishing resources have not been eased by the range of official, and often dramatic, statements that the teaching profession has for far too long accepted low standards and that an unacceptably high proportion of pupils underachieve. Low morale and inadequate salaries have resulted in an unacceptably high proportion of teachers abandoning the profession for more economically rewarding and satisfying jobs.

Into this climate of uncertainty, it was considered necessary to introduce the ERA as a panacea for all ills. The ERA, although welcome in many ways, did not address the vital issues of teacher shortages or diminishing resources. At a time of change, and of new opportunities, teacher education had to face additional problems. The movement from public sector funding and the pressures to amalgamate with other institutions while moving to a greater diversification of courses added to the chaos.

What Is Teacher Education?

Teacher education, however it is organized and funded, will always be concerned with the professional development of teachers from the moment they enter initial training courses to the time of their retirement. The James Report (DES, 1972), twenty years ago, argued for the continuing education of teachers, and proposed that teacher education should be divided into three sections or cycles: the preliminary education of the student; preservice training and induction; and inservice education and training.

The committee made two vitally important proposals: that the teaching profession should share in the training of its own members and in defining standards; and that teachers should receive a period of secondment for inservice study which would be a right rather than a privilege.

Collaboration

Recommendations of this nature for the professional development of teachers require a collaborative approach between schools, colleges, and LEAs. Collaboration has acquired many meanings in many contexts but is used here to mean working constructively together for the development of pupils' learning. Despite pressure over the years for colleges and schools to form close links, HMI was still looking for a collaborative approach in the 1980s (DES, 1983a; 1983b; 1984; 1985 and 1989). Such collaboration demands a change of attitude from all concerned. Perry, when she was Chief Inspector for Teacher Education, wrote:

> Too many teachers feel that the training system is none of their business, and of little interest to them. I have equally sometimes been taken aback by the way in which training institutions have described their contact with schools in terms which imply that they see the schools as objects of their research or temporary practice grounds for their students, rather than as equal partners in the process of professional development. (Perry, 1983)

The reasons for this lack of collaboration are complex, but some of the responsibility lies in the 'charismatic education' offered by training institutions before and during the 1960s. Training was achieved by a process of socialization: 'a master/apprenticeship relationship between student and tutor' (Bell, 1981). This approach excluded close relationships with schools and resulted in the tutors' lack of credibility with professional colleagues. Even today, the teaching profession tends to regard tutors as failed teachers who have escaped from the rigours of the classroom in order to carry out personal research on obscure elements of classroom practice. Although it was recognized that between 1920 and the late 1940s training colleges 'offered a narrow experience to students through unenterprising lecturers with limited classroom experience' (Gosden, 1989), it can be argued that tutors are selected today for their knowledge of their main subject and their practical excellence. The Council for Accreditation of Teacher Education (CATE) insists that it is the responsibility of colleges to ensure that a rolling programme of staff development in schools is developed as a prerequisite for course approval.

Some headway has been made, however, on the breaking down of barriers between schools and colleges through such projects as IT-INSET (Ashton *et al.*, 1983). IT-INSET links the initial training of students to the inservice education of teachers and fosters closer relationships between the two. The work is school-based and school-focused and provides a collaborative approach to curriculum development and review.

Teacher education for the National Curriculum should be a collaborative exercise which encourages the schools' own inservice initiatives supported by the resources and expertise of the LEAs and the colleges. Such a process requires a planned programme of professional development progressing from:

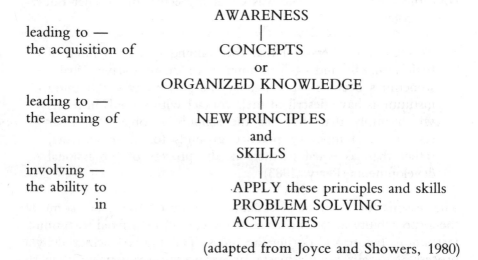

	AWARENESS
leading to —	|
the acquisition of	CONCEPTS
	or
	ORGANIZED KNOWLEDGE
leading to —	|
the learning of	NEW PRINCIPLES
	and
	SKILLS
involving —	|
the ability to	APPLY these principles and skills
in	PROBLEM SOLVING
	ACTIVITIES

(adapted from Joyce and Showers, 1980)

To date, collaboration on National Curriculum education for teachers of pupils with SLD between LEAs, schools and colleges has been fragmented and arbitrary. Occasionally colleges and LEAs have provided joint short courses for teachers at an 'awareness' level, or the college has provided the venue for the LEAs' own initiatives.

LEA Training and Support

LEA training and support for the National Curriculum implementation has, in the main, been inadequate. Usually it has involved mainstream staff in a healthy and lively exchange of ideas, but with little thought given to the needs of pupils with SLD. Such a situation is not entirely the fault of the LEAs for the original National Curriculum documents made no mention of such pupils. Regrettably there was an unwritten assumption that many pupils, particularly those with profound and multiple learning difficulties (PMLD) would be exempt from the National Curriculum. This interpretation has led LEAs to assume that if all teachers were encouraged to focus on the needs of mainstream pupils the teachers responsible for pupils with SLD would, 'by osmosis', be able to suggest their own meaningful solutions. In an unpublished survey of INSET provision for the National Curriculum in West Midlands Special Schools (Wiltshire, 1990) it was found that the Local Authority INSET was available only to senior mainstream staff. The participants were subsequently expected to use the cascade model of dissemination of information in their own schools. Unfortunately, as much of the INSET available was not relevant and was later diluted through the communication difficulties of this model, the majority of class teachers appear to have gained very little from the original 'pearls of wisdom' exercise.

School-based INSET

Anita Gadsby (see Chapter 18 in this volume) stresses the importance of school-based, school focused INSET in the implementation of the National Curriculum for pupils with SLD. It is not the intention of the present writer to duplicate issues raised elsewhere, other than to stress that teachers, and others, must be given time and opportunities to cope adequately with the suggested changes. Unfortunately, much of the National Curriculum is prescriptive and has consequently proved to be in opposition to accepted normative re-educative strategies for change.

Such strategies must entail full professional involvement, shared commitment and ownership of the suggested changes. We all, instinctively, reject change over which we have no control and good management in any context is based on involvement and clear lines of communication. A recognized pattern (or process) of handling change involves: anxiety responses; the need for time to reflect and assess; the expansion of additional skills; the internalization of the situation; and the development of new understanding.

Although much of the National Curriculum reflects accepted good practice by teachers of pupils with SLD, some adjustments are essential. A relevant route for one pupil in a particular Programme of Study may not be applicable to another child in a comparable situation. It is necessary not only to consider the breadth and balance of the learning experiences on offer, but also the depth, differentiation, and necessary cross-curricular links.

School INSET programmes should incorporate the recognized coping strategies for change that staff are likely to go through together with time for planning, implementation and evaluation in order to shape, mould and, if necessary, alter, parts of the National Curriculum. Teachers are frequently being reassured that the National Curriculum has not been written on tablets of stone and that it is likely that some aspects will need to be altered and refined in the light of experience, albeit through legislative procedures.

Visser discusses the dangers of school-based INSET and how purely subjective considerations can inhibit dynamic responses. He argues for the involvement of external agencies in order to provide a broader frame of reference as a stimulus to meaningful development (Visser, 1987).

College-based Support: Initial Training Courses for Mainstream Teachers

The approval of initial teacher training courses is given by the Secretary of State through accreditation, which then entitles students successfully completing an accredited course to qualified teacher status (QTS). Only then can they be employed as teachers in maintained schools.

The stringent accreditation of courses is detailed in DES Circular 24/89 (DES, 1989), which stresses the importance of the National Curriculum, and the need for newly qualified and appointed teachers to be able to contribute to its delivery on new developments. The circular also stresses the importance of flexibility in order that new developments are reflected in course content:

As the subjects of the National Curriculum are developed, institutions should review their course content to ensure that this need is being met, and that their courses are in line with the statutory documents, and with the non-statutory guidance which will be available. (DES, 1989, p. 17)

New entrants to the profession through 'the mainstream route' should therefore be well versed in the implementation of the National Curriculum although not necessarily its application to pupils with severe learning difficulties.

College-based Support: Short Courses, One Term Courses, Diploma and BPhil(Ed) Courses

The James Report (DES, 1972) recommended that teachers should receive a period of secondment for inservice study as a right, rather than a privilege. Unfortunately this recommendation has never been fully implemented, although in 1986 some attempts were made to promote more effective professional teacher development through the Grant Related In-Service Training scheme (GRIST). The scheme required all LEAs to identify a clear and coherent staff development policy for all teachers and to submit proposals directly to the DES in order to obtain central funding (DES, 1986).

Two distinct categories were proposed: funding to meet 'local needs'; and funding for areas designated 'National Priority' by the DES. Although Severe Learning Difficulties became a designated priority area in 1987, the introduction of the National Curriculum in 1988 has tended to divert the energies of teachers of pupils with SLD away from courses designed to enhance their personal professional development towards a consideration of the detailed implications of the new legislation. Many LEAs, therefore, have favoured short, school-based courses dealing with specific practical problems. The consequence, in some cases, has been a form of crisis management relying primarily on hastily prepared training sessions during which tutors and teachers have struggled to respond to new initiatives by immediate implementation rather than through more meaningful and firmly considered curriculum development.

Francis, arguing for the proper recognition of INSET, suggests that the professional education of teachers has taken a backward step. 'The new INSET initiatives have replaced secondments to Diploma and Masters courses in Higher Education, and made support for part-time courses, taken outside working hours, harder to find' (Francis, 1990).

At a time of rapid change it is more important than ever for institutions of higher education to collaborate with LEAs and schools to produce balanced courses in order to meet changing needs. National

Curriculum education is essential to the balance of any course and should be offered using the Joyce and Showers (1980) framework outlined earlier. It is, however, important, too, to keep these elements in perspective and the National Curriculum must be seen as one component only in the total curriculum for pupils with SLD.

In the final analysis, whatever changes need to be made to the education of pupils with SLD, meaningful developments must depend on the identifiable basic skills of educators: classroom competency; counselling; administration; organization; policy making; curriculum development; curriculum evaluation and relations with external agencies.

Teacher Fellowships

LEAs are beginning to consider the opportunities, within the framework of their own policies and provisions, for using colleges to 'support' teachers seconded to work on specific areas of the National Curriculum. 'Support' entails tutorials with specialist staff; access to library and other resources; and involvement in a college's relationships with schools, LEAs and other relevant agencies. Arrangements vary, from one day per week over one term to full-time attachment for a complete academic year.

The aims and objectives of such fellowships need to be accurately defined at the onset and it is essential for all parties to give full consideration to ways in which a scheme will benefit the teacher, the LEA and the college.

In the main, fellowship schemes have been highly successful for several reasons. Colleges, schools, LEAs and teachers are given the opportunity to work collaboratively and to produce realistic recommendations and relevant teaching material. The focus is usually multidimensional and can include curriculum development, INSET provision and research. The facilitators (colleges, tutors and LEAs) provide a critical framework which supports the teacher's own initiatives and creative responses.

A number of institutions of higher education with departments of Special Education, including the Cambridge Institute and Westhill College, offer a rolling programme of Teacher Fellowships. In every case, the LEAs consider that their involvement in, and support for, the schemes has led to an enhancement of their own INSET programmes.

Ideas Exchange

Over the past year, 'monitoring' or 'development' groups of teachers of pupils with SLD have been formed to share concerns and to offer mutual support. Teachers from a number of LEAs are involved in each group and the regular meetings provide a forum for debate and opportunities for the welcome exchange of information. Groups in some regions have used college premises as a base and college staffs as convenors responsible for the organization and administration of work in progress. This relationship has also supported teacher initiatives designed to meet regional needs.

The West Midlands group holds monthly meetings, each of which considers a single aspect of the National Curriculum. Nationally recognized speakers are invited to contribute and between 150 and 250 teachers, from eleven LEAs, attend each meeting. Smaller working parties have been formed to consider the implications of the National Curriculum's core subjects, and assessment recommendations, for pupils with SLD. The 'work in progress' reports and broadsheets are nationally available and have already provided a valuable basis for wide-ranging discussions in schools and education departments.

The work of this and other groups has been brought to the notice of SEAC, NCC and HMI and has already had some influence on National Curriculum policy for pupils with SLD.

Conclusion

Whatever effects the introduction of the National Curriculum has had upon teachers of pupils with SLD, the LEAs and the colleges, it is necessary to consider the opportunities that it offers rather than the problems that it poses. Teachers have undoubtedly been demoralized and confused by the masses of paperwork, but clearly as the acceptance of each tiny detail is impossible, the interpretation of its implications is the only possible response. Individual reactions are essential, but meaningful change can only be achieved through collaboration.

The initiatives outlined in this chapter demonstrate modest success, which has depended on good management and the involvement of all parties. Further progress, however, is dependent upon a number of essential factors. The first is the opportunity for all teachers to be involved in decisions about their own professional development. The second, and this should be given high priority, must be the freedom of LEAs to encourage creative and critical responses to the National Curriculum as a whole. But, finally, total success will only be achieved if resources are made available nationally. At present, education in Britain is short of teachers, of basic resources and of self-esteem. Sadly, money, or a lack of it, is the root of all these evils.

References

ASHTON, P.M.E., HENDERSON, E.S., MERRILL, J.E. and MORTIMER, D.J. (1983) *Teacher Education in the Classroom: Initial and In-Service*, London, Croom Helm.

BELL, A. (1981) 'Structure, knowledge and social relationships in teacher education', *British Journal of Sociology of Education*, 2, 1.

CLARKE, A.M. and CLARKE, A.D.B. (Eds) (1958) *Mental Deficiency: The Changing Outlook*, London, Methuen.

DES (1944) *Education Act, 1944*, London, HMSO.

DES (1970) *Education (Handicapped Children) Act, 1970*, London, HMSO.

DES (1972) *Training* (The James Report), London, HMSO.

DES (1978) *Special Educational Needs: Report of the Committee of Enquiry into the Education of Handicapped Children and Young People* (The Warnock Report), London, HMSO.

DES (1983a) *Teaching Quality*, London, HMSO.

DES (1983b) *Teaching in Schools: The Content of Initial Teacher Training*, an HMI discussion paper, London, HMSO.

DES (1984) *Initial Teacher Training: Approval of Courses*, Circular 3/84, London, HMSO.

DES (1985) *Better Schools*, London, HMSO.

DES (1986) *Local Education Authority Training Grants Scheme: Financial Year 1987–88*, Circular 6/86, London, HMSO.

DES (1988) *Education Reform Act, 1988*, London, HMSO.

DES (1989) *Initial Teacher Training: Approval of Courses*, Circular 24/89, London, HMSO.

DHSS (1959) *Mental Health Act, 1959*, London, HMSO.

FRANCIS, H. (1990) 'Accredit where it's due', *Times Educational Supplement*, 16 March, p. 18.

GOSDEN, P.H.J.H. (1989) 'Teaching quality and the accreditation of initial teacher training courses', in MCCLELLAND, V.A. and VARMA, V.P. (Eds) *Advances in Teacher Education*, London, Routledge.

GUNZBURG, H.C. (1968) *Social Competence and Mental Handicap*, London, Bailliere, Tindall & Cassell.

HEDDELL, F. (1980) *Accident of Birth: Aspects of Mental Handicap*, London, BBC.

Joyce, B. and Showers, B. (1980) 'Improving in-service training: The messages of research', *Educational Leadership*, 37, 5, pp. 379–85.

Luria, A.R. (1961) *The Role of Speech in the Regulation of Normal and Abnormal Behaviour*, London, Pergamon.

Luria, A.R. and Vinogradova, O.S. (1959) 'An objective investigation of the dynamics of semantic systems', *British Journal of Psychology*, 50, pp. 89–105.

O'Connor, N. and Hermelin, B.F. (1963) *Speech and Thought in Severe Subnormality*, London, Pergamon.

Perry, P. (1983) 'The training of primary teachers: Current needs and future trends', *Primary Education Review*, 16, Spring, pp. 2–4.

Pritchard, D.G. (1972) 'The development of educational provision for mentally handicapped children', in Laing, A. (Ed.) *Educating Mentally Handicapped Children*, Swansea, Faculty of Education, University College of Swansea.

Stevens, M. (1968) *Observing Children Who Are Severely Subnormal*, London, Edward Arnold.

Stevens, M. (1971) *The Educational Needs of Severely Subnormal Children*, London, Edward Arnold.

Stevens, M. (1978) *Observe Then Teach*, 2nd edition, London, Edward Arnold.

Visser, J. (1987) 'Teacher training and special educational needs', in Hinson, M. (Ed.) *Teachers and Special Educational Needs*, Harlow, Longman.

Wiltshire, A. (1990) 'The Effect of the National Curriculum on the Curriculum in Schools for Children with Severe Learning Difficulties', unpublished BPhil(Ed) Dissertation, Birmingham, Westhill College.

20   The Way Ahead

Lambert Bignell

The Importance of Participation

These are exciting and challenging times in the education of pupils
with severe learning difficulties (SLD) yet they are times when pupils
need advocacy and representation as much as if not more than they
did in 1970. Our current parliament consists, for the most part, of
members who are striving to make their marks, or maintain their
ministerial roles or are jockeying for position in anticipation of a new
government. In doing this they frequently lose sight of the intricate
yet far reaching implications of educational legislation or proposals for
pupils with special educational needs (SEN).

It is, however, a consolation to know that there are groups of
people — central and local administrators, inspectors and advisers,
voluntary organizations, teachers and, not least, the parents and disabled young people themselves — who are the 'barometers' in these
times of change. It behoves these people to make their anxieties
known quite forcibly to the DES and their curricular and assessment
agencies — the National Curriculum Council (NNC) and the Schools
Examination and Assessment Council (SEAC) — all of whom are
receptive to responses to their publications and to positive original
ideas. The plethora of literature, memoranda and regulations arriving
at schools of all types over the past two years has provided them
with an almost insurmountable reading task, particularly schools for
pupils with SLD which are invariably small. This is a necessary chore
which could rightly be shared not only by the school's permanent staff
but also by visiting staff, parents and governors all of whom have a
vested interest in the education and welfare of the pupils. Synopses of
these documents could then be submitted to all concerned to determine whether further in-depth study is warranted. Participation is one

of the fashionable words of the early 1990s and this is a purposeful, initial way in which it can be applied.

Central to this documentation has rightly been that associated with the curriculum and its delivery, for it is precisely this which causes a school to 'live, move and have its being'. It is understandable, too, that much attention has been paid to curriculum development in other chapters of this book; nevertheless a few concluding comments might be worthwhile.

One of the most exciting changes over the past twenty years has been the attitude to curriculum content and the range of experiences it offered. In 1970 the cry was all too often 'They won't be able to do that, they are mentally handicapped'. In contrast, today's attitudes are about breadth, balance, accessibility and entitlement and there is no reason to doubt that the National Curriculum will fuel further advances. Two decades ago it was usual to visit schools without detailed written curricula. It is unusual to find schools like that these days. One might ask how can a school possibly assure continuity, progression and consistency without a written curriculum.

When documents result from consultation, discussion and agreement with and between staff there is an air of unanimity and confidence which contributes directly to the school ethos, the quality of the environment and the learning and teaching. The National Curriculum has caused such schools to review and, in some cases, redraft subject areas like Science and Technology, whilst one group of teachers on a recent course explored the appropriateness of History for all pupils in their schools and were amazed at the scope the subject offered. For those schools which continue to be without a detailed written curriculum the National Curriculum has become a resource bank of information for preparatory staff discussion.

To return to the word 'participation', it is perhaps never more important than when it is associated with curriculum development. The involvement in the task of medical, paramedical and social work staff, careers and environmental health officers, employers and Further Education (FE) staff, to name but a few, as members of a 'think tank', is of paramount importance. Collectively they will contribute a wealth of ideas about the range of experiences which the school should offer its pupils. Furthermore, teachers are enjoined to canvas the views of the pupils and students themselves. Above all, parents should be invited to participate not only in the wider aspects of curriculum development but also in the individual goal planning for their children. Education is not just about the acquisition of knowledge, skills, attitudes and values for young people with SLD: it is about their quality of life and that of their families.

Teachers across the country have been concerned that Personal and Social Education (PSE) did not appear as a foundation, if not a core, subject in the National Curriculum. Subsequently it was regarded as a cross-curricular theme of the utmost importance for pupils with SLD. If it is to have adequate coverage, all timetabled subjects, as well as evening and weekend activities in residential schools, will have to be analyzed to discover what aspects of PSE they promote. It will be essential for teaching and residential staff to work closely together and where they discover areas not covered by the subjects and activities taught these will have to be timetabled in their own right.

Assessment and Testing

It is obvious that no curriculum can be effective without the means of assessing pupils' progress on it, without procedures to evaluate its quality and without a succinct and simple record system. Each component influences and informs the others. It is a matter of regret that the requirements of the National Curriculum, as they stand, in terms of assessment and record keeping are likely to make intolerable demands on teachers' time, possibly affecting their performance. There is a danger, too, that staff will be panicked into teaching to Attainment Targets, which in turn will lead to a narrow and impoverished range of experiences for the pupils. It has been said in the past that an aggregate of checklists has not constituted a curriculum. The same comment may be made of a collection of Attainment Targets.

Many innovative and successful methods of assessment and record keeping have been devised to reflect the curriculum of the schools, using photographs, audio and video tapes and more recently microcomputers. These must not be replaced by standardized tests which are soul-destroying for staff and boring for pupils. One of the most exciting developments of recent years has been the establishment of Records of Achievement (ROA) which are related to all aspects of pupils' progress. Admittedly they are time-consuming to complete, particularly those entries which are negotiated by teacher and pupil. One has only to discuss ROA with youngsters to judge their worth. These are just a few of the comments made:

We know our teachers better and they know us.

We can write about the things we like doing and the things we are best at, but we also know about our weaknesses and we can do something about them too.

We have something good to talk about when we go on work experience or to college and we are more confident at interviews.

Incidentally one of these contributors was an Olympic gymnast with Down's syndrome who, surprisingly, could not get on with people other than gymnasts, but was determined to do something about it!

Teacher assessment and moderation, for the time being, appear to have receded into the background, but they must be resurrected. The Task Group on Assessment and Testing (TGAT) stressed strongly that teacher assessment should be a fundamental element of a national system, and that it should be moderated in order to inform national standards. This is good sense, since, next to their parents, pupils are known by their teachers better than by anyone else. It is essential now that groups of teachers, using their expertise and existing practice, devise tests suitable for all pupils in their schools in relation to the core subjects of the National Curriculum. There is little experience so far of moderating such test results with pupils with SLD but there are good examples in other areas of education — for instance, the General Certificate of Secondary Education (GCSE) and the Certificate of Pre-vocational Education (CPVE). Without delay, workable systems need to be set up, used and modified before presentation to SEAC.

Pupils with Challenging Behaviour

Amongst the most difficult pupils to be taught and assessed are those with 'challenging' behaviour. Mindful of the inappropriate placement of these young children in 'mental handicap' hospitals, central government in the late 1970s and early 1980s urged area health and social services departments to make provision for them within the community. As a direct result of this, day schools for pupils with SLD began to experience an influx of youngsters with profound and multiple learning difficulties (PMLD), complicated by severely disturbed and disturbing behaviour. These came to be known as pupils with challenging behaviour. They might be described as pupils and students who have SLD with additional emotional disturbance, behavioural disorder or psychiatric illness. As a result they may be a danger to themselves or others and present a threat to the physical environment in which they find themselves. Their disorders are possibly of sufficient degree to influence the type of provision made for them.

Schools found great difficulties in managing this behaviour and either had to exclude these pupils or appoint staff to supervise them. At best they affected the curriculum of other pupils, some of whom were deprived of first-hand experience which is so vital to their education. Doors had to be locked, thus affecting independence and responsibility training. Frequently their tantrums resulted in cuts and bruises for those dealing with them or nearest to them. Many schools adopted a behavioural approach to the problem, frequently resulting in a somewhat arid curriculum, but the more enlightened employed a broad range of experiences to ameliorate adverse behaviour.

Inevitably, the exclusion of these pupils from day schools provided a growth area for independent schools in the mid and late 1980s. These are generous in staffing but heavy on resources. A dilemma exists for placing authorities as to whether this is the most suitable provision. Is it appropriate to put such pupils together in one place? At least one independent school has enrolled a mix of pupils with a view to providing models of good behaviour yet maintaining some very secure accommodation for those who need it. Central government has funded research into the problem but this so far has amounted to little more than statistics gathering and mapping exercises. As yet there is little expertise in this area and training is in short supply. Clearly this nettle needs to be grasped both centrally and locally in terms of establishing different models of provision which will inform and influence practice, placement and training.

Issues Related to Integration

Suitable provision for pupils with SLD has been a subject for lively discussion for many years — possibly ever since special facilities have been organized for young people with SEN. Should it be separate, should it be on the site of mainstream schools, should it be within mainstream schools, should it be all-age or phased in line with mainstream education, should it be day or residential? There are arguments for and against all these alternatives and views invariably change as new developments take place.

Whatever arrangements have been made one problem is invariably present — that of transition or transfer, whether it be from department to department, phase to phase, school to school or school to FE. Communications break down and continuity and progression are deeply affected. Transition is difficult for the majority of pupils whether they have SEN or not. For pupils with SLD it needs to be very carefully planned as a result of frequent and detailed consultation between all who are involved. Teachers strive hard to acknowledge growing maturity in their pupils through structured programmes leading to increased independence, responsibility and privilege. When they move on this can be so easily undermined by lack of information, lack of knowledge and under-expectation. This is most frequently true of the transfer from school to FE. As a consequence, students full of excitement and anticipation find themselves unchallenged, regressing and disenchanted.

It was regrettable that, although FE featured importantly in the Warnock Report (DES, 1978) it was not covered in the provisions of the 1981 Education Act nor was it included in the Education Reform Act of 1988. Nevertheless there are few colleges without a body of goodwill and growing expertise in the further education of students with SLD. Much of this is due to the support of the Further Education Unit (FEU) through publications and training packages.

In a growing number of LEAs, too, there is a policy concerning FE and SEN which underpins the work of college lecturers, and makes proper financial provision. In a few LEAs teachers and lecturers are addressing the question of transition. In one instance, a teacher and a lecturer have been given a year's secondment to research and make recommendations concerning the preparations and induction needed to facilitate the transfer of pupils with SLD from school to FE. There is a sense of urgency about this work brought about by the need for continuity in relation to the wider curriculum in general and the National Curriculum in particular.

Integration has a number of interpretations in the SLD field. For the pupil with PMLD it means that some or all of his or her education will take place in the general classrooms of the school. In a programme of visits to 45 schools as far back as 1983 it was found that some measure of integration was taking place in every one of them. A prerequisite of this sort of integration is that the class teachers and their assistants must have a positive attitude to the learning and teaching of pupils with PMLD. This requires training and a level of support which permits the effective education of other pupils in the class. Further, there needs to be adequate space for pupils who may be physically disabled and for the extra adults who will be supporting.

Staffing implications were reflected in the recent DES draft consultative document (DES, 1990). It was considered that there should be two teachers and three special support assistants (SSA) per ten pupils with PMLD. This ratio would permit the support described above but would also ensure that the base designated for pupils with PMLD was adequately staffed for the teaching of the highly specialized programmes which may be necessary. Such programmes would form an integral part of the overall personal curriculum for each pupil.

Integration for the more able pupils with SLD is related to their education being provided wholly or partly in mainstream, primary and secondary schools. In some cases this integration has resulted from parental pressure, often against the advice of LEA administrators and special school staff. In other cases the special schools themselves have initiated the move. In both circumstances special school staff have offered advice and support.

The best provision is made where there is a clear LEA policy which covers proper staffing, adequate resources and visits from LEA and other agency supporting services. Monitoring and reviews are carried out by a panel consisting of the parents, representatives of the school staff and the supporting services. Good practice is characterized by work which is differentiated in relation to pupils' individual needs, and which is supported by the senior management of the school and by the parents. In such schools there is an agreed policy related to pupils with SEN which embraces staff awareness, attitude and training. It is particularly important that class teachers develop the ability to devise individual Programmes of Study and that support teachers and assistants acquire the skills of negotiation and collaboration.

The National Curriculum can and should enhance continuity and progression for pupils with SLD in mainstream schools, and this is especially important if they are attending on a part-time basis. Experience shows that very young pupils gain a great deal from being exposed to good spoken language models and to a rich structured infants' school curriculum. The attainment gap between pupils with SLD and their more able counterparts widens as they grow older. At the same time the need for individual programmes becomes more and more apparent if they are to remain in their chronological age groups.

Ultimately integration must be based on the individual needs of pupils, and the balance sheet of what is to be gained and what may be lost must be scrutinized. The fact that more able pupils are being integrated into mainstream schools presents a problem for those remaining in the special schools. The spoken language of these pupils is declining. Campus development or reciprocal arrangements between mainstream and special schools may be the answer.

Teacher Education

Almost everything which has been said in this final chapter, and indeed throughout the book, has implications for teacher education. The 1980s have seen a widening in the scope of training mainly through the growth of modular courses and distance learning packages. At the same time the SLD field has not yet recovered from the decision to end specialist initial courses. Some would question the reasons for this decision and the qualifications of those making it. As the last cohorts of students complete this specialist training, schools are already suffering from the loss of a group of highly intelligent and highly committed young teachers. Fewer staff than was anticipated are transferring from mainstream schools, so there is a serious recruitment problem which LEAs and schools will need to address. One solution might be the reintroduction of teacher secondment to 'test the water' of special education.

Structured and formal induction of new teachers must be greatly expanded and as an inducement such programmes might be linked to award-bearing courses which would increase in breadth, depth and intensity as the new teacher gains in experience. One of the induction elements invariably overlooked is an introduction to the employing school's curriculum. New teachers are frequently left to implement schemes which have been devised by others. Steps need to be taken to assist the inductee towards ownership of that curriculum.

Modular courses pioneered by a consortium based at Manchester University have developed slowly, and there is a need for expansion in other regions. These courses permit trainees to 'pick and mix' according to their career development, often linked with school initiatives. Elements related to preparation for life, language and communication, working with pupils with PMLD, and the management of curriculum development and change, come to mind.

Collaboration is perhaps the key to training over the next decade or so. Teacher training establishments, LEAs and schools must cooperate in the induction and inservice training of new and established teachers. Recent school visits showed that induction, where it existed, lacked necessary coordination between schools and LEA advisers. The expertise of teacher trainers was rarely enlisted. This and the closure of specialist initial courses have led to the dissipation of many tutors and their skills.

Collaboration of a different sort has been the basis of award-bearing modular courses. Teacher training institutions have contributed elements to diploma and degree courses according to their particular expertise. At the time of writing, considerations are being given by a group of tutors to the concept of a national modular course. Students undertaking it would go to different parts of the country for different modules, thus further widening the scope of the course. At the same time four European countries, including the United Kingdom, are preparing a distance learning course on autism in anticipation of the single community.

Sharing Experience and Expertise

One of the most impressive pieces of collaboration has been that which was inspired by the National Curriculum. Mainly centred on and coordinated by teacher training institutions across the country, several hundred teachers have studied the core and foundation subjects of the National Curriculum. Where appropriate they have responded to the National Curriculum Council consultative documents. Mutual support through the sharing of experience and expertise has been a strong feature of these activities, resulting in the production of practical guidelines and the circulation of broadsheets. At the same time LEAs have organized primary, secondary and cross-phase working groups which have included representatives of special schools. Feedback from all these groups has ensured that the broadest possible experience and expertise has been applied to the schools' curriculum development. It is now necessary to establish a national database which will link teachers who have common interests and which will reduce the possibility of 'reinventing the wheel'.

There is no doubt that pupils with SLD in Great Britain are taught by some of the best educators in the world. Clearly they were stunned by the possibility that their charges might be excluded from the National Curriculum. However, shock was replaced by anger and this in turn gave way to a determination to get the best possible deal for their pupils. Two years later they view the future with much greater optimism. As each document has been published, whilst recognizing that the National Curriculum is backed by law, these teachers have gradually identified a flexible framework within which they are able to work. So, through commitment, opportunism, adaptability, mutual support and sheer hard work they have accepted the curriculum challenge. There is still much to be done, yet there is now a powerful will to succeed and provide their pupils with an education which is second to none.

References

DES (1978) *Special Educational Needs* (The Warnock Report), London, HMSO.
DES (1981) *The Education Act, 1981*, London, HMSO.
DES (1988) *The Education Reform Act, 1988*, London, HMSO.
DES (1990) *Staffing for Pupils with Special Educational Needs*, London, DES.

Notes on Contributors

Rob Ashdown is currently Headteacher at St Luke's School, Scunthorpe, a Humberside county special school for pupils with severe learning difficulties (SLD). He graduated from University College, Cardiff in 1975 with a BA in Education and continued at the Faculty of Education there to do three years of postgraduate research into the use of behaviour modification techniques with young children with SLD. He received his PhD in 1980. He trained at Bristol Polytechnic to teach pupils with SLD and has subsequently worked in the UK in schools for such pupils, apart from two years in Vancouver, British Columbia where he taught mainstreamed pupils with language disorders. Since taking up his present post he has become involved in the delivery of SLD modules as part of Humberside's modular course in special educational needs for teachers.

Lambert Bignell is a trained teacher and holds an advanced diploma in special education. Having retired in April 1990 he is currently part-time consultant to the National Autistic Society. For thirty-eight years he has been involved with young people with special educational needs. He was a headteacher in Manchester before becoming an adviser for special education in Cheshire. For the past fifteen years he has been a member of HM Inspectorate and for much of that time held a national responsibility for pupils and students with severe learning difficulties and autism. He has a strong interest in curriculum development and lectures on the subject. In his present role he is committed to forging stronger links between the National Autistic Society and Local Education Authorities.

Keith Bovair is currently Lecturer in Special Education at the University of Birmingham and was Headteacher of the Lady Adrian School, Cambridge, for children with moderate learning difficulties. He was born in Detroit, Michigan, and graduated from the University has taught children with emotional and behavioural difficulties at Ferndale High School, Michigan and received a Community Mental Health Award for his programme. He moved to England in 1977, and has been teacher in charge of an intermediate treatment unit, in Sheffield (1977–1980); Headteacher of a residential school for the emotionally impaired in Tyne and Wear (1980–1984); and visiting schoolteacher fellow in the Department of Education, University of Cambridge (1989). The Lady Adrian School received the Schools Curriculum Award for 1987.

Barry Carpenter is currently Inspector of Schools for Solihull Education Authority with particular responsibility for Special Educational Needs. Until recently, he was Headteacher of Blythe Special School in Warwickshire. Following initial training in Westminster College, Oxford he entered special education in 1976 and has taught in the spheres of both moderate and severe learning difficulties, specializing in curriculum development and augmentative communication. He completed postgraduate studies in special needs at London University and has subsequently gained a higher degree through research from the University of Nottingham. He has been course tutor to the BPhil (Ed) course in special needs at the University of Warwick. In addition, he was a tutor for the British Institute of Mental Handicap, and a teacher-supervisor for schools experience from Westhill College, Birmingham. He contributes extensively to inservice training of teachers throughout the UK, particularly regarding the education of children with profound and multiple learning difficulties. In 1986 he undertook a lecture tour in Australia. He has published several articles and papers dealing with such issues as curriculum development and integration. In January 1990 he gave the keynote address to the South Pacific Conference on Special Education in Auckland, New Zealand.

Bill Cassell has been an Area Coordinator in Leicestershire for the last two years, concerned largely with managing TVEI developments. As part of this role he has been closely involved with supporting curriculum development work in special schools. In his teaching career in 11–18 and 11–14 schools, he has at various times had responsibility for coordination of special needs provision. He is now Deputy Head in a Leicestershire High School.

John Clarke, MA(Oxon), MEd, is Senior Adviser (Monitoring and Evaluation) for Suffolk Local Education Authority. This involves the quality assurance of all schools within the LEA, including special schools, and concerns itself with external and internal review of provision and the link between review and development. Until recently, he was Humanities Adviser within Suffolk which included responsibility for the development of History and Geography, and he has written and spoken extensively about these two curricular areas within a special needs context. Apart from the implementation of the National Curriculum, his current interests include the reconceptualization of special needs and the effective schools movement.

Sue Fagg, Cert. Ed, BEd(Hons), is currently an Adviser for Special Needs with Lancashire County Council. Until recently she was Headteacher of Piper Hill School (SLD) in Manchester. Her teaching experience includes comprehensive schools and special schools (MLD, PhH and Visual Impairment). She has close links with Mencap, as the PRMH Project is based at Piper Hill School. During the academic year 1990–91 she was on secondment to Manchester University as team leader to a group of teachers addressing the challenge of the National Curriculum for pupils with special needs, specifically those with severe and complex learning difficulties. The results of this work are being published. She continues to liaise with the present secondees. As well as her interest in curriculum development and associated inservice training, she is also involved in the development of management skills and its associated inservice training. The management of change in a time of new legislation is a key area of concern and involves her in work with the North West Educational Management Centre.

Anita Gadsby, Cert. Ed, Adv. Dip. Special Education, is currently Head of St. Andrew's School, Derby, which is an all-age day and residential school for children with severe learning difficulties (SLD). She was seconded in 1986 to study aspects of curriculum delivery for pupils with SLD in integrated mainstream settings. During that time she was able to visit a number of schools in Italy to look at a totally integrated school structure. She has written papers on the role of the integration support teacher in special schools. Involved in inservice Training for the LEA since 1978, she has latterly been concerned in Management Training courses in aspects of teamwork development.

Jean Gawlinski, MA, is Headteacher of Rees Thomas School in Cambridge, a school for children with severe learning difficulties (SLD). She has taught sex education for several years to children with learning difficulties, originally incorporating sexual abuse prevention as part of a sex education programme. She researched sex education for children with learning difficulties at the University of East Anglia and introduced a programme into Meadowgate School in Wisbech, where she was Deputy Head, and more recently into Rees Thomas School. She has written about and runs conferences and workshops on sex education and Kidscape with children with learning difficulties for teachers and other professionals working in this field.

Linda Howe attended Bedford College of Education, leaving in 1975 with a Certificate in Education. Since then she has gained two further professional qualifications in the fields of management and assessment. Her present position is that of Headteacher of a mainstream primary school in Suffolk. Before taking this post she was employed as an Advisory Teacher for Primary Science, and in this capacity worked with teachers and children in special schools and in special units in mainstream schools in the western part of the county of Suffolk. She is involved both nationally and locally in initiatives to facilitate the smooth introduction of the National Curriculum. Her national work has included acting as a consultant for the Open University/NCC packs and for the non-statutory orders for Science, and running IN-SET sessions for local authorities, individual schools, (including many special schools) and for the NCC at the annual Science Education Conference. Her local work has concentrated on looking at the issues of curriculum development/entitlement for all, classroom/whole school organization and planning, and assessment and record keeping. A major project has been the sole authorship of Collins Primary Science scheme which has been produced with the aim of providing teacher and pupil materials suitable for all to use.

Nick Hughes, DEHC, MEd, is Headteacher of Fairfield School, Heckmondwike. During an educational career which includes eighteen years teaching in several schools for pupils with severe and profound learning difficulties, he has developed a general interest in all aspects of special education, including the participation of parents.

Sharon Jefferies is currently Headteacher of Newark Appletongate School in Nottinghamshire. She trained as a teacher at Trent Polytechnic, Nottingham and subsequently gained an Advanced Diploma from the University of Nottingham. She has many professional interests, particularly in interpersonal skills, sex education and anti-racist equal opportunities. She regards herself as a practising Humanist who utilizes behaviourism and who believes in the rights of the individual. She has been involved in the organization and delivery of local INSET and INSET for schools in other regions.

Ann Lewis, PhD, is a lecturer in Education at the University of Warwick. She taught for ten years in special and primary schools before taking up her present post. Major initiatives in which she has been involved include curriculum-based assessment, early identification procedures and integration. Her recent and current research focuses on analyses of the quality of child-child interaction in integrated settings. She is joint editor of *Education 3–13* and has published widely on curricula for children with special educational needs. She is involved in teacher education at initial, inservice and higher degree levels and is currently writing a book on the implementation of the National Curriculum and children with learning difficulties.

Sylvia Lindoe is General Adviser (Special Educational Needs) in Leicestershire. Prior to this she was Senior Lecturer in Special Education at Westhill College, Birmingham where she was tutor to the BPhil (Ed) course in Special Education (Severe Learning Difficulties). Her previous experience has included teaching in both mainstream and special schools.

Flo Longhorn is currently Headteacher at St John's School, Bedford. Following teaching and studying in Boston, Massachusetts, Flo worked as head of a unit for autistic children. Her first headship was at Wren Spinney School, Kettering in Northamptonshire, where her extensive work on devising a sensory curriculum culminated in her book *A Sensory Curriculum for Very Special People* and in the production of video films. She is now in the process of producing a book and video on massage for the very special child. On a personal level, she is becoming involved in the EEC educational world for 1992.

Carol Ouvry is currently Headteacher of Alexandra Priory School for pupils with severe learning difficulties (SLD) in the London Borough of Camden. She started her career as an occupational therapist and, after time out to bring up a family, during which period she ran a playgroup, she then retrained as a mature student to become a teacher. Since qualifying she has taught in SLD schools and has specialized in working with pupils with profound and multiple learning difficulties (PMLD), first as Head of a large department at Paddock School, Putney and later as advisory teacher visiting SLD schools throughout the ILEA, setting up inservice training for staff working with this group of pupils, and contributing to the induction course for probationary teachers. After a period as Deputy Head at her present school she joined the staff of Castle Priory College as course coordinator and tutor, setting up and contributing to courses for staff from all disciplines working with people of all ages with all kinds of disabilities. In March 1990 she returned to Alexandra Priory School and took up her present post. Particular interests include supporting schools through change, curriculum development and activities for pupils with additional disabilities in school and beyond, and the sharing and dissemination of expertise and information throughout the country. She has written a book, articles and papers, and currently co-ordinates the production of *PMLD Link*, a newsletter by and for teachers working with pupils with PMLD.

Brian Robbins, MEd, is Head of Hallmoor School, Birmingham. He has taught in a secondary school and in schools for pupils with moderate and severe learning difficulties. He has taken a particular interest in Mathematics and his first publication, *Step by Small Step*, resulted from working with pupils with SLD at Mayfield School, Birmingham. Whilst he was Head of Dean Hall School, Gloucester-shire the scheme was extended and the revised materials have recently been published as MATHSTEPS. Hallmoor School has been in the East Birmingham TVEI Partnership since the pilot phase and this has led to strong links with local secondary schools, a college of Further Education and industry. It also has collaborative links with primary schools and is twinned with a special school in Frankfurt. He has contributed to a number of publications including *Special Children* and *Junior Education*. He lectures regularly on Mathematics for pupils with learning difficulties.

Paul Roberts graduated from the University of Birmingham with a BA in American Studies. He then took a postgraduate Certificate in Teaching the Mentally Handicapped at Leeds Polytechnic. He has taught in schools for children with moderate and severe learning difficulties and is currently Integration Support Teacher at the Blythe School, Coleshill, Warwickshire, having also held a post as IT Co-ordinator at this school. He considers himself to be a classroom practitioner with broad curricular interests. He became interested in IT when he realized the control over learning that it offers to pupils with various learning difficulties and the sheer thrill that they get from it. He is currently a member of the National Curriculum Monitoring

Group for pupils with learning difficulties based at Westhill College, Birmingham.

Martyn Rouse, BEd, MA, originally trained as a teacher of drama but moved into special needs work early in his career. He taught in London schools for sixteen years and has worked as an advisory teacher for special needs. He currently works at the Cambridge Institute of Education where he is a tutor for special educational needs, teaching on a range of courses including the MA module on assessment. His particular interests include the development and evaluation of arrangements for whole institution responses to meeting special needs, staff development and assessment and testing. He has lectured in a number of countries abroad, and is currently a member of a planning group in the USA working with the United Nations on education and disability policy development. He is currently providing special needs consultancy to the group developing the Key Stage 3 Standard Assessment Tasks in Technology.

Philippa Russell, OBE, BA, is Principal Officer of the Voluntary Council for Handicapped Children at the National Children's Bureau. She is currently seconded part-time to the Department of Health as an Associate Director of the National Development Team for People with a Mental Handicap (with special responsibility for children's services). Her current work includes a DES funded project which is exploring ways of involving parents of children with disabilities and special needs in their children's assessment and subsequent educational provision. She has written a number of books and articles on disability and special needs and is closely involved with a range of local and voluntary organizations in this field. Most relevantly she is the parent of a son with severe learning difficulties and has lived through a decade and a half of being a parent of a child with special needs. She has recently received the Rose Fitzgerald Kennedy Memorial Leadership Award for service in the field of mental handicap.

Judy Sebba, MEd, is a tutor at the Cambridge Institute of Education. She is responsible for the Advanced Diploma in Severe Learning Difficulties and Coordinator of the National Curriculum Development Team (Severe Learning Difficulties). Previously, she worked at the Hester Adrian Research Centre, Manchester University, on various projects concerned with staff development and profound and multiple learning difficulties and has published books and papers on this work.

Her main current interest is in the area of implementation of the National Curriculum to maximize access to it for pupils with severe learning difficulties. She is also interested in applications of the effective schools research to special schools.

Carolyn Skilling shared responsibility for implementing the 1981 Education Act in Leicestershire. She subsequently became county adviser and coordinator of the extension of the Technical and Vocational Education Initiative in Leicestershire before moving to a senior post in the Birmingham Education Directorate.

Andy Tearle is a teacher with seven years experience of working with young people with SLD. At present, he works full-time within a centre for students with SLD aged from 16 to 19 years from the county of Humberside. This centre is based at Ganton Special School, Hull, where he has also worked with pupils in the 9 to 16 years age range. In both the school and the centre he has taught craft. Initially, his emphasis was upon woodwork mainly but he has developed this into a more comprehensive subject area. At an early stage, he worked on structured, developmental woodwork projects for pupils with SLD in association with Mr Joe Waller, a lecturer at Humberside Polytechnic. He did not train as a craft teacher and does not see himself as a craft specialist; in fact, he has teaching responsibilities relating to all areas of a wide curriculum. He trained as a teacher and has additional experience and qualifications relating to youth work which he finds relevant. He has been involved in inter-school working parties and the delivery of INSET on joint training days for the special schools for pupils with SLD in Humberside.

Christina Tilstone has had considerable experience in teaching pupils with severe learning difficulties and is now involved in initial and inservice teacher training at Westhill College, Birmingham. After taking an Advanced Diploma in Special Education she gained her MEd (Special Education) at the University of Birmingham, and her MA (Teacher Education) at the University of Leicester. She recently formed the West Midlands National Curriculum Monitoring Group which aims to ensure that pupils with SEN have access to all areas of the National Curriculum, and now lectures and leads workshops throughout Britain on National Curriculum concerns. She is also involved in the training of teachers of pupils with multisensory impairment and is the secretary of the national IT-INSET network. The latter provides opportunities for students in initial training, teachers and college tutors to work collaboratively on the development of the curriculum in schools.

Judy van Oosterom has had a long and wide teaching experience from nursery to secondary pupils in both mainstream and special schools, including four years in the research unit for cerebral palsied children at Queen Mary's Hospital, Carshalton. After completing the Advanced Diploma course in Educational Studies (Handicapped Children) at the Cambridge Institute of Education, she was appointed Deputy Head of the Rees Thomas School, Cambridge, until she retired in July 1983. In continuing her interest in education she runs courses and workshops, publishes materials and writes articles to promote the use of a simplified visual code using rebuses to facilitate learning both for primary school children and for those with special educational needs.

Index